Longitude Latitude, with Attitude

One Man's Quest to See the Entire World

by

Rufus McGaugh

Copyright © 2017 Rufus McGaugh. All rights reserved.

Editor: Anthony Ambrogio

No part of this book may be reproduced or transmitted in any form or by any means, electronic or mechanical, including photocopying or recording, or by an information-storage-and-retrieval system—except in the case of brief quotations embodied in critical articles or by a reviewer who may quote short passages in a review to be printed in a magazine or newspaper or published online—without permission in writing from the author.

Printed by CreateSpace, An Amazon.com Company. Available from Amazon.com, CreateSpace.com, and other retail outlets

Dedicated
to my family: Monica, Eric, and J.T.
and
to all the kids I ever taught

Table of Contents

Foreword i
A Ticket to Freedom —*or*— A Ticket Out of Nam 1
Shot up in the Que Son Valley 23
Hong Kong Tailor 37
Tacos and Nude Women in Texas 48
Imprisoned in Zimbabwe 60
How to Travel in Style 73
Russia and the Oddball Countries of Eastern Europe 76
Three Quick Takes on Three Obscure African Countries 131
Kurdistan—No Joke (Though It Ends with One) 137
Some Enchanted Islands: the South Pacific, Rufus Style 143
I Walk the Straight and *Nauru* (with a Half-Dozen Digressions Along the Way) 153
Visiting the Fake Country of Niue 182
Into Deepest, Deepest Africa: the Last Frontier of Africa 192
Rufus in Dictatorland 225
Rufus in Non-Dicatorland 242
Rufus Travels to Cuba, and Comes Back a Commie Smoking a Cigar! 253
Getting Eric 260
So I Came Up with *Another* Plan: Rufus in Libya 284

Foreword

Hodomania: an abnormal love of travel.

What makes a person not only want to travel but to visit every country in the world? I can only answer for myself.

Four pivotal and defining moments in my life made me the traveler I am today.

The first was the day I entered my first social-studies class in 5th grade at St. Leonard Catholic School in Warren, Michigan. From that moment I was hooked on everything social studies; that class planted the seed of travel in me.

I can still remember the bright-orange cover of that first social-studies book. We had no social-studies homework that night, but I took the book home just the same. I read most of the book that night. Late into the night, I turned page after page to look at the illustrations and the photos rendered in old-fashioned, grainy black and white.

I will never forget this as long as I live: I came to a picture of the pyramids in Egypt. I was 10 years old, and I thought to myself, *Someday I'm going to Egypt to see the pyramids*. I eventually did, too, in the later 1970s. However, at the time (about 1960), this conviction was not only astounding (due to my age) but also audacious, considering my socio-economic status. I was the son of a former Tennessee cotton farmer with only a 6th-grade education who migrated North. My Irish-Catholic mom from Chicago had only completed 8th grade. We were what they called "middle-class" after World War II but at the very bottom of that group. I knew no one in my family, among my friends, in the neighborhood, or at church or school who had ever made a foreign trip, anywhere. In fact, my family and I did not know a single human being who had ever traveled—even in the U.S.

I kept turning the pages and kept coming across new and fascinating sights, such as the Great Wall of China and the Roman Coliseum. And I thought, if a working-class stiff (like the one I was surely destined to become) could somehow work like a dog and save like there was no tomorrow in order to be able to see the great sights of the world, that's what I was going to do.

After graduating from high school, I entered the local community college, three miles away. That summer, a friend of mine—totally love sick because his girlfriend had gone AWOL on a summer trip to Alaska—decided he had to travel to see her. So he enlisted any of his buddies who would be up for a Michigan-to-Alaska road trip—in other words, his friends who had lower IQs.

Of course I was at the top of this extremely short list (consisting of me and one other guy). Because I was providing the transportation, my 1967 Firebird, I had one stipulation: we had to take the scenic route so I could see the sights along the way.

The very nice (and, I might now admit, very competent), AAA travel agent repeatedly warned us that it was impossible to drive to Alaska—let alone come back home—in the ten days we were allotting for the trip. But, with all the ignorance and arrogance of youth, we insisted it could be done. Not one of the three of us had ever really been much outside of Michigan, but we felt we could accomplish this feat by (1) taking turns driving, (2) not sleeping, and (3) breaking all the speed laws of every state we would travel through.

We did all of the above but, just the same, only got as far as Montana before being forced to turn back. Still, we had a blast! And we definitely were going to do it again. Instead of compromising a bit or being more realistic and practical, I went for the mother lode. I proposed that, next year, we should go to California—and we did! I will forever cherish those two trips and all their misadventures. Seeing the great sights of America—Mt. Rushmore, Yellowstone National Park, Glacier National Park, the Rocky Mountains, Mesa Verde, San Francisco, and so many others—only whetted my appetite to "see it all."

Vietnam. The war drove home to me how precious and precarious life is. Everything, especially life, can be destroyed and ended in a flash. Don't ever procrastinate or put off anything—at least anything good. There are no second chances. When you're killed, you're dead; you will never experience anything again. Death is 'way too final. Grab life; take it—everything it has to offer, because life can end so horribly and so tragically before you've had a real chance at it.

Travel. Throughout our planet, nature offers so much awesome beauty. There are so many ideal, beautiful Edens. The majesty of the Himalayas, the Pamirs of Tajikistan, the red-pink canyons of Utah, the lush green of the Azores, the plateaus of Madagascar are all very special creations of total and absolute beauty. And, if one has a love and respect for history, walking through Angkor Wat, or Bagan in Burma, or Stonehenge, or Petra in Jordan produces an eerie and profound emotional effect. At least, I've felt it when I've been there.

These were the elements that moved and propelled me to see all that was created.

Here is my story: my story of seeing the world.

– Rufus McGaugh

"Seeing so much that is beautiful, grand, and new; from these I draw my contentment."
- Henri Mouhot, French explorer, 1826-1861, who was one of the first to see Angkor Wat

"Though we travel the world over to find the beautiful, we must carry it with us or we find it not."
- Ralph Waldo Emerson

"We travel, some of us forever, to seek other states, other lives, other souls."
- Anais Nin, author and writer, 1903-1997

Rufus McGaugh

A Ticket to Freedom —or— A Ticket Out of Nam

The first overseas traveling I did was not exactly the sight-seeing kind.

I had been in the Marines for almost a year and was home on leave again—the third leave I'd been given in a year!

On three separate occasions within that year, I had received orders that I was going to Nam (and thus given the home-for-one-last-time leave that preceded shipping out)—only to have those orders inexplicably changed when I returned from my leave. It certainly re-enforced my belief that the military in general, and the Marine Corps in particular, didn't have a clue as to what in the hell they were doing.

As it turned out, this was my last leave before actually being shipped out to Nam.

On the night of the last day of my last leave before being sent overseas, I was out with three good friends, cruising around and stopping for a beer now and then at bars known to serve underage patrons. Here I was, getting ready to ship out and go to war, but I wasn't old enough to drink!

Back then, I really wasn't drinking. I went to bars so I could socialize with my buddies rather than consume alcohol; I would order a beer and drink little of it.

By 2:00 a.m., we had closed the last bar and were heading home when I made a right-hand turn on a red light—which was illegal in Michigan in 1970. I don't think I had even completed the turn before we all saw the flashing lights of a police car right behind me. I pulled over and promptly received a ticket.

I sat for a minute with the ticket in my hand—and then tore it up and threw it out the window, an action which engendered shock and disbelief in my car-mates. All four of us were Catholic-school boys and the sons of World War II veterans. With a background like that, you did not show such disrespect for the law.

Finally one of my friends broke the stunned silence and asked, "What in the hell did you do that for?"

I replied, "It's my insurance policy."

Another friend asked, "What the hell is that supposed to mean?"

"Well, I'm not going to pay the ticket. I'm shipping out for Nam, and I could get killed. Paying a ticket before you die is a real waste, so I'm

[1]

Longitude and Latitude, with Attitude

not paying it. If I do survive, I'll pay the ticket and any penalties gladly—it's my insurance policy."

At this point, my three friends were looking at me as if I had lost my mind or for the first time had actually had too many beers. "Think about it for a minute," I elaborated. "If God, or fate, or luck, keeps me alive for a year and then I end up having to pay for this ticket, that's really not a bad deal to stay alive." They all agreed that this was great logic—if it worked.

That was the last time I gave that ticket any thought for some time.

After I arrived in Vietnam, I had a harrowing baptism of fire. In 1970, the Marines could still brag that not one of their major bases had ever been overrun by the enemy. But, on my first night in An Hoa, the headquarters for the 5th Marine Regiment, the base *was* overrun when an ARVN (South Vietnamese Army) unit defending its part of the perimeter was routed by the communist Viet Cong. Day two, the first friend I made in Vietnam was killed by a booby trap twenty minutes after I met him. He was a Michigan guy, and we really hit it off in our brief encounter. We planned to hook up after his patrol. He never made it back. To this date, I feel a certain amount of guilt: I don't even know or remember the name of my first friend in Nam!

Day three, nothing happened.

Day four, my whole unit was almost wiped out by friendly fire when Marine artillery mistook us for a Viet Cong unit while we were out on a night ambush.

Then there was the learning curve and keeping busy. My learning curve sure as hell kept me busy. Let me explain.

After flying by chopper from the city of DaNang to 5th Marine Headquarters in An Hoa, I was put on a Marine truck to head out, down a dirt road, to join my unit, Echo 2/5. We arrived at a tiny outpost, a single platoon of 50 or so Marines. They lived within the confines of a small, primitive position, surrounded by barbed wire and razor wire, backed by surrounding fighting holes, with three Marines to a hole.

The truck stopped, and a staff sergeant walked out of the perimeter and greeted us. "Do I have any machine gunners? I need a machine gunner." No one answered. "Anyone want to be a machine gunner?" he asked. No one answered. He looked us over and, for whatever reason, looked at me and said, "You! You ever fire a machine gun?"

Like every Marine in that truck—and every Marine, period—yes, I had fired a short burst from a machine gun in training, but that was it. So I said, "I fired a few rounds of the M60 in training."

With a big smile on his face, the staff sergeant said, "Great! You're our new machine gunner!" Everyone on the truck laughed, but neither they nor I knew if I had just hit the jackpot or was getting screwed royally.

I had no hesitation or concern about learning to operate and fire a machine gun; I had been quite proficient with any weapon the Marines had ever put in my hands. I always thought that was pretty good because I had never fired a gun prior to my service in the Marines. So I got off the truck and went into the perimeter, where I was taken over and introduced to "Guns"—the machine-gun squad.

They brought out one of the M60s—an awesome weapon—and someone mentioned, just in passing, that it had to be cleaned every day and that cleaning it would be one of my most important duties.

I am very conscientious and hardworking, so I saw no problem whatsoever. But then the bombshell was dropped that didn't seem to faze anyone but me: someone mentioned that the M60 machine gun had 69,237 moving parts that had to be meticulously taken out and apart to be cleaned and oiled.

I almost fell over dead with a heart attack! I am the most incompetent human being on Earth when it comes to mechanical ability. I can't fix anything. I can't repair anything. I can't take anything apart, and I certainly can't put anything back together again, no matter how simple.

What was I to do, the biggest dunderhead on earth? Well, I hunkered down, and, by some miracle, I learned to take the M60 apart and clean it. (Because of my initial shock when I heard about the sheer number of all the moving parts, I may have exaggerated the actual number. Once I calmed down a bit, became a bit more rational, and actually started doing the job, I realized that the number of moving parts to be taken out, taken apart, and cleaned was not quite 69,237. It was 69,236.)

Each day I attempted to clean that damn thing, learning slowly (some would say slower than any Marine in Marine Corps history—but fuck those guys who said that). Now, on one level it was not so awfully important or crucial for me to learn this procedure, at least for the immediate present because, after becoming a member of a gun team, I would, like every other Marine, start at the bottom of a three-man gun team. The "top" gunner would fire the M60 machine gun. The A gunner would direct the fire of the gun and feed the gun belts in. And then there was me, the "ammo humper."

Now, you might think that "ammo humper," the third member of a Marine gun team, does not sound like a very important, illustrious, or prestigious position, but, let me assure you, you are absolutely correct; it isn't. Other names or terms the Marine Corps could have used to identify this team member might be *mule, jackass, slave, coolie, serf,* or *drudge.*

Once I had joined Guns, the other guys on the team—knowing that I had not gone to gun school to learn and train on the machine gun as they had—were very helpful and patient while I struggled to surmount the learning curve. I think the word on the street—or at least the rice paddy—was that I had probably set a new Guinness World Record in time taken to learn and master this weapon. But I did it! By the time I moved up to A-gunner and then gunner, I was proficient and knew what the hell I was doing. "Guns up!"—a hearty cry from the other Marine grunts and riflemen when in a desperate situation or a sharp fire fight—is a yell no gunner or gun-team member can ever forget. When the Marine riflemen started howling "Guns up," that's when we would move up to lay down a withering and devastating line of fire.

I had only been in-country for a couple of weeks when I received a form letter from Macomb County informing me that the fine for my illegal right-hand turn in the city of Mt. Clemens had not been paid and was now overdue. I tossed the letter; I had other things on my mind, and paying a stupid ticket was not one of them.

A week or so later, another letter from the Macomb County District Court arrived, informing me of the seriousness of not paying the fine. It too was tossed. This one-sided correspondence continued for some time, always with the same result on my part: tossing the letter. Then the Second Battalion of the 5th Marines changed its Area of Operation to the Que Son Mountains, taking me along with it.

The Que Sons were low, sharp, steep mountains in the northern area of South Vietnam. Nobody lived in these mountains; no one ever had. During the war, however, the North Vietnamese Army was moving through these mountains, and the Marines were sent to stop them—if we could find them, for these mountains were really thick jungles. We would not only have to contend with the elevation but the thick vegetation. A man could stretch his arm out and lose sight of his hand in the thick green foliage. There were no trails; we hacked our own.

The first three Marines acted as point and carried machetes to slash through the nearly impenetrable jungle. Every succeeding man in the file carried a knife or bayonet to continue to cut through the jumble of flora. Since I was in Guns, we were at the very back of the column, and it never ceased to amaze me that I still had to hack at vines, creepers, brambles, and thickets to go forward, despite the fact that 40, 50, or 60 Marines had preceded me.

Me on a "Search and Destroy" operation in the jungles of the Que Son Mountains of South Vietnam. I had just been promoted to gunner from A-gunner on the M-60 machine gun.

These were the Search and Destroy missions that Vietnam became associated with and so famous (or infamous) for. This war was not fought in set-piece battles with combatants facing off against each other. This was guerilla warfare where the enemy remained hidden, and his main strategy was hit-and-run attacks, sneak attacks, using the civilian population as cover by day and darkness as cover by night. We would first have to find this elusive enemy before fighting and destroying him. We found ourselves in a paradoxical situation: fighting a lethal and determined enemy who never seemed to want to fight.

Appearances to the contrary, the NVA (North Vietnamese Army) and the communist Viet Cong were always probing and attacking our positions—only to retreat minutes after a fire fight would begin. Their tactic seemed to be to make a few, quick, lucky hits, inflict a few causalities, and then run off. Seldom, if ever, did they mount a massive attack. Instead, they attempted to cause us death by a thousand cuts.

Getting in our food, medical supplies, ammo, or replacement troops was very difficult in these mountains and became even more so when the monsoon rains and clouds made visibility and flying even more difficult. Getting out our sick, wounded, or dead was the same. Often—if our food was running low or we were completely out of C-rations, living in now-wet, sopping jungles, up in mountains whose trails turned to slippery and impassible mud ruts that quickly turned into rivulets or streams—our standard of life and health took a severe dive. Now, besides the quirks and danger of war, we had to contend with the sicknesses of pneumonia, malaria, and fevers, along with something called immersion foot (also known, since World War I, as trench foot), where a guy's continually wet feet got so bad that he had to be hospitalized.

And yet the long arm of the law still reached me. Receiving yet another form letter from Macomb County about my ticket while I was living in such miserable conditions did nothing to improve my mood. This time, however, the form letter had changed. This letter now notified me that the District Court had been informed that I was on active duty in the U.S. military. *Great*, I thought, *I'll get a break!*

No, I would not, as it turned out. For (as the letter went on to explain) the Court had an arrangement with the armed services. This arrangement, at least as it was threateningly implied, in this new letter, allowed for me to be arrested by Marine MPs and sent back to the States to stand trial for the civil infraction of making an illegal right-hand turn on a red light.

I chuckled a bit as I read this letter. It sounded drastic—almost draconian—but it was improbable that the Marines were going to arrest me out in the furthest reaches of a war zone, up in mountainous jungles, and then fly me all the way back to the United States to ensure I paid a 25- or 35-dollar ticket. It didn't even make sense; I couldn't help but laugh.

My partner in crime, my gunner, Tim Rider, who had the most improbable nickname in the annals of Marine Corps history ("Timmy Wimmy"), heard me laugh.

Before continuing this story, let me digress for a moment so that the reader fully understands what a bizarre but factual tale s/he is about to read. I have always felt very fortunate that my three best friends over in Nam survived. I don't think many Marines can make that claim. Tim Rider, Mike Botkins, and Dave Graves are three of the finest men I have ever met. We all went through a lot of shit together—and we all made it. Confronted by any enemy or dangerous situation where guts and courage were needed, I would choose these three guys over anyone on Earth. This assertion is meant as a tribute to the bravery and tenacity of these guys.

On patrol in the An Hoa Valley, South Vietnam. My gunner, Tim Rider, is carrying an M60.

Now let's move back to Timmy Wimmy, my gunner, and the guy who probably spent more time than the rest mentoring me, patiently trying to teach the most special-needs Marine in that war—me—how to disassemble the M60 machine gun and then reassemble it so that it would work and fire when needed. Tim—whose last name, as I mentioned, was Rider—had actually picked up an earlier nickname that I am sure he was more comfortable with, "Easy Rider," after the 1969 hippie biker film starring Peter Fonda and Dennis Hopper. It was a pretty good nickname for a cool-headed guy who could handle himself in any tough situation.

Then some stupid lifer (i.e., a career Marine) overheard a mess of us talking and calling each other by our first names. This idiot lifer felt such conduct was unprofessional for a Marine and that we should address each other by rank only. In other words, Mike should be Corporal Botkins; Tim should be Lance Corporal Rider; and so on. We all thought that was one of the nuttiest things we had ever heard and said so, which incensed the lifer, who then angrily claimed that we sounded like a bunch of sissies, calling each other by our first names. Instead of backing off, we did our best to make an absurd situation even worse by immediately calling each other Mikey Wikey, Davey Wavey, Timmy Wimmy, and so on.

We accomplished our intended goal, which was to cause the stupid lifer to go ballistic and make an even bigger fool of himself.

The childish and silly nicknames for the most part only lasted for that incident, but Timmy Wimmy was 'way too cool to drop, and most of the guys continued to use it for a while, if for no other reason than to piss the lifers off. Eventually, calling Tim Rider Timmy Wimmy pretty much died out altogether—except with me. I kept it up because, like George W. Bush, I like and enjoy nicknames and have one myself: Rufus.

So there you have it: two men—with very low IQs, little talent, and few brains (one who avoided military service, the other who joined the Marines)—like nicknames. One becomes President and one becomes the author of a book.

Back to our story. When Timmy Wimmy—Mr. Wimmy to you—heard the laughter, he wanted to know what was so funny. I can assure you, there was little humor and little to laugh about in Vietnam, so laughter of any kind was rare. I read the letter to Tim and gave him the background to it, and he too laughed and thought it quite amusing, especially the absurdity of me being packed off to the States to pay a ticket. Pretty soon, the whole platoon was in on the news and quite excited over my good fortune. It's not often that being arrested and going to jail is considered a good omen, but, from our position, it sure was!

Among my fellow Marines, a great discussion and debate ensued—all about what I should do, what the best course of action for me would be. Everyone, to the man, agreed I should not pay the ticket under any circumstances. That led to the debate about what I ought to do if a superior officer *ordered* me to pay the fine.

All along, I had a sneaking suspicion that that was how the situation was going to play out: some superior officer would give me a direct order to pay my fine, and that would be the end of it. In fact, I felt it wouldn't even go that far. The District Court of Macomb County would simply have the military deduct the money from my pay and be done with it—probably without anyone even bothering to discuss the situation with me. As it was, I was now in a slave-like position, taking orders all the time from everyone. I was so low ranking that there was nobody really below me whom I could have ordered around even if I had an inclination to do so.

Once everyone in the platoon universally agreed that I would not pay the ticket but would voluntarily go to jail (the only one having second thoughts about that last part was *me*), the next big discussion took place, this one delineating all the better aspects and more favorable perqs of doing time in jail or prison. Somehow, everyone had made the leap from non-payment of ticket to jail time, thus getting out of the war and harm's way. Everyone else thought prison was a marvelous and ideal way to escape the harsh jungle conditions and cheat death itself.

Again, all this incarceration talk had me a bit unnerved. I really didn't want to go to jail! First, jail under any conditions didn't exactly fit my profile, personality, or values. Second, I was quite certain that going to jail would do little for future job prospects if and when I returned home. Third, as dumb and misguided, weird and twisted as it may now sound, at least as viewed in today's light, I was exactly where I wanted to be: serving my country honorably, not embarrassing myself and going to jail!

So, while everyone else was having a fabulous time discussing my future as a potential member of the U.S. penal system and extolling the pampered privileges and life style I no doubt would soon enjoy, the idea was not sounding so great to me. When I expressed my concerns, I was floored by the sheer number of my fellow Marines—who, prior to this, I had just assumed were everyday, average high-school graduates, like me, living in some suburb, city, or out on some farm—who now revealed their first-hand experience with incarceration!

I was beyond shocked.

For, while I may not have enjoyed any part of being a member of the military establishment and couldn't wait to get out—in fact, being a Marine revealed an essential truth about myself: I was born to be a civilian and couldn't wait to be one again—nevertheless, I still considered the American armed forces to be part of that pantheon of near-sacred intuitions that made us a nation: the flag, Mom, apple pie, democracy, freedom, and all that stuff. And here I was serving with a bunch of former hoodlums whom my country had sent overseas to win the hearts and minds of the people and make the world safe for democracy. What an eye opener for this altar boy who was still not swearing or drinking yet!

(Having been a public-school teacher for 41 years, I can help the reader understand my lack of cussing and carousing by using the appropriate pedagogical vocabulary: I was, and am, what is known in educational circles as a "slow learner." Before the fad for "political correctness" overwhelmed our country, the people who taught me had a different label for me: *retarded*. I can assure the reader that, despite my slow-learner status, I long ago overcame my former reluctance to curse

Longitude and Latitude, with Attitude

or imbibe. Having been a public-school teacher for 41 years, I do 'way too much of both.)

So a number of Marines started talking in glowing terms about the advantages of county jails over state prisons while the rest of us stood there in wide-eyed fascination. These guys who all had advice for me were the guys the Marine Corps had warned us about from day one—sea lawyers. "Sea lawyer" was the disparaging term for any Marine who had a less than a stellar record and was always giving unasked-for advice to other Marines about how to get out of assignments, how to break rules, and what their "rights" were. These characters now started advising me to choose to do county time over state time—as though I had some say in it and could pick what jail or prison to go to.

This unpaid traffic ticket was looking worse and worse with every subsequent statement. What had seemed like a half-hearted lark to get out of the war for a week or so was now looking more and more serious. It was a place I really didn't want to go to.

Just when I thought that it couldn't get any more absurd or ridiculous, Alfie, who hailed from North Carolina, took me aside and gave me some lifesaving advice on how to survive the rigors of a stretch in a county jail. I cannot remember now just exactly what that advice was, but, even then, it sounded pretty farfetched.

My gunner and friend, Corporal Tim Rider, aka Timmy Wimmy, saw the expression on my face and offered some non-criminal counsel to me: "You know, I'm not sure if you want to be listening to anybody who's been up the river—and especially not to the only person I know who has done jail time with his own father in the same cell." *Good advice*, I thought.

All the same, it was settled: Rufus would go to jail—and that was final! Pretty much everybody let me know that they were counting on me to do the right thing and escape this hell hole. If I didn't do it after receiving all this expert advice, the guys were surely going to be disappointed in me.

Still, I was certain that Rufus-as-jailbird was never going to happen. It was too outlandish. Besides, knowing my rotten luck, I would probably be blown up into a million pieces by some rocket or bomb before being lucky enough to escape the war in such a ludicrous manner.

*****

I became famous! This was just too good a story for a bunch of bored Marines to keep within a single platoon. This incredible story spread by word of mouth throughout the 5th Marines. Everyone was wishing me the best: that I would go to jail!

Once, another Marine unit, up in the mountains, was crossing through our position, and their point man asked the Marines in the first fighting hole they came up to, "Is this the outfit that has the dude going to jail over the speeding ticket?" (From beginning to end, everyone always got that part of the story wrong. They all thought it was a speeding ticket. After trying to correct guys the first hundred times, I finally just let it go; after all, the kind of ticket wasn't really important. It was the *principle* of the thing.)

The Marines in the fighting hole assured him that this was the very unit with the "lucky son of a bitch who was going to jail back home and get out of the war."

Of course, by this time, everyone was indulging vicariously in their own fantasies about my impending imprisonment. Now I was hearing about real sheets on jail bunks, three squares a day (not great, but better than cold C-rations), and family visits—even visits from your girlfriend! Unfortunately I didn't have a girlfriend.

It turned out that these other Marines wanted to meet me. I was called over, and, for the next twenty minutes, as an entire platoon of Marines passed through, each man shook my hand, patted me on the back, and declared, "We're rooting for you, man!" or "Best of luck, buddy!"—or else they gave me a big smile and said something like, "Man, oh, man! Some guys have all the luck." It really touched my heart. I had no idea so many people wanted to see me go to jail!

This adulation continued for a few more weeks until, one day, when I was cleaning the gun and the other Marines were going about their business of cleaning weapons and such, a sergeant ambled over and said, "McGaugh, the Captain wants to see you!"

This was not good. Something was wrong. I must have screwed up somewhere. It's just like school. You never go down to the assistant principal's office to receive a scholarship to Harvard or to be notified that you get to skip all your final exams. You go to the assistant principal because you messed up and are now in trouble. It's no different in the military.

Immediately, I tried to think of what mistake I could have made. I hadn't made any, as far as I could remember. Maybe it was a crime of omission: something I had forgotten to do. I drew a blank there also. Desperately, I silently appealed to all my buddies, giving them the "What's wrong?" look. They all shrugged. Nobody could think of a thing. The only thing we all knew for sure was that, when the Captain

Longitude and Latitude, with Attitude

wanted to see you, it wasn't to present you with the Medal of Honor or to inform you that you had been promoted to four-star general.

I checked my .45 pistol to make sure it was clean, then started walking to the Command Post—slowly, so I could stall and try to think what I might have done. Every time I passed a group of Marines, I would imploringly look to them for a clue as to what this was all about. They all shrugged; they had no idea. I could see many were a bit nervous for me.

I checked my .45 pistol a second time. (Keeping my .45 clean was the one thing I was a bit lax about, but it was fine and would pass inspection.) And then I was there, at the Command Post.

Captain Ford was very busy, talking on the radio, surrounded by a couple of senior NCOs (Non-commissioned officers), and signing some forms or papers.

Back then, there was a lot of animosity between the older, senior NCOs and the regular, lower-ranking Marines. Self-deprecatingly, because of the lack of respect or decent treatment we received, we called ourselves peons. That should give you an idea of what our condition was like. I knew the two NCOs would be of no help to me.

Our lieutenant was standing close to the Captain, scowling at me, but that meant nothing. I had served under some good officers in the Marines, but this jerk was not one of them. Everyone in the platoon despised our lieutenant, and no one had any respect for him. He returned the favor by showing no respect, courtesy, or even concern for the troops under him. The fact that he was scowling meant nothing; he was always scowling. This lieutenant was such a perverse character that he would have been angry even if I had been brought before the Captain for doing something good. (And I certainly couldn't think of anything great or good I had done that would make the Captain want to see me.)

I was not in a very comfortable spot at all.

I finally made eye contact with my last hope, our Navy corpsman, Doc, who was just one of the guys, and a good one at that. When none of the lifers were looking, Doc just shrugged that he didn't know what was going on. So I stood there in total discomfort, unable, for the life of me, to imagine what I could have done.

As I continued to stand there, I surreptitiously began making subtle moves to straighten out my uniform a bit. It had holes in it; it was filthy from the mud and animal shit of the rice paddies. I had not had a shower in probably two weeks. I needed a haircut and hadn't shaved in days. I looked like hell—just like everyone else. But I started standing at attention and doing everything I could to make myself a little more presentable.

Finally Captain Ford got off the radio. For a moment, he gazed at the horizon as if he were gathering his thoughts. Then he looked at me as if he had just noticed that I was standing before him. His face now took on a quizzical expression; he turned to one of the lifers and whispered. I am sure he was asking who in the hell this Marine standing before him was and why he was here in the first place. The NCO whispered something short in reply, and the Captain turned and faced me and gave me a good looking over.

By this time I was standing ramrod straight at attention, which no one ever did in Nam; this was not a parade ground. Captain Ford must have noticed how I was standing and said, "At ease, Marine." I let up a bit but was still standing pretty erect and straight, so the Captain repeated his order.

So this is how they talk to you before you go in front of the firing squad or are thrown in the brig, I thought.

Captain Ford said, "So you're the Marine who got the speeding ticket?" Like everyone else, he got it wrong. It was a ticket for an illegal right-hand turn on red, but his mischaracterization gave me an opening to perhaps weasel out of this predicament. I told the Captain, that I didn't know anything about a speeding ticket—which was kind of the truth.

The Captain held another whispered consultation with the NCO, then faced me again and amended, "You got *some* sort of ticket back in the States; is that right?"

I figured this was the time to stop playing cute or dumb because it would probably just piss the Captain off and make things worse. However, I acted as though the incident was such a long-ago event that it was hazy in my mind and the details were difficult to remember—despite the fact that it was all the other Marines and I had been talking about for months and a story that I or someone else had repeated at least a hundred times a day.

I knew what was coming next. My superior officer, Captain Ford, would give me a direct order to pay the ticket, and he would be done with this tiny, insignificant administrative matter in a minute or two so that he could go back to running an entire Company of Marines and fighting a war. I also think everybody standing there, me included, knew that I better pay that damn ticket or I would be digging fighting holes, burning shitters, and filling sand bags around the clock as punishment if I decided to get on my high horse and refuse to pay it. Defeat was looming before me; just one direct order, and this whole crazy fantasy of going home—well, to jail—and getting out of a war and sleeping on sheets with normal food was over.

Longitude and Latitude, with Attitude

"Have you really thought this through, Marine? Have you given any serious consideration as to what your actions might be?" the Captain asked. He was dead serious.

I was still hanging in there by a thread, trying to figure out some way to salvage my deluxe journey to a five-star county jail, when I replied, "Well, Sir, I figured I could pay that ticket when I get home." Then I laid it on really thick, trying to impress the Captain and still weasel out of this predicament by saying, "I have a far more important duty right now with my assignment here within the platoon, and I can take care of that ticket at a later date." I waited to see how that grandiose—or total-bullshit—story would fly.

The Captain walked toward me and said, "Son, I don't think you understand what the consequences could be!"

Son! Well that was something I wasn't expecting. That actually sounded pretty good and positive. The Captain continued, "What they're going to do is fly your ass off to a rear base, maybe even all the way to Da Nang, and then they'll bring out two, three officers, probably a major, maybe a colonel—nah, they won't bother with no colonel for the likes of you. Anyway, they'll surround you and scream and yell and demand you pay that ticket. Now, you listen to me, son! You don't back down—even to a colonel. You hold your ground. You're a Marine. You made it through Marine boot camp. You been through all kinds of shit over here, so you ain't afraid of nothing. You stand your ground—and go home!"

Holy shit! The Captain was on my side! Even the other lifers were smiling and laughing over the good news and my happily-ever-after fate. The lieutenant was still scowling, but he was a prick anyway.

Dismissed, I slowly walked back to my position with really mixed emotions. I guess most people would have been happy. I don't know about you, but getting imprisoned for a traffic infraction wasn't what I wanted to do. War or no war, no matter how bad the conditions were here, going to jail just didn't seem like the right thing to do, even if my commanding officer gave me a pass on it. I guess there are certain things I just don't want to do in life—lying, cheating, stealing, and going to jail, among them.

This situation had been on-going for months now, and I reached the conclusion then that it definitely wasn't going to end with me celebrating my "good luck" in a county jail. I was pretty sure I would finish my tour of duty before following any course of action that would result in jail time.

As I ambled back, everyone avoided eye contact with me and said nothing. Nobody wanted to be seen as a friend or accomplice of the trouble maker who had just been upbraided by the Captain. For, after all, if I was going to be sentenced to all kinds of shit details and any of these jobs needed *two* men, the lifers would surely assign one of my friends to accompany me. So everyone shied away from me; they all made themselves scarce.

I got back to my fighting hole, and even Timmy Wimmy ignored me—for a bit. Finally, with his back to me, and in a low voice, he asked, "What went down?"

I said, "You're not going to believe it. The Captain is on my side. He said not to pay the ticket."

Tim jumped up and cried, "You're bullshitting! He didn't say that!"

"Yes, he did."

Well, Tim was so excited and surprised and was making so much noise that pretty soon most of the platoon came over to our fighting hole to listen (with some disbelief) to the amazing news that the Captain backed the plan.

Everyone was now rejoicing and celebrating—Rufus was definitely going to jail! You would have thought I had won a multi-million-dollar lottery or a full scholarship to Harvard—and they needed me right now! Nope. This was better; I was going to jail—with the Captain's blessing!

*****

Eventually all the excitement died down, and we once again were caught up in the sheer drudgery and brutality of war and day-to-day existence in a very harsh terrain and climate. Days, and then weeks, slipped by, and my good fortune of potentially doing time back in the States was starting to look more and more like a pipe dream. Still, on those rare occasions when a chopper would actually fly mail out to our secluded mountain post, most of the Marines gathered around, hoping and looking for a couple of Marine MPs to cart me off for an all-inclusive vacation to the county jail.

On one such mail run, there were no MPs but a big backlog of correspondence that came our way. I had a number of letters, mostly from my family, especially my mom. The aftermath of mail call was always a quiet time, with everyone reading letters from family and loved ones and getting information about what was happening back home. I've always been a stander, so I was standing, opening my letters and reading, when suddenly —while perusing a letter from my mom—I said, "Fuck!"

Now, you might remember, since I mentioned it previously, I didn't swear—not at the time—not even *damn*s or *hell*s. It had nothing to do with religion or being moral. I had read an article while in junior college that swearing was a sign of a poor vocabulary—perhaps even low intelligence. As a person who was trying to improve himself and educate himself, and be one of the first in our family to have a college education, I took that article to heart. So I worked at not swearing.

When my gunner, Tim Rider, heard me utter that obscenity, he sat bolt upright. He knew something was up. He turned around to me and asked, "What's up? What's wrong?"

I said, "You're not going to believe this. My mom paid the ticket."

Shocked disbelief played over his face. "No! She didn't! Tell me she didn't!"

In her letter, my mom said that a letter from Macomb County had arrived at the house, demanding payment for the ticket. She described the letter as "very threatening," so, because she and my dad—and I love this part—didn't want me to get into trouble, they paid the ticket.

"*Get in trouble?*" (I may have said all of this aloud instead of just thinking it.) "Mom, I couldn't be in any more trouble, ever, than I am now. My small platoon of 40 or 50 Marines is surrounded by maybe two or three NVA divisions, which is something like 40- to 60-thousand hard-core fighters who want to kill me! And you're worried about a traffic ticket? And that I might get into trouble? Mom, it just can't get any worse! And now my ticket out of hell has just been cancelled because of the check you just turned over to some stupid District Court I've never heard of in Macomb County, Michigan! What a bust!"

Within minutes, every Marine in my platoon was at Guns' fighting hole. This was a crisis, an emergency! Some paced to and fro with nervous energy; others cursed. A few were attempting to salvage the situation, reverse this heinous deed by my parents. A number of Marines wanted me to walk over to the Command Post, request mast (i.e., speak to the Captain), tell him what had happened, and see if he could radio Da Nang to get word to the States to tell my parents to stop payment on that check.

That didn't sound very practical or reasonable. The deed was done. The horse was out of the stable, and I—and all my buddies—would just have to learn to accept it. It was a nice little story and fantasy while it lasted, but it was over and time to face reality and get on with our job. It was too good to be true, anyway, and too goofy to have ever worked.

Marines were patting me on the back and saying "Tough luck" and "Too bad." If you had been there, you would have thought that I just got news that my dad had had a heart attack or Grandma had passed away. I was actually nonchalant about it, so I really didn't need any cheering up or sympathy. To be honest with you, I was glad it turned out the way it did. I didn't want to go to jail. Even more importantly, I didn't want to do anything dishonorable or cowardly. Yes, I couldn't wait to get out of the Marines, and I had given up on this futile war long ago, but I wanted to honorably fulfill my duty, to do what I had signed on to do. I didn't want to get out of even a bad war, an immoral war, like a weasel. If all's fair in love and war, maybe all's fair in getting *out* of a war, but I didn't want to go that route. You can decide about the wisdom (or lack thereof) of such a stance, but that is how I felt then and still do now.

"Check sent; case closed" should mark the end of this particular story, except for what happened next. It might also explain why those of us who fought the Vietnam War referred to back home, to America, to anywhere but here as "the world." In conversation, we never, ever, said, "When I get back to Pennsylvania" or "When I get home" or "When I get back to the States." It was always "When I get back to 'the world'"— probably because of the *unworldly* environment we now lived in. Nothing was normal, civilized, cultured, decent, humane, or natural. The norm was the absurd: a booby trap blowing a leg off, green pus from your immersion foot, ears cut off the dead Viet Cong, corpses charred black by napalm, executions, and an alien culture no one could decipher. In perhaps the greatest ironic twist in warfare, past or present, the people we were trying to rescue, the Vietnamese, were the lethal and destructive engine that dropped us one by one.

So I was eventually standing apart, pretty much ignored by the rest of the guys as they continued to debate and lament my disastrous fate— that I would not be going to prison. For lack of a better term, I was in a contemplative mood. For the others, the mood up to now had been a "festive funeral mood": despite the sad circumstance, everyone had a positive attitude. Their feeling was something like this: "Well, we didn't get our buddy out of here, but who gives a fuck! It's good to still have him around, and we'll continue just as before. It don't mean nothing."

I'm not sure if I can even explain the expression "It don't mean nothing" as the Marines used it in Vietnam. It was a fatalistic utterance indicating that everything pretty much sucked, but we would, through sheer determination and guts, surmount it—a can-do attitude, if you would.

I was already missing the sheets on the county jail bunk. In about two hours I would lie down in the mud with a poncho over me, already sopping wet but somehow getting even wetter during the night. But it don't mean nothing.

That is exactly the mood I was in when suddenly I noticed things start to tense up a bit. The change was very subtle, but the volume of conversation dropped and a number of Marines had that look. Something

Longitude and Latitude, with Attitude

was up. Sideways glances and a few M16s coming up just ever so slightly.

Whatever it was, it was behind me. I turned slowly and casually—it was Ski.

Ski was a threat and a problem. To this day I don't know what his first name was. His last name was a long Polish name, so he was just Ski to the rest of us.

No one knew what to do about Ski. He wasn't just far out; he was *gone*—totally. I had met Ski my first day in, with Echo 2/5. He was acting as something of a Supply Sergeant. I was told to report to him for what I would need and did so. He was very quiet and said little. That was OK. I didn't join the Marines or go to Nam to make friends.

Somehow in that very short encounter it came out I was from Michigan. Ski was also from Michigan. In fact, he had been born and lived a pretty short distance from me. We spoke for a few minutes. Guys from the same state always latched on to each other for no other reason than it gave some semblance of home.

I then went back over to Guns and happened to mention that I had spoken with Ski, and you would have thought I had said I was the President's son or had previously lived on Mars. Up to this point, everyone had been civil but not friendly. No one wanted to get close to the new guy until he proved himself. No one wanted the emotional connection of another friendship that could shortly end in death. But I now had everybody's attention.

A number of questions were put to me about my conversation with Ski, and the guys seemed to be very intense in their interest. In fact, I started overhearing a lot of "Hey, Paul, or Hey, Mike, did you hear Ski talked to the new guy?"

This news would stop other Marines in their tracks. They wanted to hear every word. That day, in my new unit, I probably met a larger number of guys than usual—not because they were interested in *me* but rather in my conversation with Ski. Once they had gleaned everything they could from me about that exchange, they totally lost interest in me.

Let me give you a little background on Ski—on what he was like, what happened to him, before I got there.

Somewhere along the line, Ski lost it, totally. The war and combat broke him. By the time I joined the outfit, Ski was in a holding position. The Marines were in denial and had no idea at that time what to do with a totally psychotic and shell-shocked individual.

This was the Dark Ages of mental health. The Marines felt that, if they just isolated Ski from everything and everybody, they would run the clock out on his enlistment and then release him back into society, where he would no longer be their problem. The Marines were not eager and really had no stomach for medical discharges based on psychiatric problems, or dishonorable or bad-conduct discharges for Marines who had served and fought. They really didn't know what to do with these guys except wait 'til the end of their tour of duty and then dump them back on the streets of America. Until that time, Ski had been given a stress-free and easy job with no combat involved, and everyone hoped that would work.

Now, from what I gathered upon arriving, every Marine in the platoon thought that was bullshit. These guys might only have been high-school graduates or even dropouts, but they had enough common sense to know that Ski was a danger to himself and to others—that meant us. The word on the street—or again, in the rice paddy—was that Ski was nuts and was going to do something really bad, probably to himself—but, then again, he just might decide to take a whole bunch of others with him. To put it in the most crude and basic English, no one wanted a fucking nut case killing them in some rampage.

My first night with Echo 2/5 was spent within our perimeter. The other Marines were giving me a break and wanted to ease me in as slowly as possible. That night the Marine ambush had been successful, and a number of Viet Cong had been killed. Someone suggested cutting the ears off of the dead Viet Cong. That seemed like a wonderful idea to most of the Marines on that ambush. Problem: To the everlasting embarrassment of every Marine on that ambush, no one had a knife. What in the fuck kind of Marines were these guys with no knife, no famous Marine Ka-Bar, not even one of the cheap-ass bayonets the Marines issued us? We razzed and ribbed those guys about that for months.

Anyway, we all know that necessity is the mother of invention. These Marines opened a can of C-rations—they at least had a can opener!—and took the top lid and cut an ear off one of the Viet Cong, and I guess it was hard going amputating an ear with a lid of C-ration Ham and Lima Beans. Once the ear was off, no one was quite sure what to do with it now, so they brought it back to our position. As it turned out, Ski wanted it.

Now, Ski had a number of problems. Supposedly he had been accused of stabbing a Vietnamese villager to death, shooting a surrendering Viet Cong, and perhaps committing another murder. It was all very murky, and it wasn't as if Marine Legal was keeping us grunts abreast of what was going on.

So, anyway, Ski was now in possession of one Viet Cong ear. What was one to do with such an item? Ski certainly knew what a perfect gift it could be, so he melted down a candle and sealed the ear in wax and mailed it to his mother—yes, his mother. And it wasn't even Mothers' Day! What a guy!

Everything was going well until the wax seal broke. In San Francisco, postal authorities, using their noses and noticing the return address was a war zone in Vietnam, decided to take a gander and discovered the infamous ear. You would think that the Marines or someone in the Pentagon or some doctor or psychiatrist in the Navy might have been alarmed or perhaps even thought that this guy needed to be out of Vietnam and into a mental institution. No way! Ski stayed with us, but we became more and more wary of him.

So behind me comes Ski, ambling down the path toward us in his usual incoherent and very anti-social way. As more and more Marines began to notice him, there was more and more tension.

Ski continued forward, but of course he would speak to no one. The last time anyone remembered Ski speaking was to me on that first day. Since then, not a word. We were used to it. In fact, we probably preferred it that way.

Ski walked directly behind me where I couldn't see him without turning around. But I could feel his eyes on my back, and I knew how he was. His gaze was 'way beyond the thousand-yard stare. He looked and moved as if he were on drugs, but there were no drugs out here.

He stopped. More tension.

He spoke. For the first time in months.

Incredibly he spoke to the newest guy in the platoon, whose name I can't remember. He was a short guy with big glasses and an already receding hairline. He was nervous and very anxious to fit in. No one unfortunately was giving him the time of day, and he was pretty much being ignored. Sometimes we just knew. I'm not sure how, but we did. He never made it. A short time later, he was killed. I can't even remember how or any of the details—another guilt to lay on my mind.

Anyway, Ski looked at the new guy and asked, "What's going on?" The new guy, desperate for a friend or at least someone acknowledging his existence, gave Ski the 60-second version of the ticket story and the end result that my mom paid it.

Ski stood there in almost a drunken stupor, except there was no liquor where we were at, either. We were beyond the pale of civilization and mankind, period. He rocked and wavered a bit, almost trying to gain his balance, and, after hearing my story, said, "You know what I would do?"

The new guy, happy for any sort of discourse, said, "No, Ski. What would you do, Ski?"

"I'd blow that fucking bitch away."

Stunned silence. This was over the top even for a bunch of war-tested Marines. I mean we were talking about my mom, for Christ's sake!

No one directly looked at or stared at Ski—best not with a rabid dog—but the tension was now palpably thick. Because I could not see Ski behind me, my first thought was that maybe he was issuing some sort of macho challenge to see what I might say or do. I am not the toughest man on earth, but, having said that, I don't take any shit from anyone or back down from anyone.

So I began to turn toward my adversary, Ski, to see where he wanted to take this. If he wanted a fight, he would get one.

My Marine buddies, knowing what an idiot I was in such encounters, immediately started taking action. A good friend a short distance away saw me turn and told me, "You have nothing to prove; let it go." In front of me, a dozen buddies were now taking their safeties off their M16s and ever so slowly lifting them a bit.

I was doing nothing dramatic or brave, just turning around—and I was being covered by virtually every man in the Marine platoon—but turn I did. If Ski wanted a shit-kicking contest, I was not in the least cowed by him or his insanity.

Once I was facing him, it became obvious that he was not looking for a fight. He was in another world, or in his own world. He was in a very bad way. He could barely stand, and who knew where he was going by himself with an M16 when the rest of us would only ever leave the perimeter with a full squad armed to the teeth. Ski was no threat to me at the time.

I attempted to defuse the situation—if it even needed defusing—with humor. I said, "Well, you know Ski, my mom has been pretty good to me all these years, so I'll just let it go." There was a pause, and Ski responded without looking at me, staring off into the horizon, "Do what you like, but I'd blow her away."

"War is much too serious a matter to be entrusted to the military."
- Georges Clemenceau, World War I leader of France

"It costs ten to fifteen thousand lives to train a major general."
- Marshall Joffre, Commander-in-Chief of French forces in World War I

Longitude and Latitude, with Attitude

"As I slide down the banister of life, I'll always remember Vietnam as the splinter in my ass."
– Graffiti from Vietnam, 1970

Zippo Warfare (burning enemy hootches [huts] down). This was considered by some to be a war crime. When the television show "60 Minutes" aired a program on "zippo warfare" many Americans were shocked and dismayed and support for the war was further weakened.

Rufus McGaugh

Shot up in the Que Son Valley

It was about two weeks before Christmas, not that anyone in my entire platoon gave a shit. Just existing and surviving was about as much as anyone could gather strength to muster. I don't recall a single Marine even mentioning the word Christmas, let alone getting excited about it. Nothing would change; we would still be sent to vast jungles to patrol and engage in Search and Destroy missions in the Que Son Mountains of South Vietnam. We would patrol, set up night ambushes, and in the darkness of night wait in anticipation for the enemy to hurl themselves at our isolated positions.

For 20 or 30—sometimes 35—days, we would live like savages or prehistoric men with no sanitation, toilets, tents, sleeping bags, or decent rain gear. Every step we took carried a potential hazard—a land mine or booby trap. Every draw, cave, ridge, or ravine within the Que Son Mountains was one more spot for a deadly encounter with a cunning, well-armed, well-supplied enemy.

My fellow Marines were not depressed so much as listless and fatalistic; every one of them attempting to do their job, survive, and go home after their 13-month tour of duty. At the same time, anyone who saw us or spoke to us might have been surprised, almost shocked, by our optimism. Maybe it was "optimism in hindsight": We had survived every obstacle and hardship thrown our way, so, no matter how low morale sank, we retained a sense of achievement—we had lived another day. One Marine, years later, would describe our time in the Que Son Valley—"the booby-trap capital of the world"—as the Alamo with survivors.

It was December 11, 1970, and Echo 2/5, my unit, was in a very good position, relatively speaking. We were still in a war zone but back in a rear base—LZ (Landing Zone) Baldy, to be exact. At the rear, we had had our first shower in weeks, and a mess hall. The mess hall was flooded four-inches deep with stagnant water and served horrible food, but it *was* a mess hall. The office pogies (those lucky enough to have an office job in the rear) had stolen all the metal trays for their own personal use, so the grunts (infantry) were forced to tear up cardboard C-ration cases to use as trays.

I can assure you, from personal experience, that the watery beef, potatoes, beans and other unidentifiable objects, when placed on cardboard, do not float for long before drowning. One had to eat quickly, trying to keep the floating jumble of food *on* the collapsing cardboard

Longitude and Latitude, with Attitude

tray while at the same time making sure the waterlogged cardboard did not also become part of the meal.

The office pogies had also stolen all the glasses and cups. Now, the Marine Corps, using its institutional history (almost 200 years of putting Marines into combat and then feeding them), came up with an intriguing, unique plan to solve this problem.

Of course, the intelligent solution (even if one had no intelligence whatsoever, as was often the case with any number of Marine officers and senior NCO's) would have been to use simple common sense. All that some officer would have had to do would have been to order those thieving desk-warriors to surrender their stolen trays, glasses, cups, etc., and return them to the mess hall. Then Marine grunts (the ones who had actually been out in the bush engaging the enemy in hostile terrain instead of pushing paper behind the lines) would have had something to eat on instead of soggy cardboard. This solution would have meant that we also would have had something to drink out of instead of—are you ready for this?

To drink at the mess hall, we used, dirty, unwashed Coke and beer cans. This "solution" was actually ingenious, in its own sick way. At the mess-hall entrance, there were metal garbage cans that had never been used for real garbage. Instead, they held old, empty cans of Coke and beer. So, when we arrived at the mess hall, we simply grabbed one of these cans that had been used by countless other men but had never been washed. As gross and as disgusting as that might seem, at least we were then able to drink whatever beverage the mess hall served that day, whether it be milk, lemonade, or clean water.

Sitting down in the mess hall was always a gamble, especially during the monsoons, when it rained non-stop for months. With the monsoon rains, the water level in the mess hall started creeping up, from above-ankle height to sit-down-and-you-now-have-a-wet-butt level. So we sat or stood, wet or dry (mostly wet) and enjoyed our delectable meal of various floating objects (some of which, sadly, drowned on the soggy cardboard), which we ate with our fingers, jungle knives, and bayonets (yes: *bayonets*—because the fucking office pogies had stolen all the utensils, too).

Our last act, upon leaving the mess hall, was to toss the old, dirty, used beer can or Coke can into a row of garbage bins stationed at the exit. When these bins were full, the mess-hall workers would simply pick them up and cart them around to the front of the mess hall to begin the whole procedure all over again. (Hell, we were practicing recycling long before it caught on at home!)

As bad as all this sounds, it was universally accepted by every Marine in the Marine Corps, from the lowest private to the highest-ranking general, and universally believed to be a vast improvement over the much-hated and -despised canned C-rations that we had to eat while operating out in the bush (the jungles or rice paddies).

Most people reading this account (unless they've been in the armed forces in a combat zone) might consider these conditions—a cold shower once every three or four weeks and then meals at Café Marine (an eatery that carried zero Michelin stars but was unsurpassed when it came to negative stars, even by the enemy Viet Cong health inspector)—a case of roughing it, but we Marines always regarded these two days at the rear as R & R. (That's "rest and recuperation," in case you don't know. You can see why, after my tour of duty in Vietnam, *whatever* godforsaken lodging I stayed in—in whatever Third-World country—would have seemed like luxury accommodations.)

Perhaps I should also note that we were also in new clothes—well, not really *new*, but clothes that were not rotting off our bodies like the ones we had just discarded before heading to the showers. After being airlifted to this rear base, our bodies covered and smeared with three to four weeks of sweat, body odor, mud, and human and animal feces from the rice paddies, we were treated to a shower. Forty—sometimes 50—of us men, after arriving at our quarters, would strip naked. Our old clothes were so filthy and ripped—with some parts, such as sleeves and pant legs, outright missing—that they were burned.

Dysentery, diarrhea, and other intestinal diseases had many of the men in such a state that, while on patrol, they did not bother to pull over to go, but—while walking through the fetid rice paddies—just leaked liquid shit. Somehow, none of us ever wore underwear, sick or not—so that was one less item to soil or burn.

The clothing issue illustrated another interesting way the Marine Corps supply system operated. After our showers, we returned to the tents we were to sleep in. A jeep would arrive with a wagon loaded with clothing. The driver would dump the clothing, making a huge pile. Then 40 or 50 naked Marines would attempt to make order out of this chaos.

As I mentioned, the clothing was not new. Had it belonged to Marines who had rotated out of country? No one knew or really seemed to care. The shoddy, filthy rags we had been wearing were gone, to be replaced by uniforms that were, if not new, at least satisfactory.

Another strange aspect of this supply system was that these uniforms—what we called "utilities"—were all chaotically arranged without regard to size and with no attempt made to keep complete uniforms together. Shirts and pants of all different sizes were mixed in with odd bits and parts of esoteric military clothing, including sleeping shirts. ("Sleeping shirt" sounds like something Hugh Hefner of *Playboy* Magazine would wear in his palatial mansion, but, actually, it was a military sweatshirt to be used when you were sopping wet and soaked to the bone trying to sleep under a poncho.)

So we would go about our mission, trying to find a shirt and pants that were our size or close to it. Sometimes, if a buddy had an unusual size, such as extra-large, you might keep your eye open to help him out.

After all this time, I don't know if I should be outraged or make a sick, dark joke about it, but the most disturbing thing about this free-for-all clothes drive was when you would find a shirt with a massive, jagged hole in it, the periphery of which was covered in blood stains. I mean somebody had died in that shirt! And the Marines wanted one of us to wear this slightly used article of clothing!

The funny part about it—well, I guess you had to be there to enjoy the humor—was watching the reaction of most of the Marines. The Marines may be a macho group. They may be a tough group. But they definitely are a superstitious group. All these guys would walk a wide path around such a shirt. Basically, they would keep the distance one might use around someone with an especially bad case of leprosy. I like to say I'm afraid of nothing, but I have to admit those shirts would creep me out. I would find myself thinking, "Christ, that could have been any one of us—me included!"

You would think that, if you were in a war zone, you would be thinking about this issue a lot. Actually you don't. Personally, I think the longer we were exposed to combat, danger, and death, the more we became inured to it. I don't know of one Marine I served with who was cocky or over-confident. The danger and the number of people getting hurt, wounded, and killed had now just become a part of normal day life. This is how we lived.

Bottom line: this "back at the rear" was about as good as it got for a Marine grunt. It still sucked, but, considering the alternatives—which were all bad and sometimes led to people dying—it was not so awfully bad. We now had free time and were not directly in harm's way. This meant we could go back to the showers for our second, third, fourth, and sometimes fifth shower in a vain attempt to get the dirt, grime, mud, and fecal matter off and out of our bodies. We could get a haircut and a shave (since most of now looked like dirty, long-haired hippies with beards rather than a poster picture of what a Marine was supposed to look like). We could listen to music, read, get our packages from mom, and write letters to the girlfriends who were never going to wait for us despite the oaths and vows of fidelity they'd made when we had last seen them.

Best of all: beer—plenty of it and dirt cheap. The colonel bought us cases of beer; Captain Ford would buy us beer; our platoon commander bought us beer; and *we* bought us beer. I am writing this account 40 years later, and it is only now that I have become a true aficionado of beer—a connoisseur, if you will. And it almost brings tears to my eyes that, in my time of need, when people were actually trying to kill me, I was not a user of this wonderful beverage that just might have soothed me a bit and reconciled me to the fact that I was hated by every Vietnamese in both South and North Vietnam.

I am sure it was nothing personal on the part of the Vietnamese. Maybe it was because Richard Nixon was president and the Vietnamese hated him so much that killing me was the closest thing to killing him. (Rufus the surrogate Nixon.) Who knows?

Today, many years later, every single night of my life ends with me sitting on my deck, or down in the basement, or getting together with a group of friends at a bar, drinking beer—and nobody is even trying to kill me anymore! In my greatest time of need—when people *were* trying to kill me, all the time, and everywhere I went, I had not discovered—I did not appreciate—this nectar of the gods. I was still drinking Coke! There I was at the late age of 21 drinking Cokes!

It gets worse! I didn't smoke. I still went to church and believed in God. I didn't even swear! I was a complete fucking loser! (Now, when I look in a mirror and see this pessimistic, callous, cynical creature that my mom called Doll Boy, Father Rancourt at St. Leonard's Catholic Church called "Giggles, the Altar Boy," and the nuns called Smiley, I cringe. Whatever happened to that person?)

Big surprise here: I also didn't do drugs, not even marijuana. I used nothing to medicate the trauma of Nam. That's all right. I'm always trying to pass myself off as a hard ass, and I guess in some strange way I lived up to that image without the help of booze or drugs or anything else. I now feel my reward for that abstinence is to make up for lost time by drinking beer every night of my life, except on those rare occasions when my wife and I go to a nice Italian restaurant; then I just switch to red wine.

Unfortunately, not everyone in the Marine Corps was walking the straight and narrow as I was, and drugs were a big problem. They were actually easier to obtain than alcohol. And the time to do drugs was this down time. Every illegal drug known to mankind was here—cheap, and easy to get. I once watched a Marine use a needle and syringe to inject heroin into his head.

During these 24 hours or 48 hours of relative peace and some relaxation, most of my comrades were doing drugs or drinking. Some slept. Others withdrew into themselves. I read. Always a nerd!

The next morning would be boring, safe, and frustrating. We could stay at the rear but were not allowed to stray too far. Because, although this second day was described as a day of rest and recuperation, we were in standby mode; we had to be ready to perform as a quick-reaction force. We were not allowed out of sight of the Marine choppers sitting yards away from us. If any Marine unit, anywhere in our AO (Area of Operation) got into trouble or needed help, we would immediately enter into Operation Sparrow Hawk. That meant we were the cavalry that would ride out—fly out—to rescue a beleaguered unit.

If we were lucky, nobody got into trouble, and we rested. When we did get the call to action, more often than not, after hearing the Marine choppers coming in with more Marine grunts, Charlie—the Viet Cong—retreated. On a few occasions, we had been fired on by the retreating enemy, but, usually, upon landing, we had little to do other than to accept the gratitude of fellow Marines who had had a narrow escape.

Here I am on Hill 510, Que Son Mountains, Vietnam

Very late one R and R morning, we got the call that a besieged Marine Recon unit was in a hell of a fight and desperately needed help. We were on our way. We ran to our assigned choppers, loaded down with weapons and ammo. Three Marine choppers carrying about 15 Marines each were airborne in minutes. I was on the lead chopper as A-gunner to the machine gunner, Tim Rider (you remember him as Timmy Wimmy), one of my best friends. As usual, the longer the flight, the more nauseous I got.

I soon had other things to make me sick. First I heard the cacophony and noise of a gun battle below us. Then, suddenly, rifle and machine-gun rounds started whizzing through the thin skin of the chopper, peppering it with hundreds of holes. The pilot lurched the chopper from side to side as he descended, in an attempt to avoid the enemy fire.

Then even more rounds penetrated the chopper, miraculously missing everyone. As the enemy Viet Cong poured on more and more fire, the chopper abruptly changed direction, going back up, lopsidedly, throwing many Marines from their seats to the floor.

The pilot tried to bring the chopper down again, quickly, and we were hit unmercifully by heavy enemy fire.

Hundreds of rounds were now pouring into our chopper, leaving small jagged holes in the side of it. Many of us were trying to dodge or otherwise evade the barrage, but it was futile and useless.

We had become a giant target for the enemy. It's awfully damn hard to miss a big Marine chopper at relatively close range—especially if the pilot gives you chance after chance. And the pilot continued his insane tactic of lurching the chopper about as he attempted to land us in the midst of a frenzied fire fight.

This nightmare of a ride seemed to be never ending. The chopper was swaying, and then lurching, punctuated with bursts of acceleration in an attempt to get out of range of the worst of the barrage.

I had now served with these Marines for almost four months—a lifetime within the confines of war. I had never, ever, seen these guys panic, show fear, or lose it, but now even they had had enough of this pilot's stupid and ill-advised tactics. Nearly everyone was screaming "Up!" or "Get us down!" To a man, we either wanted to get on the ground to fight—or get the hell out of there. This middle ground—neither landing nor flying away—was suicide. We were figuratively sitting ducks waiting to be slaughtered without ever getting a shot off.

Finally, it looked as if we were going to land. All the Marines now turned toward the back cargo door of the chopper, weapons ready and safeties off, some screaming or bellowing, not in fear but in anger fed by uncontrollable adrenalin and testosterone.

Within the confines of this relatively cramped space, packed with 15 or 16 Marines, some now screaming in full-throttle rage, I saw an electric cord over my gunner's machine gun. I was not sure if he had noticed it; it would surely trip him, or worse yet, yank the machine gun out of his hands. With the noise of the chopper's blades and its turbulent motor, the door gunner blasting away with his 50-caliber machine gun, the pilot and co-pilot barking commands, the grunts howling in attack mode, and the thundering, piercing gunfire that was ripping our chopper apart, I knew Tim would never hear me. So I reached for the electric wire.

Just as I touched it, my entire body felt as if it had been electrocuted and hit by a Mack truck all at the same time. The hair on my head stood up while my toes stretched completely out.

Then I went flying.

Up and back I was flung, as I was struck by that invisible Mack truck. I hit my head, hard, on the upper reaches of the chopper, knocking my helmet off. From that height I slid down the chopper wall, as if in slow motion. To this day, I cannot explain the surreal, slow-motion part—that's just what I remember.

Then things speeded up. The chopper lurched once again, and my descent down the inside wall of the chopper was reversed: I was jarred upward again.

Then I tumbled down as the chopper simultaneously lurched up, and I came crashing down on my left knee agonizingly hard. An instant sharp pain radiated out of that joint in all directions.

As I cradled my left knee, the chopper jerked forward and down, and I fell backwards this time, striking the back of my head on the thickest and most heavily armored part of the chopper, the floor.

I was in a bad way but had not yet discovered the worst of it. My knee was swelling; the pain was great—but now I felt burning in that leg above the knee. Still lying on the floor, I pulled myself up enough to check what damage might have been done—and that's when I saw the real injury and the real damage.

I had shrapnel wounds down my ass, thigh, and leg all the way to the broken knee cap. The meat was missing where a number of holes had been scooped out of my ass, thigh, and leg.

From having nearly knocked my brains out when I flew up and hit the side of the chopper wall, I felt as if someone had hit my head with a sledge hammer. Now everything was spinning, and my vision was blurred and hazy.

"What the hell is going on?" I remember cloudily thinking. I understood the pain and had comprehended—even in my current condition, engulfed in the chaos of a fire fight—the severity of the shrapnel wounds, but the vision/focus problem was unfathomable. Everything around me was spinning, and this fucking, lurching, swaying chopper was not helping me to orient myself at all.

The chopper was now gyrating with a crazy swaying motion, side to side, as I attempted to see just how bad the shrapnel wounds were. Trying to sit up, I suddenly just collapsed like a stringed puppet, falling back, hitting my skull on the thick metal chopper floor again.

I felt as if I were going out—almost going to sleep. It felt very peaceful, as strange as that may sound.

And then I fought as I never fought before! I was passing out, and despite the piss-poor state I was in, there was no way I was going to let that happen. That would surely be a death sentence. We were crashing. There was no way this chopper was ever going to make it. And, when it did crash, I could not be passed out or unconscious.

Most chopper crashes I had witnessed ended with the chopper going up in flames. I did not want to burn to death. There are various ways to die, and being immolated was surely one of the ways that I did *not* want to die.

Even if there were no fire, I did not want to be in an exposed, helpless position, unconscious on the floor, so that, if the enemy invaded the chopper, they could come in and slit my throat.

I had to stay conscious. Passing out would make me a dead man. So I put all of my stamina and perseverance into that goal. I have great stamina and will power, and I was now putting forth every effort in my body and every ounce of self-control to keep alert and not go out.

I didn't make it.

I came to, confused—my blurred vision making me even more confused because, at first, due to that hazy vision, I did not even comprehend what was before me; I couldn't tell what I was looking at. (It was the ceiling of the chopper—something I had never bothered to look at or notice before.)

Just about when I figured it out and now remembered why I was sprawled on the floor of a chopper, the helicopter reeled back. The nose or the front of the chopper went up, and the tail or back end slanted down.

This movement caused a flow of blood covering the metal floor to rush toward me. I did not know at the time that two other Marines up ahead of me had also been shot up. I thought, "My God, this is all my blood!"—which was a real wakeup call.

For, if this *were* all my blood, I knew, from training, that I needed to get a tourniquet on my left leg, something I was not anxious to do under

Longitude and Latitude, with Attitude

any circumstances. We had been trained and warned to be very cautious and selective about the use of tourniquets, due to the fear that, if the tourniquet were left on too long, it would result in amputation. However, I didn't want to bleed to death, either.

In the chaos and pandemonium, I knew no one could help me, so I started to tug on my belt to remove it for a tourniquet. To this day I am not sure what stopped me, but I hesitated—probably because it was such a drastic action.

My left leg by now was completely numb. Worse, I couldn't move it; it just lay there, still attached to my body. Neither my mental commands nor instinctive physical motion could move my leg.

Finally, through sheer mental determination, I made that damn leg move. I stood up—weakly and awkwardly, but stand I did.

Through the shrapnel-hole wounds of my pants I could see some bleeding, but the red-hot-metal shrapnel that had torn and then penetrated my body had also cauterized many of the wounds. Although my leg, hip, and ass were oozing various colors of body fluids, red blood was only one of many. Surprisingly, even to me, I felt somehow I could go on. Besides, wherever my gunner, Tim, went, I—as his A-gunner—went with him. It was an unwritten, unbroken rule: that's what you did, unless you died.

I was wobbly. I was wounded, but I was ready to go, not out of any heroics but only because there didn't seem like a whole lot of other options.

There was another very important reason. By this time, I was already sick of Vietnam, war, the military in general, and the Marines in particular, but I had great loyalty to the guys I served with—where they went, I went.

After what seemed like an eternity, the chopper finally landed. We charged out, not only to engage the enemy but just to get out of that damn chopper.

As I exited the chopper, I passed the other two wounded Marines. They were sprawled across the floor, both with leg wounds like me. There was nothing we could do for them. They were on their own. We could only hope they were not injured too badly, or, if they were, that the chopper could get them medivac'd to a hospital in time. This situation was out of our hands. We had a more pressing and deadly mission to pursue at present.

The chopper had been somewhat dark, so the bright Vietnam sun was a shock to the eyes as we disembarked through the back of the chopper.

Enemy fire was now at its worst because now the Viet Cong had a huge ground-level target to pour the lead into. Each disembarking Marine was figuratively the fish in the barrel that the VC were shooting at. How could they miss?

The chopper was taking the brunt of it. I was just stepping out of the chopper when I was stung in the right hand—more shrapnel! It was not a horrible wound by any standards, but it stung badly. Considering my circumstances, I gave it little consideration.

To tell you the truth, I was surprised the fire fight was continuing. Usually by now, between us and the choppers, the Viet Cong would be retreating or gone.

From inside the chopper, all the enemy fire seemed to be coming from our left side. When I disembarked, my hand had been hit from the left. So, with my next step, I was already starting my own reconnaissance as to exactly where the enemy had positioned themselves. We would need this information to accurately return fire once we had set up our "360"—the circle we would form to face out to the enemy and fight.

Thus, with that next step, I turned to look left—and it was bad.

I could see many, many muzzle flashes—more than I had ever seen before—coming from the tree line.

There were a lot of VC out there, and, at this point, they weren't backing off. Even worse, as I scanned their position, I could see that their line of fire continued to stretch and stretch down the terrain. I kept turning and turning my neck, witnessing in near disbelief this incredibly long line of Viet Cong which seemed to stretch forever! I had never experienced so many of the enemy engaging us in a set-piece fire fight.

I got hit again. This time in the face. The weird part: I didn't get hit on the left side of my face, the side that faced the enemy fire, but on the right side, because I had been turning my neck so sharply that I had exposed that right side.

A hot piece of jagged-metal shrapnel cut into my right cheek. Again the wound had been instantly cauterized, so there was actually little blood. The bad news, however, was that I had a razor sharp shrapnel slice down the right side of my face. This wound was somewhat L shaped so that, as I ran to take cover, the flap of skin with the meat of my cheek attached kept flapping back and forth.

The fire fight now was not destined to last too long. Now that the grunts were on the ground, they could actually fight, and this changed the whole situation. We were now entrenched and were planning on going nowhere—other than forward. And that is just what we did. We killed and captured some enemy along with some weapons. In an unusual twist, we actually captured the communist anti-aircraft gun that had done such horrific work on our chopper and that had wounded me and the other two Marines.

"Extraction" by chopper in the Que Son Mts., South Vietnam.

After the smoke had cleared, I was medevac'd to a hospital, where I went through four weeks of being patched up and having shrapnel removed. About midway through my hospital stay, the doctors decided that any remaining shrapnel would cause more damage coming out than being left where it was—in me. That was fine with me until after I was discharged, when I later became a traveler.

The remaining metal shrapnel in my leg, knee, ass, hip, and thigh would cause me all kinds of grief going through the old airport metal detectors—especially in foreign countries. Of course, if you were on the other side, as a spectator, my predicament would have provided you with lots of cheap entertainment as I endured near sexual assault by security agents: hands up in the air, spread eagled, patted down, and cavity searched, all the while answering many, many curious questions posed by Security.

The gash on face, on my right cheek, was covered over with a big bandage at the hospital where my recovery took place, and, by Marine standards, that was good enough. However, you can well imagine that rough treatment like that would not do wonders for my face, especially for how it would end up looking (hint: not good). But the Marines had an answer for that, reminding me that I had joined the Marine Corps, not a beauty pageant. Even I had to admit that it wasn't much of a face to begin with. Nevertheless, at least prior to being wounded, I had no scar running down the right side of my face or a small lump of shrapnel protruding out of it.

Just a few years after I was discharged and back home, my face had to have medical attention and be operated on. The shrapnel left in my face had caused the lump to get bigger. The lump developed into a cyst, and then the cyst became inflamed and infected and oozing, so I bit the proverbial bullet and had surgery.

They fixed my face. Unfortunately there are many mean people out there who express shock when they learn that the face they are looking at has been "fixed"—as if to say, "And this is the best that they could do?"

Me, I hate to brag, but, after the surgery, I was once again the best-looking guy in the platoon. The other 40 or so Marines disagree, but you have no idea what an insecure and jealous group they are. If by chance you ever run into any of these guys and they don't immediately admit that I am the best-looking guy, don't believe any of them; they are also a bunch of awful liars.

The broken knee cap never healed correctly, causing me, to this day, much pain. The shrapnel did a lot of nerve and vein damage to the left leg, so, a few years after the face surgery, I had surgery on that leg to remove the veins that had been most damaged. Other than that, I am fit as a fiddle and one hell of a good-looking guy!

(My wife, her family, my family, and all our friends might tell you that I am not really good looking at all. In fact, all these people describe me as a goofy-looking Irishman. All I have to say is, "Who are you going to believe, all those liars, or me?")

War will exist until the distant day when the conscientious objector enjoys the same reputation and prestige as the warrior does today.
    – President John F Kennedy

Call it Peace or call it Treason
Call it Love or call it Reason
But I ain't marchin' anymore
    – Phil Ochs, American folk singer

Weapons are disastrous implements, no tools for a noble being. Only when he cannot do otherwise, does he make use of them.
    – Lao-tse, Chinese philosopher, 6th Century BC

Longitude and Latitude, with Attitude

Stand-down on Hill 34, May 1971. I was the machine gunner on the last Marine combat patrol in Vietnam. This picture shows the end of the patrol and the end of the Marine Corps' role in that very long and disastrous war.

Rufus McGaugh

Hong Kong Tailor

It was 1979, I had been a teacher for a few years—on crap wages, I might mention. My first year's salary was $8,496, less than half of what, according to the Census Bureau, was the median household income in Michigan ($19,223) at the time. For two years before I started teaching, I had been a struggling college student living in a Detroit ghetto, in a $50-a-month flophouse. This flophouse had the charming and somewhat upscale name of the Billinghurst Hotel, but a flophouse for transients and winos it was. Still, I survived; I was able to pay my tuition with an inflation-wracked and much-depreciated G. I. Bill and a part-time janitorial job.

I spent the two years before college in the Marine Corps, earning—after two promotions—$155 a month. During my 10 months in Vietnam, I earned an extra $65 a month in combat pay. As you can clearly see, I had not exactly set the capitalist world on fire with my earning ability. Then, through a quirk of fate, when it came time for my first real job after college, I chose just about the lowest-paying profession one could find.

The pay didn't matter so much. At that time, as now, I had no expensive tastes, hobbies, or activities—save one: travel. (And the summers off that teaching afforded allowed me to indulge in that activity.) Looking back over a long career of travel, I now realize I would have done much better and would have saved a lot of money if I instead had bought and maintained a yacht or developed a gambling addiction.

On January 1, 1979, President Jimmy Carter recognized communist China diplomatically. This meant that Americans for the first time in nearly half a century could travel to China—and I would be one of the first! Even before WWII, due to the Chinese civil war, this country had been closed to Americans. President Carter's new policy was a rapprochement between two enemies. The U.S. had aided the Nationalist side during China's civil war. When the Nationalists were defeated in 1949, the U.S. entered a Cold War with China. Just a few years later, communist China would enter the Korean War to fight against the U.S., nearly defeating U.S. and South Korean troops. Later, during the Vietnam War, China was a major backer and supplier to communist North Vietnam. So there had been very bad blood between the two countries.

In any case, that very summer, through Wayne State University, my old alma mater, I snagged one of the available slots for making a visit to this newly opened country. Being one of the first Americans in communist China was a rare and unique experience—but that story will come at another time. It's the Hong Kong part of the story I wish to relate to you presently.

The end of our two-week visit to the Forbidden Kingdom had us exiting China into British Hong Kong. At that point in my life, Hong Kong was pretty low down on my list of places to someday visit, mostly because Hong Kong then was not—and now still is not—a country. Back then, Hong Kong was simply a British colony or possession, and not a very big one at that.

As a British possession, Hong Kong consisted of one single city, a small peninsula (Kowloon), and a number of small islands. Even the history of this colony was deplorable; Britain gained it through the odious Opium War in the 1800s. If many Americans feel a special shame over the United States' role in its treatment of Native Americans or over the issue of slavery, Britain could quite well match that with its past treatment of China. Today we are accustomed to hearing or reading about the war on drugs. This war is fought to stop the making, supplying, and use of addictive drugs. The Opium War, fought from 1839 to 1842, was an act of oppression by Britain against China to enable British merchants to sell drugs to Chinese citizens. When the war ended in a British victory in 1842, China, weakened and defeated, not only had to allow the British to sell addictive opium to its people but was forced to cede Hong Kong to the British, eventually (in 1898) giving the United Kingdom a 99-year lease on the territory.

I knew the history of Hong Kong and knew it had a number of interesting attractions, but, since it wasn't a country, it wasn't a place I would go out of my way to visit. At that point in my travels, I had been to just over 50 countries, so that meant I had a long way to go to achieve my goal of seeing every country in the world. Colonies, islands, commonwealths, and dependencies would just have to wait.

As usual, I had done little research or reading about the places I would visit. That's just my way. I feel that, before I leave for any trip, I am reasonably knowledgeable about the country or countries I am planning to visit. I prefer to learn "on the job"—during the trip itself. And then, once I am home, I do my reading and research about all those people, places, and things that piqued my interest while I was traveling. From the little reading I had done about Hong Kong, I determined what I wanted to do when I was there: see Victoria Peak, get to any of the outer islands I could, and ride the Star Ferry through one of the greatest and most spectacular harbors in the world for the equivalent of a nickel.

Doing my research, I discovered something that would alter my plans and end up as the greatest shopping fiasco of my life. In a tour book that amazingly caught my eye, I stumbled onto something that had the potential to save me a lot of money and put an end to my days of looking like "Joe Shit, the ragman."

I feel I should give readers a little background about my wardrobe, attire, and total lack of fashion to help them understand the disastrous outcome of this story. I never really ever put any effort into dressing well. As long as I was wearing pants, a shirt, and shoes, I was ready to go. I couldn't care less if anything matched, went together, or was horribly out of date. My lack of concern about clothing had caused a number of middle-aged women teachers on the staff at my school to take a motherly interest in my scandalous attire—scandalous only because it was so bad.

A classic example of Rufus' Scandalous Attire was the ensemble I wore to school one day consisting of a pair of green pants and a white short-sleeve see-through shirt. Visible beneath that transparent white shirt was a green t-shirt—of a very different shade of green from the pants. As on previous occasions, a female staff member discreetly took me aside and very nicely informed me that I was once again making a fashion statement that no one else had ever made—nor *should* make.

One morning, I walked halfway to school before noticing that I had on one brown shoe and one black shoe. (My socks *never* matched.) I was able to go back home and remedy the situation. But, another time, I got all the way to school before noticing I had two different shoes on. That day, I just gutted it out and stood behind my desk all day so the kids wouldn't see the mistake and be laughing all class period.

I successfully managed to conceal my error that day, but the very next day I was greeted by student laughter—all of it directed at me, even though I was proudly shod in two shoes of the same color. My pupils even pointed to what they were laughing at, but I didn't get it. They started making jokes about my situation, and I still didn't get it. Eventually, the whole class joined in on the merriment at my expense, and I kept hearing the same word: *floods. Floods*? What was this all about?

Finally, one brazen student, pointing to my pants and laughing, asked me if I were expecting a flood. I looked down and noticed for the first time that my pant cuffs ended about an inch or two above my shoes. I remember thinking, *What's so bad about that?* until I noticed that not only all the boys but also all the male teachers had pants that were much longer, with cuffs that touched their shoes.

I looked at my pants yet again, reappraising the situation, and now estimated that they ended a little more than an inch or two above my shoes—maybe three! Not short enough for a flood but enough to go wading in.

The last straw occurred on Back-To-School Night, when I had to meet all the parents. I had never owned a suit in my life except my Holy Communion suit in second grade. As I got older, my parents had enough money for a sport coat for me for Easter, funerals, Confirmation, and other such events. I would wear my sport coat for two or three years before outgrowing it and looking ridiculous the last year. For Back-To School-Night of my rookie year of teaching, I wore my 9th-grade sports coat! The problem was, I had a gown a bit since 9th-grade—not a lot, but enough, especially in the arms. So that night proved to be a struggle for me. I stood in front of five classes of parents in my very tight sport coat—the color and pattern of which no one in America had seen for a long time—while I constantly tugged at the coat sleeves in a vain attempt to cover my very exposed shirt sleeves.

Now it wasn't just the female faculty and staff who discreetly admonished me. Even their male counterparts diplomatically suggested that, now that I was teaching in a good school system in an upscale community, it would probably be a good idea to break down and spend a few bucks on a suit.

The article I had read mentioned that the best place on earth to buy a suit—if one were not independently wealthy—was Hong Kong. The same quality, designs, materials, and craftsmanship that could be obtained in the custom tailor shops of London, New York, and Milan could be had for a fraction of the price in Hong Kong. At the time, Hong Kong had 5,000 tailors in the city, and there were three or four tailor shops on every block.

So I hatched my plan. I would drain my bank account and buy a decent suit in Hong Kong. Further reading revealed that it would take two days for the fittings. Perfect! The Hong Kong part of the trip was scheduled for three days. That would give me two days for the suit and one day to run around like a maniac and see and do everything there was to see and do in Hong Kong.

When I told my dad about my plans, he reached into his wallet and gave me sixty dollars, saying, "Here, add this to what you are taking and buy a good suit!" This was the first time my dad had ever given me any money other than what he'd given when I was a little kid for ice cream or something like that. Like I said, we—the family—didn't have a lot of money.

I was pretty touched by this action and said I would pay him back or might not even need it, but he brushed me off and told me to just get a good suit. So now I was on a mission.

Once we arrived in Hong Kong, after two fascinating weeks in China, I immediately put my plan into action. We got to the city late at night, so I hit the hay right away in order to get up at the crack of dawn to make an epic one-day tour of Hong Kong. I accomplished everything that I wanted to do, saw everything I wanted to see that day, and returned to my hotel after midnight, hot and exhausted. I skipped eating and went to bed.

The next morning I again arose at first light and took to the streets of the city, hell-bent on getting a tailor-made suit. Amazingly all the shops had their doors open for business at 5:00 a.m.! Having no idea as to which particular shop I should give my business to, I ambled into the very first one I came to. After receiving a very formal greeting, including a very dramatic bow, from the man who appeared to be the tailor/owner, I was informed that, unfortunately, a fitting for a suit took *three* days. Making a dramatic bow of my own, I left, assuming this guy was not the typical fast-paced tailor who could do the job in the usual two days.

But I got this same message in tailor shop after tailor shop.

After visiting nearly a dozen tailor shops and receiving the exact same message in all of them (that a tailor-made suit would take three days), I was flabbergasted. Something was wrong—and, unfortunately, what was wrong was the information in the tour book I had read about buying a suit in Hong Kong.

Persistent as always (family and friends like to use the word *stubborn*), I forged ahead to perhaps find the one tailor in Hong Kong who would put a suit together in two days.

A few shops later, it was starting to sink in that I was on a futile expedition. I decided to make one last attempt and, if that did not succeed, to drop it and just buy a suit when I got home.

I walked into yet another Hong Kong tailor shop, which looked no different than the others I had already been to, and was greeted by the proprietor, a Mr. Yang. As had all the other proprietors, he bowed ceremoniously as I entered his storefront shop. And just as the others had, before we engaged in any conversations, he insisted we introduce ourselves first, which I thought was a bit formal. But, when in Rome...

This might just be the time to mention that Mr. Yang, like all the other Chinese tailors, was having a hard time pronouncing my name. Those of you who have not traveled through East Asia (or seen Asians portrayed in movies) may not know that many Asian people have a difficult time making the "R" sound, especially if they learned English as an adult. Some simply skip *R*'s, but most replace the R sound with an "L" sound. This replacement causes some humorous spellings and pronunciations. (While traveling through East Asia, I once saw a business in Bangkok, Thailand, named "Moon Liver" after the American song "Moon *R*iver.")

Long before this trip, I had given up trying to get people in this area of the world to correctly pronounce my name. For the last two weeks I had grown accustomed to being "Lufus" rather than Rufus. I was not too happy about it (after all, not only does "Lufus" sound ridiculous but it is also 'way too close, phonetically, to "loser"), but no one meant me any ill will by it, nor was there anything I could do about it.

The conversation with Mr. Yang was proceeding as all the others had: he could not—even with the help of the other two tailors in his shop—make a suit for me in two days. I thanked Mr. Yang for his time, turned, and started on my way out. That is when Mr. Yang halted my departure. "Lufus! Lufus, don't leave! We may not have enough time to make you a custom-made suit, but we could make you a tailor-made shirt!"

Believe it or not, Mr. Yang actually caught my attention with that proposal, which was just short of a miracle, considering that I am the sort of person who would normally never spend a nickel on clothing or even have any interest in clothing outside of that elusive suit I couldn't get. Due to the ever-present state of my poor finances, my first question of course was, "How much?"

"We could make you very nice shirt for $22, Lufus," Mr. Yang answered.

Now, if you think about it, even back in 1979, $22 for a custom-made shirt by a professional tailor was not a bad price. And I had, up to that minute, been ready to spend as much as $175 on a suit. But now I was going to have to go back to the States and spend that amount there. I didn't have cash to throw away on a shirt. After all, a suit is a suit, and a shirt is a shirt. Upon hearing the price, I almost had a heart attack right on the floor of that tailor shop. "Twenty-two dollars!" I exclaimed loudly. "I could buy four shirts for that price at Kmart!"

"Kmart?" Mr. Yang quizzically inquired. "I do not know Kmart. What is Kmart"?

"The greatest store on earth," I replied. "It's where I buy everything."

"Well, Lufus, I don't know this Kmart, but the price I give you is of course for the finest cloth. Perhaps we could use a lesser-priced material and lower the price."

I was all for that. I had actually gotten my hopes up and was thinking that it would be pretty cool to come back home and start strutting around in a custom-made shirt and just happen to casually mention to people that it was professionally made in Hong Kong. I would finally have something in the way of clothing to brag about.

I spent the next 20 minutes or so with Mr. Yang as he showed me different materials and fabrics. One was $18, another $16, and finally one was $12. Sadly and embarrassingly, a $12 custom-made shirt by a professional tailor was still out of my price range, or at least more than what this cheapskate was going to pay. But Mr. Yang was not budging on the $12; that was as low as he was going to go.

I don't give up on anything easily, so I didn't leave. I was thinking, or perhaps plotting, when I spotted it. Over against the back wall were three huge rolls or bolts of cloth in three different colors. The material looked like cheaper cloth. I walked back to the big rolls and turned to Mr. Yang and asked, "How much would a shirt made of this cloth cost me?"

Mr. Yang at first stood as though bolted to the floor, and said nothing. Then confusion washed over his face and finally he started laughing uproariously. "Lufus, that cloth is 100% polyester. Nobody wear that garbage anymore!"

Well, maybe—then again, maybe not; it might just depend on what the price was, which is exactly what I asked Mr. Yang.

Mr. Yang, before answering, looked horrified. "Lufus, nobody wear 100% polyester anymore. I know you very cheap, but, please, just a dollar or two more, and we make you nice shirt."

"How much?" I asked, not budging from the giant rolls of cloth.

"Lufus, don't do this; shirt will not look good!"

Again: "How much, Mr. Yang?"

Finally he gave me a price: $10. I countered with $4. Mr. Yang said $8 was as low as he could go. I explained that, on my budget, I couldn't go over $5. Mr. Yang pleaded with me, saying, "Lufus, I know you very cheap man, but, please, I need for bottom price, $7."

We agreed on $6.

Now, all we needed to do was choose a color from one of the three big rolls of cloth: brown, blue, or green. I chose the 100%-polyester blue for my custom-fitted, tailor-made shirt.

Next on the agenda was the tailoring, which was actually pretty neat. Mr. Yang had one of his backroom tailors come out with a cloth measuring tape. He measured my neck, stomach, arms, biceps—the whole nine yards.

All the while I was being measured, I was thinking, *One shirt would be fine, but two shirts would be even better! I mean, you can't wear the same shirt to work every day if you want to show off and brag. Plus, there just might be another deal in all of this that could work to my advantage.*

As his assistant measured, I asked the proprietor, "Mr. Yang, if I were to order two shirts, what kind of deal would you give me?"

Mr. Yang stood there totally expressionless, but I could sense the gears turning in his head. Mr. Yang was a cagey character, yet he knew he was up against a formidable adversary when it came to bargaining and negotiating. There was silence, and Mr. Yang, surely realizing there was little wiggle room, said, "Six dollars also for second shirt." I countered with five. Mr. Yang said that, because I was such a nice person and such a good customer, "Lufus, you get special rate only for you: $5.50 for second shirt."

I was in my killer bargaining mode now, and was going for the jugular. Five bucks or cancel the second shirt was my final offer.

Now this is where it gets truly embarrassing. Two grown men entered into intense and harsh negotiations over fifty cents, with neither giving any quarter (ha-ha) or mercy to the other.

After much haggling we finally agreed on $11 for the pair—$6 for the first and $5 for the second (or $5.50 apiece, whichever allowed Mr. Yang to save face; I didn't care). I had won! My superior negotiating skills gave me the supreme victory in the fifty-cent negotiations. Why was I not on Wall Street? I am sure that, to this day, the lowest episode of finance to ever besmirch the reputation of the financial hub of Hong Kong was the day I walked away with my four-bit victory. Let's hear it for capitalism and American exceptionalism! Let economic freedom and unfettered free markets ring forth through the world!

Anyway, I picked another material—this time, brown—and sealed the deal with a handshake: two custom-fitted, tailor-made shirts of 100% polyester for the price of $11, to be paid in Hong Kong currency. Mr. Yang, now all smiles after the intense negotiations, was effusive. How this guy could still be making a profit baffled me, to say the least. I was wondering if he had a trick up his sleeve or might even be up to no good. But, then again, what sort of scam can you pull off involving $11, fifty cents, polyester, and two shirts? Mr. Yang, as he shook my hand for the sixth or seventh time, said my two shirts would be ready early next morning.

I left the shop feeling somewhat consoled. I would not get a suit, but I could get one when I got home. Even better, maybe, I would have two snazzy, well-fitted shirts that I would be able to wear much more often than a suit. Things were looking up.

There was another bonus to all this, too. The entire transaction at the tailor shop had taken a little more than an hour. I now had another full day to explore Hong Kong. I headed back to my hotel to consult my tour book and maps. I grabbed my key at the hotel desk and took the elevator 'way up to my room, where I had a great view of the city. Like most hotels and office buildings in Hong Kong, my hotel was a tall skyscraper, and I was up somewhere around the 30th floor.

I got to my room, put the key in the door, and, as soon as I walked in, my room phone started to ring.

This was very unusual. Back in 1979, cell phones did not exist, and calling overseas was expensive and difficult. I knew absolutely no one in Hong Kong, and absolutely no one back in the States knew where I was. Well, certainly, no one knew what hotel I might be in. This was very perplexing.

I walked over to my phone, picked it up, and said hello. Someone on the other end of the phone was speaking to me, but his Chinese accent made him difficult to understand over a mechanical device. Finally I said, "I'm sorry. Who is this speaking?"

"Lufus, this is your tailor, Mr. Yang!"

Now, that was really strange! Why would the tailor be calling me? I said, "Mr. Yang, what can I do for you?"

"Lufus, because you such nice man, and long-time good customer, I have special deal for you!" Long-time customer? I just met the man an hour-and-a-half ago!

Cautiously I asked what this "deal" was.

"I put monogram on your shirts, if you like, Lufus."

What did this guy think I was, the biggest chump on Earth? So I let loose on Mr. Yang. "Oh, no, you don't! I wasn't born yesterday, you know. We have a deal: two shirts for $11, and that's final. I'm not paying one extra cent—got it?"

"Lufus, Lufus, calm down before you have heart attack," Mr. Yang pleaded. "Monograms are"—and because he could not make an r sound—"fee." This now only added to the linguistic confusion.

"You mean the monograms would be *free*?" I asked.

"Yes: *fee*," he said.

Well, linguistically this was going nowhere. So I tried another approach. "In other words, no more money for a monogram, correct?"

"Yes, Lufus, that is exactly what I said."

Well this was a new, nice little twist. Just think, I would be strutting about school and the neighborhood not only in a custom-fitted, tailor-

[45]

made shirt, but one that was *monogrammed* too! So I said, "Sure. That sounds great."

Mr. Yang's next question was, "Lufus, what name you want monogram of on shirt, first name or last name?"

Well, that was easy. Over the years, I had pretty much lost my first name (Donald) and my last name (McGaugh—check the title page of this book) to my nickname, Rufus. I had picked up that nickname when I was nine or ten years old and my goofy adolescent friends and I were giving each other monikers such as Rufus, Dufus, Goofus, Pervie, Dirty Al, and Peahead.

At the time, we thought those names were hilarious. The unfathomable part is that those nicknames stuck, and we still go by those names to this day! Whenever someone smirks at my nickname, Rufus, I always counter with, "Well it could be worse. You could be calling me Dufus or Peahead right now."

Hardly anyone called me by my first name, Don, and most students and their parents were completely unaware of my last name. The entire school community, kids included, knew me as, and called me, "Rufus." So no big surprise when I told Mr. Yang, to use the only first name I had given him, Rufus. Mr. Yang's next words would live with me (as I write this, it's been almost four decades now)—sometimes in the way of sweaty nightmares. "Okay, Lufus, we use first name."

Click. Even at the moment, I sensed that something was wrong.

Certainly, something was not right, but I couldn't put my finger on it. The entire rest of the day, as I used ferries to go to other islands, I kept getting flashes of a premonition that something (the best-laid plans of mice and Rufus) was going to go awry.

As usual, I came back to the hotel after midnight, exhausted from that day's excursions. Late the next morning (so as not to seem too eager), I arrived at Mr. Yang's tailor shop. When I entered the shop, Mr. Yang—bowing gracefully, all smiles—shook my hand. Turning to the back room, he issued a command to bring forth the newly created tailor-made shirts.

One of the workers stepped out with two shirts, one blue and one brown, on brand-new hangers, walked toward me, and bowed. He then stood erect with one shirt in each hand while Mr. Yang continued to make small talk, which was distracting me. I was trying to pay attention to Mr. Yang for politeness' sake, but I also was attempting to inspect these two shirts to see if Mr. Yang was literally trying to pull the wool (or, in this case, the polyester) over my eyes.

I kept inspecting the shirts, and everything seemed okay. Mr. Yang asked if I was satisfied, and, just as I started to answer in the affirmative, I saw it! I couldn't believe it! How could these idiots have done this to my brand-new tailor-made shirts? But there it was; there was no getting around it. Closer inspection only made matters worse. This flub was something that could not even be corrected or somehow hidden.

There, prominently on the left shoulder of both shirts was a finely stitched monogram of the letter "L."

I was now the proud owner of the only two "Lufus" shirts in the world.

For the next 30 years, I would wear them to school when teaching the Hong Kong unit and tell this very same story to my 7th graders, which would result in the best laugh on a teacher they would ever have in their lives (better than when I wore "flood" pants). The two "Lufus" shirts and the story behind them would become near legendary within my community.

Tacos and Nude Women in Texas

Easter of 1982, four of us headed out to do a backpacking trip in Big Bend National Park in Texas.

As usual, on the last day of school, I bolted out the school door and barreled my way down the freeways to get to Chicago, where my three companions lived. Without much more than a "Hi," I jumped into Bruno's van with my backpack and equipment. We would now take turns around the steering wheel of the van for the next 20 to 22 hours, driving non-stop, to reach our destination: Big Bend National Park in southern Texas.

Surprisingly, this year's site had been my idea. Usually it was Mark or Bruno who did some research and then picked out what they hoped would be a unique and beautiful area to pack 'way back in for some great natural beauty. One of the reasons I had decided on Big Bend National Park was that my reading (in the days before the internet) had led me to believe that we could backpack and then canoe the Rio Grande River on this same trip. Besides backpacking, we were all avid canoeists.

Once we got to Texas, we discovered that canoe-rental establishments were not very available, unlike Michigan where they are plentiful. The stretch of the Rio Grande on which we could canoe wasn't very long, so we just gave up on that part once we arrived.

No canoeing turned out to be the first disappointment we suffered after making that killer drive to southern Texas. Then another blow was dropped on us.

Big Bend, Texas, is, of course, nothing like Michigan. Michigan is the "Great Lakes" state. These Great Lakes contain one fifth of all the fresh water on planet Earth. Inland streams, rivers, lakes, ponds, and wetlands abound from one end of the state's two peninsulas to the other. If that were not enough water for all of God's living creatures, He did his best to often soak us in downpours of rain or snow. We definitely have water in Michigan! But Texas has dust. Lots and lots of it.

They gave us this disappointing news at the ranger station—preparing us, I guess for the *next* discouraging piece of information: There was no way in hell—which, by the way, is four degrees cooler than Big Bend at this time of year—that we could hike or backpack for six or seven days across Big Bend, which is desert and semi-desert land, without stashing water along the route. We were not pleased about this, but there seemed to be no alternatives.

The rangers advised us that we would need to carry great quantities of water, and water—in case you didn't know it—is very heavy, especially when there's a lot of it and it's on your back while you're traipsing across deserts and climbing mountains in Texas right at the Mexican border. Also we would need to use our maps and compass to find and locate those few spots where water dripped out of the rock. If we did that, we would be able to make it!

It took a while, but we managed to stash water along the worst of the trail and then began our expedition. Our route had us immediately heading straight up, ascending two mountains to gain our desired elevation and keep us on our planned path. Each night we would place our empty canteens and water bottles under dripping rocks to refill them. After we set up camp each night, it would take hours for all the canteens to fill with water. And you had to be attentive to the process, watching for one canteen to fill and then replacing it with the next empty one. Since we carried an average of three canteens apiece, that was twelve canteens we had to fill each night!

On our second day, we had to ascend yet another mountain. It was tough—and, again, pretty much straight up—but the amazing view was worth it. Across from us, cliffs presented a panorama of dazzling colors: red, orange, yellow, pink. They were so beautiful that we decided to make camp and spend the remaining daylight hours taking in the sensuous pleasure of this rainbow of rock colors. All of us were transfixed, standing before this brilliant edifice. Every few minutes, the position of the setting sun would change and enhance the color scene before us—a theater built by God!

I was quite content with what Mother Nature and God had created, but the other three felt some improvement was needed. The device used to enhance what the Almighty had designed was mushrooms. I am not referring to the mushrooms you and I might have on our pizza or the ones you might happen to find in a Campbell's soup can. I am talking about hallucinogenic mushrooms, the kind that make you kind of weird.

You have to remember that my traveling companions were a bit younger than me and had learned the joys and attributes of hallucinogenic drugs when they were about three or four years old. Whenever backpacking, canoeing, or skiing with these guys, I always felt I was the nanny, or the school teacher that I was, to these young, twenty-something juvenile delinquents.

Canoeing was always the best, providing the rest of the crew with fabulous entertainment. After a long, hot day paddling through the snags and obstructions of a swift Michigan river, it didn't get much better than to see Mark and Bruno canoeing backwards, attempting to paddle against the current to go upriver—all thanks to the miraculous mushrooms they had ingested.

So, what God could not do, or did not care to do, Mark, Bruno, and Matt would: improve on Big Bend.

For the life of me I can't see how anyone can even get mushrooms down. Hallucinogenic mushrooms grow only in cow or horse manure—not real soil or dirt, but animal shit! To say the mushrooms pick up that aroma is an understatement. When you open up a plastic bag of hallucinogenic mushrooms, you are suddenly transported to the Kentucky Derby—the stables. And this is even before you ingest them and get high!

To gag this lovely essence-producing concoction down, the boys used Kool-Aid, mixed into our precious and limited supply of water. And there they sat, for some time, admiring one of the most beautiful sights America has to offer, giggling and sometimes, after losing their ever fragile balance, falling backwards to the ground, only to find that mishap quite perplexing and amusing.

The final insult to my intelligence as this nonsense proceeded was for the three of them to implore me with the impeccable logic that comes from eating mind-altering substances, "Rufus, come and do some mushrooms with us; it makes the scenery beautiful."

I called back to them that, from my perspective, they were idiots! It was already beautiful without hallucinating. I might go so far as to say that, in my opinion, God had done a pretty good job on this sight, and it needed no artificial improvement or enhancement.

Despite having three mushroom-induced goofs as companions, I did have a great time seeing some very spectacular and beautiful country. Toward the end of this backpacking trip in which we had not seen one other person for a week, the trail passed alongside the Rio Grande River, which is the border between Texas and Mexico. At that juncture, the Rio Grande was very low and could have easily been crossed or forded on foot.

It was also at that juncture that we spotted some Mexicans on the other side of the river. The Mexicans got our attention and hollered something over the river, but we couldn't make out what they were saying. So the Mexicans walked across the river to us.

There was a Mexican village on the other side of the river, they told us—much to our surprise—but it was out of sight, hidden by the mountains. It was very close, they said, and they would like us to visit. None of us were too interested until they mentioned that the town had a little restaurant where a Mexican woman made great homemade tacos.

After eating freeze-dried food, jerky, and crackers for a week, that didn't sound too bad. Then the Mexicans played their four aces: there was also a bar that had *cerveza*—beer! That sealed the deal and we were ready to emigrate to Mexico before it became so fashionable to go the other way. It was truly amazing how this was turning into an all-inclusive vacation.

Just then, four Mexican men with donkeys appeared and wanted to ferry us across the shallow Rio Grande. For fifty cents, we could keep our feet and boots dry. Everyone thought this a perfect idea, but me. Now just put aside how cheap I am—guilty: I'm a guy who likes to hold on to his quarters. Also, ignore the fact (as I did) that I was a Vietnam vet who had put up with and suffered from a year's worth of wet feet in rice paddies and monsoons: I'm a guy who can stand to get his feet wet without complaining about a little water. No, simply consider that this situation offered me the chance for some payback on these clowns who for years had been calling me "Joe Shit, the ragman" because of my sloppy old clothing and my beat-up backpack and equipment.

My companions were all wearing expensive, waterproof Gore-Tex boots while I stood there in my $22 Kmart Blue Light Special boots. So I let them know what a bunch of sissies, punks, and wussies they were. I called their manhood into question and had quite a good time doing it.

As they mounted the donkeys and then started to cross the river, I had to get a few more jabs in. "Hey, you jackasses on the Mexican asses over there," I shouted from my side of the river, "make sure you lift up your footsie wootsies so they don't dangle in the river and wash all the softener out of your girlie socks."

I was having a great time giving those guys hell. As I prepared to wade across the river—like a *real* man—I noticed something: the fourth Mexican. He was older, and, just by looking at him, you could see he had had a hard life. He was standing next to his donkey, looking forlorn with no fifty cents coming his way. *Damn!* I knew what had to be done, but I had to be sneaky about it after all the hell I had given those guys.

When the poor Mexican man asked me again if I wanted to ride the donkey across the river, I said yes but stalled. There was no way I was going to let those guys see me crossing the river on a donkey after all the insults I had just laid on them.

Eventually, I got on the donkey and crossed the river, saving my Kmart boots the indignity of getting wet. I got off the donkey before we quite finished the very short distance to the town, hoping the others would not notice my nice dry boots. The Mexican man held his hand out for the fifty cents, and I gave him a dollar. He asked if that was for the return trip back to Texas. I said, "Naw, I'll just walk across the river. You don't have to hang around." He was happy with that.

Longitude and Latitude, with Attitude

When I reached the village, I didn't see the other guys anywhere. People noticed how I was looking around, and, probably because this little town never gets any visitors (I understand that the last tourist here was Cortes in 1519), were able to figure out who I was looking for and to point me in the right direction.

The restaurant was actually a very tiny patio attached to a very small and poor house. The Mexican lady running this operation was all hustle and bustle, charm and friendliness. On the patio she had a small card table with folding legs that would seat four people, which was fine for us, as we had brought no guests along other than the donkeys.

The thing I admire and respect in my friends is that they all have their priorities straight—even when they are on mushrooms! The first order of business for us four dirty, stinky, smelly backpackers who had survived seven days on freeze-dried food and crackers was to take care of our thirst. We used the one single Spanish word in our vocabulary that we knew or cared about, *cerveza* (beer). But then the ground gave way beneath us and a thunderbolt was hurled from above with the placid announcement that there was no beer here! How could this apparently nice lady, who had seemed so wonderful just moments before, stand there with a smile on her face and deliver such news to us?

We now seriously considered murdering the Mexicans who had lied to us about getting beer over here. Our thought was that any beer-drinking jury on either side of the border would acquit us. The Mexican woman now started to become a bit concerned and alarmed. I guess she had never seen four grown men sobbing and crying uncontrollably. She quickly put an end to this scene with the news that the building across the road was actually a bar. It certainly didn't look like a bar! We immediately and simultaneously agreed that what we needed was not one, but two cold beers each, to start us off.

Two of the guys walked over for beer and returned with eight hot-as-a-Mexican-desert beers. This was a bit of a letdown. When I think of beer, I think cold, especially in a Mexican desert. Before we could all start crying and wailing like a bunch of big babies again, the Mexican woman attempted to calm us down with a motioning gesture with her arms and hands. She summoned a little Mexican boy, gave him his marching orders, and he flew down an unpaved rock road of one of the poorest and most depressing towns I have seen anywhere. There were maybe six or eight buildings, and they all looked like hell. A few minutes later the Mexican boy returned with ice. *Yes!* There *is* a God—and he lives in Mexico!

(*Note:* In fall 2016, Donald Trump's campaign distributed a press release which claimed—they had it on good authority—that a young, pregnant Mexican girl by the name of Maria and her husband, José, an unemployed carpenter, sneaked across the border into Arizona for the sole purpose of having an anchor baby and gaining U. S. citizenship! Say what you want about Donald Trump, but he got this one right. This is exactly why we don't want any murdering, rapist Mexicans illegally entering our country. This anchor baby that Maria and José gave us is a nut case running around calling himself God.)

The next order of business, of course, was food. We felt kind of silly asking for a menu at such a place, so we attempted to show off all the Spanish we had learned in high school, college, and Taco Bell by enquiring about burritos, enchiladas, and so forth. To each of our enquiries we received a polite shake of the head: no.

What! Was this a Chinese restaurant? No—but somehow we had all neglected to use the word *taco*, and that's what she had—the only thing she had. That was fine with us. We were not especially picky or expecting gourmet dining in the deserts of Mexico.

The next decision was to decide how many tacos to order. We floundered around a bit on this issue since we had no idea of the price or size of the tacos. The Mexican woman signified that the tacos were 20 cents each! On hearing that news, everybody ordered five tacos apiece, except me. I'm a light eater and could never eat five tacos.

The other guys started giving me hell then. "Buy five" they said. "It's only a dollar! Even if you don't eat all five, you're not exactly out a lot of money." So it was five tacos each. One of the other hogs could eat what I couldn't finish.

The food came quickly, and the beer was only just starting to cool, but thirst for our beloved beverage won out, and so we began our feast.

Once the food was placed on the table, we noticed that the tacos were not very big, about two or three bites each. Just the same, at 20 cents apiece, they were a great bargain because they were very good! We must have looked like a pack of hyenas on a kill because the first twenty tacos were gone in no time. It was time to re-order and have that second Corona that had been sitting on ice a bit longer than the first one.

We now fell into a deep and serious discussion about how many tacos we should order this time around. They were delicious. They were homemade. They were cheap, and they were small. Even I wanted more. Ten tacos each, please! That would now add up to sixty tacos! We weren't even sure the woman could make that many. She was totally unflustered by our order and went back to the kitchen.

It was about this time that somebody noticed that I did not have wet boots after my courageous and heroic crossing of the treacherous rapids of the mighty Rio Grande on foot. It was now my turn to catch hell. That, thankfully was interrupted by a very wise and observant member of our party who made the amazing and astute discovery that we were not only out of food but out of beer! The task of getting more beer was entrusted to me, probably because everyone had notice that I had paid for nothing yet.

Before I left, a big discussion ensued over the number of beers to bring back for each of us. The desert heat had convinced us that the numbers one and two were not good numbers, so we settled on three beers each. Minutes later I was back with twelve scorching hot Coronas. The Mexican lady was one step ahead of us and had already sent the little Mexican boy to get more ice. I have to tell you, these Mexican beers were great, even the warm ones.

Our food was now here—40 tacos! Minutes later these too were gone! Time to re-order. So, after consuming sixty tacos, we were ready for more—not to mention that the beer was getting low again. I'll tell you! There's nothing like going through a tough, manly backpacking trip and enduring all kinds of deprivations—lack of food, lack of water—as we were dealing with now, requiring us to walk across the street for more beverages and strain our vocal cords ordering another batch of tacos.

Forty more tacos arrived, and I don't think I have ever been happier in my life. There was another beer run, and somehow another twenty tacos arrived. If I got my math correct, that was 120 tacos we had now devoured.

Finally, all this debauchery had to end; we had to get a move on. We had to get back to Texas to set up camp. No freeze-dried food tonight, although all of us were probably ready to be honorary members of Weight Watchers and would have been granted immediate entry to the Betty Ford Detox Center.

We crossed the Rio Grande, three on donkeys and me attempting to walk. With the way I was walking I was concerned that I might drown in the ankle-deep water. But they don't call me an intrepid explorer for nothing. Besides, those 30 tacos I consumed must have given me ballast. I made it across, and thus lived to tell the tale (to you).

We had concluded our trip, and it was time to make that horribly long and boring drive back home. Buddy Bruno had another idea, however. He had heard of a hot springs in the park, and he wanted to see it and use it. I just wanted to get going and get home. But Bruno had his heart set on it. We were already here, so another hour or two wouldn't kill us and off we went.

After a brief 20-minute drive, we were there. We parked the van, and a sign informed us that a 10-minute walk down a short trail would lead us to the hot springs. In slightly larger lettering, the sign also warned that nudity or nude bathing in a national park was prohibited and unlawful. Off we went and arrived to a large pool of hot water. We were the only ones there. Big Bend does not get many visitors compared to other national parks due to its remoteness and the hot climate. There was absolutely no one around for miles and miles. Still, another sign at the pool's edge reiterated, in no uncertain terms, the prohibition against nudity.

The guys held a hurried discussion, and everyone decided to get out of their stinky, week-long sweat-soaked clothing, including underwear, except for me. I actually sometimes follow the rules (more or less). My reasoning had nothing to do with obeying some obscure law. My concern was that someone—anyone—might feel uncomfortable coming to this hot spring and coming upon four smelly guys with no clothes on. We were going to be in nice warm bath water up to our necks, and no one could see anything anyway, but, just the same, I kept my underwear on.

People had actually left bars of soap behind. We had a nice bath and damn well needed one. This would be the first time we would drive home clean and smelling good! We were really enjoying this luxury; it was therapeutic for our sore muscles and feet. Then we saw someone approaching. Our first thought was that it was a park ranger because we had seen so few people in this park over the last week. Whoever it was had a ranger-type hat.

The others started to make a move toward their clothes to at least get their underwear on so as not to end up with a ticket or worse. All four of us kept watching the approaching figure closely. If it was not a ranger but a guy, the others would continue their *au naturel* bathing. If it was a girl or woman, the underwear would go on. Try as we might, we couldn't discern if the individual was male or female.

Finally it was a bit too late to take any action when the person got to us. It was a young woman in jeans, long-sleeve shirt for protection from the blazing sun, and a sort of baseball cap to shield her face from the harsh rays. She greeted us with a hello, and a bit of small talk took place.

We asked what her plans were. If she was going to get into this hot spring, three guys needed to get their pants on. She said not to worry about it. She planned to hike the trail she was on, return, and perhaps then take a soak in the hot springs. I assumed that was a hint that the guys ought to get their pants on. There would be plenty of time and

Longitude and Latitude, with Attitude

privacy to do so before her return. As she hiked down the trail and out of sight, everyone thought this would be a good time to get their pants on, except Bruno— that dirty little pervert.

Twenty minutes later, the young gal returned. She stood before us and asked how the water was. We responded that it was wonderful. The young lady then said, "Well, in that case, I'll join you."

At that moment I experienced and was treated to one of the great wonders of God. This precious young thing did a striptease down to her birthday suit, the likes of which I will probably never, ever witness again. She was a truly a beautiful specimen of the female form.

Standing before us was this beautiful sublime nude Venus. Here was Eve before the fall as Adam first saw her, before clothes were invented, and before there were perverts like the four of us. With her long golden-blonde hair cascading down her back as she gave us a full-frontal view of what causes men to get married, she slowly entered the pool. This was no rush job on her part—I hate having my sex rushed, even if the sex is just looking and drooling down my chin like an imbecile. Big Bend had now just moved into the number-one spot of national parks for me.

I don't want to brag or anything, but I happened to have quite a bit of experience with beautiful young nude woman in my bachelor days: they all came to me each month by way of *Playboy* magazine. This splendid beauty could have been the Playmate of any month she chose.

The other guys acted normal; they surrounded this naked delight like a school of piranhas and were ever so polite and attentive to anything this delectable prize might happen to say. I, on the other hand, just hung back at the furthest point of the pool and minded my own business. I was doing my best to restore my sight and trying to stop my heart from beating so hard and fast. Keeping your distance and being very quiet around a beautiful young blonde nude might explain my 44 years of bachelorhood more than another chapter or even a whole book would.

On one level, the torture of this situation only got worse. As I listened to the conversation, it quickly became apparent that the young woman was not not only knock-dead gorgeous but a very nice, sweet, and a friendly person. *Damn!* Some people get it all! Sometimes I get a bit depressed because I'm not real smart, so I go and look into a mirror— and I get even more depressed. This ravishing beauty, on the other hand, probably *never* got depressed!

Actually, I thought my three buddies were even bigger losers than I was. They were falling all over themselves trying to impress this glorious and enticing young lady. What did they hope to accomplish in the next

20 to 60 minutes in a national park in Texas? It seemed pretty futile and fruitless to me.

That same thought must have passed through the hapless minds of these love-sick, smitten piranhas surrounding this shapely young lass because one of them finally asked, "Where you from?"

"Michigan. Ann Arbor," she replied.

Oh my God! She just about lived in my neighborhood if you consider a neighborhood to be about 50 square miles. Ann Arbor is less than an hour from where I lived in Detroit, 45 minutes if you speed—and I definitely would do some speeding to get to this appealing goddess.

I pulled myself out of the self-imposed lethargy I was ensconced in, at the far end of the hot spring, to dazzle this young damsel with my charming personality (I had given up in the looks department years ago. And I think I left my wits in my pants. So charm was the best thing going for me.). Via quick, sharp glances, I insinuated to the other three losers that they should beat it. Chicagoans all, they were hours and hours away from this pretty girl, whereas I was practically in the neighborhood.

It was only because I have a near minor from my college days in physical education that I let my eyes linger on her well-developed upper body. The longer I stared at these amazing upper attributes, the more I knew the drive would be worth it. I had never been very active in the dating scene, but this serendipitous beauty made it worth the effort to engage.

My idiot companions, however, could not take the hint to get lost, so I soldiered on. "Are you in school or working?" I asked because she looked pretty young.

Miss Universe said she was working but then paused. "Well, actually, I'm on disability from work."

With my keen, hawk-like eyes, I could discover no disability in this flawless beauty—even though I looked *very* hard, I can tell you. Whatever her disability was, I could live with it because it certainly had nothing to do with this fine body standing naked before me.

The other three clowns acted all concerned and solicitous once they heard her admission. Someone asked what sort of disability had caused her to be out of work. I didn't care what it was; I just wanted to be married to her, preferably by a justice of the peace before we got out of Texas tonight.

"Well, I had a nervous breakdown" she answered.

Not good, I thought to myself.

"Actually I had a series of serious nervous breakdowns," she confessed.

This was even worse, maybe a deal breaker, I thought. Then my eyes went back to that long, beautiful blonde hair and that very well endowed chest, and I decided that my crusade and true mission in life was to get intimately involved with those who suffered from nervous breakdowns. Right there, on the spot, I had an epiphany: I knew my mission was to comfort those who suffered from the dreaded nervous breakdown, especially those with a body like this one!

She continued, "My job is so stressful, so tense, so nerve wracking, and so overwhelming, that it is very common and almost expected to have a nervous breakdown like I did."

Wow! Nobody knew what to say. I was champing at the bit to get to the justice of the peace, so we could start honeymoon therapy sessions as soon as possible at the very first motel we came upon. Actually, in one of the very rare moments when I was not fantasizing about having sex with this incredibly well-built and voluptuous beauty, I did kind of wonder what in the hell kind of job she worked at. Was she an air traffic controller; did she work in a nuclear-weapons laboratory, or what?

My job as a middle-school teacher—which I loved—would probably pale in comparison to whatever she did. I loved the kids at middle-school level, but I am sure people who have very prestigious or distinguished occupations probably don't think much of what I do. I loved teaching my passion in life: history, geography, politics, and travel—but it was the kids I enjoyed and loved the most. However, it was so hard to concentrate on all that when I had the most beautiful woman I had ever seen standing two feet from me in warm water, totally nude!

Finally someone else asked, "What kind of work did you do that caused you to have a series of major nervous breakdowns?"

"I was a middle-school teacher," she answered.

Slowly, I worked my way back to the far end of the pool until we decided to finally leave.

Moral of my trip to Texas: I enjoyed the tacos more than the nude women.

Postscript: In a very long, long life, I am very sad to say that I have had many more experiences with tacos than nude women.

"I think on-stage nudity is disgusting, shameful and damaging to all things American. But, if I were 22 with a great body, it would be artistic, tasteful, patriotic, and a progressive religious experience."
   – Shelley Winters

You know the good part about all those executions in Texas? Fewer Texans.
  – George Carlin

Imprisoned in Zimbabwe

The school year ending in June 1982 was no different than all the rest. I bonded with and fell in love with (in a proper teacher-student way, you understand) 150 or so seventh graders and then sent them off on their summer vacation. I spent the next day, a teacher-duty day, working on final grades and wrapping things up. By the end of that day at Brownell Middle School, a ritual would play out that had been taking place since 1979 and would continue for almost three more decades. I would say goodbye to my administrators and colleagues, and they—knowing that I was off to "somewhere"—would joke with me and urge me to be careful and stay safe.

By this time, I was already traveling to countries that most Americans would not recognize or had never heard of, such as Kazakhstan, Zambia, Sao Tome and Principe, and other odd and exotic places. My rejoinder to faculty and staff was always, "If I'm not back and at my desk on the first day of school, send out a search party, call the State Department, or start a bake sale for my ransom." This declaration of course brought many disclaimers about how I would not even be missed and many comments along the lines of, "No way! We're going to enjoy the peace and quiet," or "I think the principal is already interviewing your replacement." As you can clearly see, I worked with a bunch of comedians, clowns, and individuals who thought they were quite humorous—always at my expense.

I was 33 and single, and, as usual, I had a big summer ahead of me. I would leave the next day on a four-week road trip through the West with an old college friend. A few days home and then a five-week journey through southern Africa. The first country I would visit was Zimbabwe, formerly Rhodesia. Zimbabwe had been independent and free only since 1980, for just two years. Prior to that, the black inhabitants of this land had led a miserable economic and political existence. Whites, primarily British, who made up only 3% of the population, had imposed a deeply segregationist Jim Crow-type of government and society upon the majority-black population. Under this apartheid-styled regime, the black citizens were denied most basic human rights. Liberty and freedom were only words, not the reality, for these black Africans.

I arrived in Zimbabwe in July after a long and difficult journey: Detroit to London; a very long layover; then, in the wee hours of the night, another long flight to get to Zimbabwe. By the time I arrived, I was beat, exhausted, and jet lagged.

I arrived at my hotel in the capital, Harare, around three or four in the afternoon. I checked in and really wanted and needed sleep. But I knew that, if I went to bed, I would sleep for eight hours, and, when I awoke, it would be midnight or after. What was I going to do then? My whole schedule and day would be thrown off. So the best solution seemed to be to gut it out, and stay awake.

To do that, I needed to keep moving. So I went out to the streets of Harare and walked—and walked. In a few hours I had exhausted all the sight-seeing possibilities that Harare had to offer. I don't think anyone in the history of mankind has ever deliberately made a trip to Harare to see the place. There's nothing there, nothing to see. Harare is just the step one must go through to go on amazing safaris and to see one of the true wonders of the world, Victoria Falls.

I continued to aimlessly walk around with no map or any plan other than staying awake. Eventually I arrived in an upscale residential area where, evidently, the rich lived. In front of one sprawling home, "Zimbabwe House" was painted in white on some rocks. The place had a number of guards or soldiers hanging about the entrance. I assumed it was the Prime Minister's house or official residence, similar to our White House.

I walked over to the front of the property and asked the first soldier I came across if this indeed was the Prime Minister's house. He immediately displayed an angry attitude, barking out in a loud, mean voice, "Why do you ask?"

Whoa! I don't need an expert or a psychologist to tell me this guy is bad news, so I attempted to exit this situation just as quickly as I could. This guy was looking for a fight. I explained that I was just interested, a tourist, and that, if it were the Prime Minister's house, perhaps there were tours, as there were at the American White House.

The soldier snapped back, "You presently are not in your country, the United States!"

I decided to skip telling this grouch that I was fully aware of where I was and where I was not, just to avoid any further conflict, when suddenly he shouted something, and—the next thing I knew—I had four soldiers surrounding me, their fixed-bayonet rifles pointed at my head.

The soldier who started it all left me this way, entered a guard shack, and got on the phone. Soon, a police car arrived. (I was actually happy about that. I figured the police would be more professional and better trained than this rag-tag group of illiterate soldiers.)

The police handcuffed me—that was a first!—put me in the back seat of a squad car, and sped off with me to police headquarters, where I sat, shackled, for an hour or so.

Longitude and Latitude, with Attitude

Then a number of guards showed up and led me through police headquarters to the Central Prison—not a jail: a *prison*. The funny thing about the prison—well, to be honest with you, at the time there was nothing funny about the prison—is that it looked exactly like all the prisons you have ever seen in any Hollywood movie. In other words, not nice, homey, or welcoming but stark and intimidating.

The guards marched behind me as we walked down these long, ominous prison hallways. Everything—walls, floor, and ceilings—was made of concrete. Every 30 or 40 feet there would be a single, naked light bulb hanging from the ceiling.

We finally reached our destination, which was apparently behind a very large metal door. One of the guards took a key and unlocked the door. It took his full strength to open it. Another guard removed my handcuffs, and a third motioned for me to enter through the now-open door.

It was hard to see because of the near darkness, but I cautiously proceeded through the door when suddenly I was pushed quite roughly from behind and figuratively went flying into the room. The door slammed shut behind me, and I found myself alone, in a very large room with nothing: no chair, bench, bunk, or anything.

Up to now there had been no rough stuff, but that violent shove into the room was a wakeup call about the possibilities that might unfold. So I was on guard.

I was in this room for many hours. I did a reconnaissance of it and explored it pretty well. At that moment, I wasn't planning a prison break because, for one thing, I really didn't have any experience in that field, and, for another, this Alcatraz that I now found myself in seemed intent on keeping me right where I was, without much hope or possibility of escape.

Without warning the large door to my cell was thrust open, and a parade of agents filtered into my cell. There were a lot of them—12 or 15 at least! Without uttering a word to me, they encircled me.

They were all black Africans who seemed to be very new to their jobs. They all wore shirts, ties, and sport coats or suits—but of very inferior quality. These native men had probably been bush fighters who had been promoted—rewarded with what was probably regarded as a good job, with good clothes and a decent salary.

I am sure it was a far cry from the deprivation they had suffered previously, when the white Rhodesian army was trying to track them down and kill them with the cutting-edge-technology weaponry of the day. Just the same, their wardrobe looked like it had come from a bad

Salvation Army depot. You know it's bad when I, aka "Joe Shit, the ragman" of fashion, comment on how poor someone's clothing looks. Nevertheless, neither they nor I was there for a fashion show or to make a fashion statement.

They were making another kind of statement. I hadn't been within their circle for very long when each of the agents made sure I had noticed his shoulder holster with a weapon in it. Because no one spoke and I sure as hell wasn't going to start any conversation, the silent atmosphere made the entire incident even stranger, weirder, more tense.

I did have a concern that others in my situation might not have had. Back when I had been in the Marines, I had witnessed a similar spectacle. Twice I had seen a Marine tied up and strapped to a pillar or column in the barracks to then be tormented and physically abused by other Marines. The plight of the bound Marine resembled the pictures I had seen in Catholic school of Jesus' torture during the Stations of the Cross.

The first time this happened, I was obviously perplexed but kept my mouth shut and kept a low profile. The fact that the event was occurring directly across from my bunk, only 15 feet away, didn't stop me from becoming invisible and disappearing. I wasn't sure what was going on, but I wanted no part of it.

I finally got up the gumption to ask one of the older and more senior Marines what was going on. The way he told it, any young, hot-headed Marine who entered a new outfit and started acting smart-ass, know-it-all, and obnoxious was an insult to the tight group of Marines he'd joined—a group of men who had served together for a long time and had formed a very cohesive unit, tight-knit and loyal to each other. They felt that these young loudmouths, needed to be taken down a notch or two. Thus the torture. I made an immediate mental note to start keeping my mouth shut more often.

My current predicament reminded me of the second time I had witnessed the pack take a Marine down. The circle of Marines had surrounded him, waiting to exact retribution. He didn't go down without a fight, but there were just too many adversaries—and they exacted their retribution all right. Now I felt that I was in a similar circumstance.

I think being in that circle actually helped me become the greatest social-studies teacher on Earth, for I don't think another teacher in the universe can explain to students as well as I can what it felt like to be Custer at the Little Big Horn or what it must have been like to be at the Alamo.

My only strategy was to keep moving so that the back of my head was never positioned in front of the same agent for very long, so that none of them could take good, perfect aim with a club or his pistol. I figured that my constant movement would keep the agents a bit uneasy, which would work to my advantage. I tried not to think about the obvious: there were at least 12 of them and only one of me—plus they had all the guns.

You can imagine my shock when the first question put to me was, "Why did you blow up the Zimbabwean Air Force?" A few days earlier, their air force had been blown up, but I can assure you I was not the one who did it. I remembered reading about it before I had left on this trip, but I had no idea what in the hell that had to do with me.

The question was so disconcerting that, for once in my life, I was at a loss for words. Mentally stumbling about to find the correct answer—meaning one that would demonstrate my innocence in this affair and thus allow me to escape what was looking more and more like a very bad situation—I made what was probably the worst and most poorly planned statement of my life. "I didn't blow up your air force; in fact I didn't even know you had an air force."

No sooner had the words come tumbling out of my mouth than I realized what a blunder I had committed—and what this remark must have sounded like to my captors. Here was this white guy from the United States, with its very long history of institutional racism, standing in front of a dozen or more black Africans, insinuating that perhaps the ignorant, uncivilized, savages of Africa were probably too dumb, unsophisticated, and educationally and scientifically un-schooled enough to have an air force.

If these agents had interpreted my potentially racist remark *as* racist, they gave no indication that they did. Just the same, I immediately started to do some backpedaling—and some sweating. "I'm sure your air force was a good one, but I had nothing to do with blowing it up."

Silence—a long silence. I held my ground and was ready.

The station chief, or whoever he was, now stepped forward, stopping within inches of my face, and started an interrogation, punctuated now and then by a stray or random question from one of the other agents surrounding me.

I answered the questions as they were fired at me, no matter how arcane or weird. And they asked me a lot of arcane and weird questions, I can tell you!

Still, things seemed to be going relatively well—if being held in a foreign prison surrounded by a bunch of gun-wielding characters who were just a little pissed off because their air force had recently been destroyed—by me—could be considered going well.

With my short attention span, hyperactivity, lack of the normal human emotion of fear (see "Shot up in the Que Son Valley," above), and ability far beyond those of mortal men to say something very stupid at the wrong time, I decided to compound my earlier faux pas. I was bored with this whole silly *Dragnet*/Inspector Clouseau charade when it was obvious (at least to me) that I had not blown up anybody's air force recently—or ever. So, as if my earlier, somewhat racist but certainly pejorative statement was not bad enough, I went for the jugular: "I demand to make a phone call to the U.S. Embassy." *How do you clowns like that!* I thought. *You don't know who you're messing with! I know my Miranda rights.*

This tactic always seemed to work in just about every movie I had ever seen, but my interrogators apparently hadn't seen the same movies. However, if I was trying to get everyone's attention, I certainly succeeded. Not only did I capture their undivided attention—after all, I *am* a teacher—I precipitated a psychological event, causing most of the agents' eyes to just about pop out of their heads at my audacity.

Their shocked reaction was not one of awe and compliance (they didn't hurry up and hustle me to a telephone); it was something completely different—illustrating that, obviously, these fools *didn't* know who they were messing with: my grandiose and imperious statement caused hysterical laughter and total disbelief.

Their risible response suggested that I could, if I wanted to, have had a great second career in Zimbabwe television on their equivalent of *Comedy Central*. Here I was, in a prison, surrounded by armed men, not asking, or pleading, or begging, but *demanding* and giving orders. My only protection, my only defense was to live by my wits—which meant I was defenseless. Even my Swiss Army Knife was back in the hotel room!

I had just become the laughing stock of the Zimbabwe Central Prison, perhaps the entire Zimbabwe penal system for all I knew. Surely they could see that I was not a terrorist, saboteur, or enemy of Zimbabwe but a rising comedian, and they would let me go, right?

The answer I received was not what I was hoping for. "You may not make any demands while in our prison. You are a prisoner undergoing questioning. You may not make a phone call to the U.S. Embassy or anywhere else. You are a prisoner of the state of Zimbabwe and are being charged with a serious crime: the destruction of the Air Force of Zimbabwe and war against the people of Zimbabwe. *We* will decide your fate," pronounced the station chief.

Very well be that way, if you want!

Longitude and Latitude, with Attitude

It was time for me to regroup and try to come up with a better strategy—if I wanted to continue living.

The interrogation went on and on. The idiotic and moronic questions put to me by one of the agents made it painfully obvious that he was one of the most pitiably ignorant human beings on Earth. I might have endured and even survived his stupidity, though, if it weren't for the fact that (as he made quite clear) he *knew* I was the terrorist who had destroyed the entire air force of Zimbabwe.

Since my guilt was a "proven" fact, accepted by at least one member of the team, my job was to try to convince the others that I was just a mild-mannered social-studies teacher and traveler, and a very, very, very, very, very, very innocent *non*-terrorist who had *NOT* blown up their air force.

Over the course of many hours, we discussed all kinds of interesting personal facts and global events. The discussion and interrogation included U.S. imperialism, racism in America, my role in the CIA, how long I had worked for the FBI, other clandestine operations I had been involved in, my spying activities, my preference in explosives and other weapons, who my confederates were, whether they were still on the continent, how many other African countries I had helped to destabilize, what assassinations I had been involved in, and if most of my commando work was in the field or generally restricted to planning, and administration.

I have to admit, as a social studies guy, that I thought this political seminar was going quite well; the discussions were thought provoking and interesting beyond belief. I was really enjoying them, actually starting to savor them (although the anti-Americanism didn't always sit well with me)! We were getting along, the way good friends do—except they had all the guns and I didn't! That tiny detail and just one other little thing put a small damper on our wonderful conversation: the agents' insistence that I had been in the middle of all of these terrible events!

Now, I like to think that I am a pretty persuasive guy who can lay on the charm when he has to, and that's just what I did. I was so charming that I was certain it would just be a matter of time before we cleared things up and I was on my way—probably with an apology from my new associates, as I now considered them, since everything was going so smooth and friendly like.

But, of course, nothing can ever go perfectly. Unfortunately, there always has to be that one person who is just intent on ruining things. Here, of course, that one person was the ignorant idiot of an agent who had to continually offer his useless, two cents' worth, which was always negative. Whenever I felt my charm offensive had swayed the entire group, Agent Moron would always be there to sow that seed of doubt.

"Who did you come to Zimbabwe with?" barked Agent Nitwit.

"I am traveling alone; I came by myself," I answered.

"You expect us to believe that!" he screamed skeptically. The thickening and expanding vein running down his forehead showed raw emotion. He was sweating profusely, and I thought he was going to have a coronary. No such luck.

I was unsure why my traveling solo to Zimbabwe would be so strange. Many people travel by themselves, and I had met many of them during my travels. *Nothing unusual there*, I thought. So I answered, "Who was I supposed to come with—the Pope?"

That answer threw Agent Idiot into a total fit of confusion while the other agents laughed or smirked at his stupidity. I took that as a good sign but didn't push it.

Things continued to go well when Agent Dimwit took another stab at uncovering my secret plot to annihilate Zimbabwe and its air force. "What is your profession?" he shouted.

Well, that was an easy one, and I answered promptly that I was a teacher. There was an audible murmur of approval. Finally I said something right. I did not know it at the time, but, in both Africa and Asia, teachers are not considered to be low-life, underpaid, lazy cranks, as they are in America. Teachers are highly respected and revered.

The whole negative and threatening atmosphere was now starting to ease up. But, naturally, Agent Blockhead was not done with me or convinced; so he had to make a follow-up counter move. "Prove it!" he demanded.

Now, proving it presented a bit of a problem. I was sure these guys were in no mood for one of my astounding and fascinating lectures. I guess I could have picked up a piece of chalk to write something on the blackboard, if there had been a blackboard or chalk in my prison cell. It was an easy question, but there was no easy way to answer it. Then it hit me; I could.

The reason why I could produce the proof is not only embarrassing but will put yet another nail in my coffin among family and friends by illustrating just how damn cheap I really am. I had learned early in my travels that students and teachers get discounts all over the world, especially at museums, palaces, castles, art galleries, and almost anything that is educational or intellectual.

I am not an intellectual or educational man. I am a cheap and thrifty man. My thrifty cheapness would lead me to value and have near worship for school-picture day. On school-picture day, teachers were requested to also have their pictures taken for the yearbook. Later in the year, when the students' pictures came in, the teachers received their pictures—but we didn't have to pay for ours.

Nearly every teacher just tossed their free middle-school pictures. Not Rufus! For, within that packet of pictures were small pictures that I could use for visa applications and, best of all, a school ID card just like the one the kids received. That ID card got me into a lot of museums and galleries at discount prices. So my ace in the hole was a Brownell Middle School ID card that no self-respecting teacher on Earth who had any self-esteem or pride would have been seen possessing—except me.

I reached into my pocket—slowly—as every agent watched with rapt attention, and, with great relish, revealed my Brownell Middle School ID card that proved I was a teacher. That meant I was out of trouble and that they were not going to execute me for blowing up their whole fucking air force! I was home free!

Well, I was—until Agent Muttonhead grabbed my ID card right out of my hand, where just seconds ago I was flourishing it with so much happiness and hope.

That's when I learned that Agent Bonehead had either not been at the top of his third-grade reading class or was even dumber than I thought (maybe both; they weren't mutually exclusive). This man could not read a single word on my ID card without help—and they weren't hard words! In fact one of the longer words was "school." At first he was stumped and not just by the reading part. This man was now very confused, angry, and perplexed as he stared at the ID card. The other agents were now more informal and relaxed. I was going to take a walk! No sooner had that thought entered my brain than Agent Pinhead abruptly renewed his attack—and this time it was scary! "We got him!" he cried out.

Oh shit! What now? Agent Tomfool pushed his way through the other agents to confront me nose to nose. Brandishing the ID card in front of me, he said, "Yes, it says 'Brownell Middle School,' and, yes, it has your picture on it, and, yes it has your name on it, but it does not say you are a teacher there!"

Don't even ask me how I can be a smart-aleck even in a dangerous and threatening situation. It probably has something to do with lack of both brains and common sense. But my answer was, "What? You think I'm a seventh grader with a mustache?" The other agents showed this fool no mercy as they guffawed and laughed at his stupid antics until the station chief had to restore order.

By now, the station chief's whole demeanor and tone had changed. Respectfully, deferentially, he and the rest of the agents began calling me "Professor." In their eyes, I had gone from the lowest of the low to the most high.

I attempted a few times to explain that I was a middle-school teacher, not a professor, but they were having none of that. Calmly but forcefully, they insisted I was "Professor," and that is how every agent now addressed me—a few even bowed.

The station chief apologized for any inconvenience I may have suffered and was sorry for the disruption of my trip and occupation of my time. He would have his men drive me back to my hotel. Was there anything they could do for me? Would I care for a glass of water or a Coca Cola?

Amazing what a few minutes' difference made in my position and fate!

*****

The next day I flew out to Hwange National Park in a small plane whose manifest consisted of me and the pilot. After landing on a dirt runway out on the savannah in the middle of nowhere, I was taken to a safari camp by jeep. I was issued a tent at the small compound, and that evening, around the fire, I had the opportunity to meet the other clients who were to be on this safari.

There were only six people: a Canadian, an Australian, a New Zealander, a German, a Brit, and another American. Over the fire and a few beers, I recounted my last 24 hours that had mostly been spent in the Central Prison of Zimbabwe. By the time I finished, there was total silence.

Finally, the Australian said, "Rufus, if that had been me and I had gone through what you just have, I would have had my ass on the first plane out of this country and flying home with my tail between my legs." The other five guys all agreed. One by one they expressed the opinion that, had it been one of them, they would be gone.

The German said, "Rufus if I had just gone through such a harrowing and nerve-racking experience as yours, I personally would not be in any mental shape or condition to continue traveling, certainly not in this country."

The Brit was probably the most vocal in his disbelief that I was continuing on. "Rufus, how can you, after what has happened to you, proceed with a trip within this country?"

"Easy" I replied. "First, it's over; it's done. It's the past. Secondly, I *paid* for this safari, and, by God, come hell or high water, I'm going on it. I'm not going to lose my payment for this trip; I work too hard for my money for that to happen. Call me frugal or whatever, but not even the threat of imprisonment and a firing squad is going to deter me from a paid trip."

This group of various nationalities from various nations around the world then unanimously declared me the cheapest and biggest tightwad on the planet.

Postscript: How I Was Attacked, Killed, and Eaten by a Leopard

Spoiler alert: the title is a bit misleading. The leopard didn't eat me. He did get his chance to kill me, however!

One would think that—after being thrown in a prison in a Third-World African country, being accused of blowing up its air force, and escaping with life and limb intact—everything that followed would be easy or anti-climactic. Not for me. It just kept getting better—or worse, depending on how you look at it.

After narrowly escaping a firing squad, I casually continued my journey, assuming the worst was over and out of the way. What else could possibly happen? I was about to find out.

After my work release from prison (and I was never quite clear on the details—whether I was on parole or probation), I had three full days at the beautiful Hwange National Park of Zimbabwe. Rather than stay at one of the larger, grander (more expensive) American or European camps, I had made my reservation at a small camp run by a local small-businessman. The set-up consisted of simple walk-in tents with a cot, simple home-style meals, and beer out of an ice chest. It was pure luxury compared to the backpacking, mountain trekking, and mountain climbing I had done.

When I arrived, the owner greeted me personally and showed me to the tent site, offering me my pick of the seven or eight tents set up there. Since they were all the same, it didn't matter to me which one I slept in, so I arbitrarily chose one that looked as good as any of the others.

I had dinner that night, then stood around the fire having a few beers (and telling my safari mates about my imprisonment, as related above) before going to my tent. Now that I was a free man and no longer incarcerated, I slept like a baby.

The next morning, I was up and out of my tent very early. I saw the businessman who owned the camp walking in my direction, his head down, as if he were studying the ground. I walked toward him, and, as we met, we exchanged good mornings. I asked what he was looking at so intently. He in turn asked me to look at the ground and tell him if I could see the tracks.

The large tracks were hard to miss. I was staring at them when he asked me, "Do you know what kind of tracks these are?"

I had no idea. I was still, at this stage of the game, trying to learn all the different animals, especially the various breeds and species of gazelles. (One of the things you start realizing when you visit Africa is that there are a lot more animals out there than you think. It's not just elephants, zebras, lions, and giraffes. There are all kinds of strange and unusual animals that I had never heard of, such as gemsbok, springbok, hyrax, Oryx, hartebeest, kudu, and more.)

The owner was worried and quite excited. "These are leopard tracks!" he exclaimed knowledgably. "They are vicious man killers!"

Wow! A leopard! Right in our camp, strutting about like he owned the place!

The owner continued following the tracks through the camp over to the tents. The tracks circled one tent. Amazingly, as we continued to follow the leopard tracks, we ended up making three circles around that solitary tent. The owner looked up at me, his face white and full of astonishment. "My God, that leopard was stalking the poor sucker who was sleeping in that tent last night!" he fearfully exclaimed.

"*I* was the poor sucker sleeping in that tent last night!" I bellowed.

I was a bit contrite after this initial, inadvertent outburst, so I asked in a quieter but still insistent tone, "Should I be concerned?"

The situation was now awkward for the owner after his impulsive, fear-mongering appraisal, and he was, momentarily, at a loss for words. A few discomfiting seconds passed before the owner (not sounding very reassuring, I might add) responded. "Don't worry; I'll have one of the staff keep a watch on your tent at night."

Did this idiot really believe I was going to fall for his made-up, spontaneous bullshit? First of all, he didn't have much of a staff to begin with, and they were on the go and working what seemed to be 24/7 shifts. I have never been able to determine or discover how my own country's myth that black people are lazy and don't want to work ever started. That racist fable seems to have traveled quite well to Africa, where you also hear it among some whites. Whether I'm in America or Africa, it sure seems to me that I see an awful lot of black people doing really hot, hard, and difficult, work, usually of the crummier variety that society has to offer.

In any case, this guy was not going to have one of these local native people—who were up hours before I arose at sunrise, toiled all day in the camp, and were still working in the camp kitchen after midnight—sitting up the rest of the night babysitting Rufus. It was humanly impossible.

So there was my problem—how to continue living and not end up in the digestive system of a hungry, man-eating leopard.

The next two nights, I can assure you, there was very little sleep going on in one of those seven or eight tents—mine. Every broken branch, every snap of a twig, and every brush of vegetation against the side of my tent had me ready to do mortal combat with an enemy that I would not be able to defeat.

The few times I did drop off to sleep, after so much sleep deprivation and through sheer exhaustion, I would have graphic and gory nightmares of me traveling through the intestines of that leopard who had his sights on his next meal, which, unfortunately, meant me. I did not even have the satisfaction that my vicious and horrible death would be a shared or mutual experience, for that liar of an owner never placed anyone outside, or near, my tent for protection from a savage and atrocious carnivore intent on dining on my corpse.

There are two possible conclusions to this story. "The end," or "The leopard never got me."

"A journey is like marriage. The certain way to be wrong is to think you control it."
   – John Steinbeck

"A mind that is stretched by a new experience can never go back to its old dimensions."
   – Oliver Wendell Holmes Jr., Justice of the U.S. Supreme Court, 1902-1931

Rufus McGaugh

How to Travel in Style

Although I like to think I am the most normal person on Earth, I guess that, when one looks at my life, one finds many aspects of it that are not what one would call normal.

A perfect example of this is the fact that I did not get married until I was 44. And, if you have been reading this book, it should come as no surprise that I did not have one honeymoon but two. (In other words. any excuse to make yet another trip.)

My wife, Monica, and I married in the spring of 1993, and, that Easter, having a week off, we made what I often describe as a mild-mannered, plain-vanilla, driving trip down South from our home in Michigan. We spent our time hiking at wilderness areas such as Cumberland Gap in Kentucky, touring historic sites such as Charleston and Fort Sumter in South Carolina, and experiencing charming cities such as Savannah, Georgia, and St. Augustine, Florida. A great time was had by all, especially my wife, who always felt my choices of where to go and then my mode of travel, once there, were over the top.

*****

Just before we married, we had taken a three-week trip to Europe. On that trip I received an A+ as a travel guide but an F- in choice of accommodations and dinning. For some strange reason, my wife was opposed to staying in hovels where the heat factor (no air conditioning—not even a fan) was equal to an iron-ore blast furnace and one was tormented and bitten by mosquitoes all night.

Very early on in this trip, my soon-to-be wife informed me that my ideas about dining or eating were even more insane than my ideas about accommodations. I in turn explained that the dining experience I was providing was total proof of my expertise in the art of travel and had served me quite well for 43 years. I hate to brag, but, once I explain my method of fine dining, you will surely feel that you are in the presence of real genius.

My plan was to get up in the morning, as early as humanly possible, and, if the place we were staying at offered a FREE breakfast, to definitely take advantage of it—for a number of reasons. The first reason was that—as usual—we were starving on my plan. The second reason was that it proved to all those dirty, rotten atheists in the world that there really is a God. (What could be better proof of an all-loving God than the fact that he was not going to let two very nice people starve to death just because one of them happened to be very cheap?) Finally, we were going to need that breakfast because our next meal was probably going to be breakfast *tomorrow*.

Now, because we were staying in the cheapest dumps I could find in all of Europe, the usual complimentary breakfast that is offered universally by every hotel on the continent never seemed to materialize. No problem; I'm not a breakfast person anyway. (Additionally, the "no-breakfast" situation at these establishments extended to such other non-essential items as pillows, sheets, blankets, or soap, which also never seemed to show up in our room.)

So, to make a very long story short, we usually did not have breakfast. My spin to my wife on this was, "Hey, we're in Europe, for Christ's sake! We don't want to sit around eating a bowl of cereal or a croissant when we can be out seeing things!"

Now, my wife does not have the outsized personality that I have, and by that I mean she is a very nice person, so she reluctantly followed my lead. When she plaintively asked about at least getting some coffee, I assured her that was no problem. At the train station or on the way, there were a million places to get a quick cup of coffee on the run, which was true—but, as it turned out, in three weeks we never had enough time to get any.

Now for lunch. It has always been my policy—even when I had the money—to skip lunch.

—First of all, I don't even know why I wrote the preceding sentence because I never seemed to have enough money for lunch, but, if I had, the policy would still be in effect: no lunch. My view of lunch is that only a complete dork or fool is going to waste a precious second of daylight sitting around eating food when he could be spending his time standing in excruciatingly long lines to get into palaces and castles and great museums.

Bottom line: we skipped lunch. This might explain why, over 40 years after being discharged from the Marines, I am basically at the same weight I was then. It also explains (and I don't want to brag here and make the rest of you guys look like you married a demanding, intolerant, selfish, self-centered shrew) why my wife is a saint—a saint whose martyrdom will come about through starvation, but a saint nonetheless. (Best of all, I don't have to worry about ever having a fat wife, unlike most of you schmucks reading this!)

By this point, we had skipped two meals, and, of course, the big question—at least for my wife, because I couldn't care less about eating—was what to do for dinner. Always at the ready, I demonstrated to my wife what over 20 years of travel experience had done for me when it comes to securing the one and only meal we would have this particular day. It really is a stroke of genius, if I do say so myself. First, the plan called for us to get a train to our next destination so we wouldn't waste any precious time on our trip, despite the fact that it was now 6:30 p.m. At 6:30 p.m., during summer high season, every hotel in every city in every country of Europe has already been spoken for two hours earlier.

Three hours later (9:30 p.m.), when we finally arrived by rail at our next destination, we began our nighttime wandering through another city, looking not for just any ol' hotel—but a cheap one. Usually, through some miracle and the blessings of a higher power, we usually—but not always—found some dive where we could rest our bodies. And, finally (here's the best part), usually it was by then around 11:00 p.m.; we were dead-dog tired, and too tired to eat, so the final tally for money spent on food for the day was zero. (Even better than the old *Europe on Five Dollars a Day*!)

And there you have my formula for How to Travel in Style. For complete success, continue with this plan throughout the entire trip, and you will not only save time and money but will ways have the answer to the question, "How can you afford to travel so much on your salary?"

Obviously, my ingenious plan for saving money on food while traveling must have impressed Monica after the fact (after we'd come back to the States and she finally got some nourishment) because, after all, she married me, didn't she?

Russia and the Oddball Countries of Eastern Europe

I have only myself to blame. It was my idea. Early in the marriage I had come up with this ingenious plan (slightly different from my ingenious plan described in the previous chapter, "How to Travel in Style") to both travel and keep our marriage together. And unfortunately my wife was following the plan—in the travel department, at least. The marriage was a whole other ballgame, with me slipping in the popularity polls each passing year.

My plan, which I thought was brilliant, was to alternate who got to pick the travel destination each year. One year I would choose where to go, and the next year Monica would get to choose where to go. I added the caveat that the person not choosing the destination should be a good sport about it and not complain or ruin it for the other.

So far, the plan had worked out well except for the fact that I had earned a Green Card and legal alien status in Canada from visiting there so often. My only fear was that Monica would keep planning *more* trips to Canada, where I feared I would eventually die of boredom. (For more on our Canadian—*yawn*—"adventures," see the chapter "I Walk the Straight and *Nauru*.") So, when Monica said she wanted to go to Poland (both of her parents and both sets of grandparents were Polish) and Russia, I could have jumped for joy. She had actually chosen two real foreign countries!

The Poland part was obvious, but Russia was surprising. That was a bit outside of her comfort zone and very unlike her. So I asked, "Why Russia?"

Her response was bit unusual: "Oh, I've always thought it was an interesting place. I don't know much about it, so I thought I would like to visit it." I was elated. Evidently my lust for adventure was rubbing off!

Just about when you think it can't get any better—like when you find out that you're not going to Canada—it did get better. She suggested that, if we had enough time after doing Poland and Russia, I should choose another country or two to add to our three-week trip. Had this woman truly lost her mind? She had now been married to me for four years and had learned she could not trust me—about anything! (The only thing I had never done was to commit adultery; I would never do that. But—other than that one exception—I seemed to have dropped the ball in every other department.)

Our marriage seemed to be one betrayal after another. I had not only spent all my money on travel but most of hers, too. I had led her to believe before marriage that I had a good job and could support a family. That was a lie; I was a teacher. I told her I had money in the bank—and savings. I did, from September to June. Then I would blow it all traveling and come home broke. Back in the good old days—before marriage—I would return from a summer-long trip and eat at my mom's for two weeks until I got my first pay check.

I told Monica we would have fun traveling together, but we often traveled as if we were a couple of escaping Ethiopian refugees. I have already devoted an entire chapter to the suffering, malnutrition, and starvation she had gone through on the first of our trips, but the following anecdote is worth mentioning: Once, in Monica's presence, a good friend of mine told about the time I took my mom to Greece and how, when we rode around in our rental car, I would follow behind the big trucks that transported oranges. Each time these trucks would hit a bump, a few oranges would bounce out, and I would stop to retrieve them. In a half hour, I had a dozen oranges, and dinner would be six oranges each. Sometimes, to supplement our diet, we helped ourselves at an olive grove. This is how bad it was. My wife's only comment was, "So you treated your mother and fed her better on trips than you do me!" Olives and oranges would have been a step up in some of our earliest trips together.

After all this, she was going to trust yours truly to put her trip together. It was the first time in our marriage I felt she truly needed psychiatric help.

I started working with my travel agent, and we came up with an itinerary that had us in Poland for about four days, visiting Warsaw and Krakow. We would fly to Russia for five or six days and basically spend most of our time in Moscow and St. Petersburg. That left 10 or 11 days to continue to travel, and, if Monica didn't want to use those days, I sure did! I was conniving and plotting like a dirty rat about what to do with those 10 days or so. But, before I got too far, something very unexpected happened.

One morning, the office at school called up to my classroom during my preparation period and said I had a phone call. I went downstairs to the office, picked up the phone, and the first thing I heard was, "Hey, Rufus! This is your old student Ian MacNeill!" Now, this was a surprise! I had had Ian as a 7th-grade student about 10 years earlier and then his sister Leslie a year or so later. Both were great kids!

"Great to hear from you! What's going on?"

Longitude and Latitude, with Attitude

"Well, I was at Greatways Travel in Grosse Pointe this weekend, and your name came up. The office mentioned you were going to Russia this summer, and I wanted to invite you and your wife to visit with me and my wife, Laura."

"You're in Russia?" I asked.

"Yes, I am," he said. And so we sealed the deal right then and there for a visit while we were in Moscow. Now all I had to do was finish off the itinerary. A short time later, after sneaking in every oddball country I had not yet been to in Eastern Europe, I presented my masterpiece to my wife, who, with only a cursory glance at the list, gave her approval.

It was now time to get down on my knees and say many prayers to God for having created Catholic schools (which both my wife and I had attended for nearly all our education). Besides having a total monopoly on all vacancies in heaven, the Catholic Church had also used its lobbyists to make sure no apostate Protestant heathens got in. To achieve this monopoly and keep everybody else out, the good nuns who taught us always preferred a good religion unit over useless and frivolous units such as social studies, science, music, art, or literature, a practice which resulted in many students graduating from Catholic schools totally ignorant in some academic areas. My wife was one of those. She is brighter than me on an IQ scale but has big gaps in areas such as history and geography. Due to this lack, she had just signed up to visit some of the more bizarre countries on Earth. Just trust me, when I say that even the most seasoned travelers have not been to the list I added to Poland and Russia.

That list included Turkmenistan—never even heard of that one, right? Then it would be off to Belarus. Then Macedonia—not Alexander the Great's Macedonia but the fake, knock-off one that has a UN seat and has pissed off Greece and the real Macedonia. Next would be the brand-new and never-heard-of country of Slovenia—no, not Slo*vakia*: Slo*venia*. (Have I confused you even more now? Good!) The grand finale would be Albania—a country which, once we arrived in Europe, everyone warned us about, telling us horror stories about our probable fate (to be raped and murdered—not necessarily in that order). This itinerary was like a rogue's gallery of the weird.

My family shrugged; they were used to the outcast type of countries I had been visiting for years. Monica's family, especially the extended tribe of Polish aunts, uncles, cousins, etc., had a collective nervous breakdown. Up to this point, the Polish side of the family had begrudgingly accepted me—the Irish renegade— and my somewhat unorthodox ways. But, now, they were not a happy crowd. Nevertheless, in late June of 1995, Monica and I set off on our greatest adventure. (Spoiler Alert! As you will see, we ended up having a serious problem or issue in nearly every single country.)

Poland: The Lady and the Tram

We started off with Poland, my wife's ancestral homeland. We flew into the capital, Warsaw, and I immediately assumed my role of tour guide and map reader.

Things were going pretty smoothly. Monica was enjoying a traditional European city, and I was awed by all the positive changes that had taken place since my previous visit, during communist times. We mostly walked but used the trams or streetcars for greater distances within the city.

At one point, Monica noticed that, although we were riding the trams a lot, I never bought a ticket; she asked me about that. I had to explain to this naïve and novice traveler that buying tickets for the public-transportation systems that existed throughout European cities was for suckers. Only fools would spend their precious and limited money subsidizing other countries' mass transit.

To cap my argument, I used the ironclad logic that I am so famous for: "Hey, Monica, these countries are going to get every nickel and dime out of us before we leave, anyway. Riding for free just extends our stay a bit longer. There isn't even a moral issue here. When we fly back, three weeks from now, these countries will have all our money, and we'll be broke, so the end justifies the means."

Re-reading these last words now, I have come to the conclusion that I was on very shaky ground with my ethical rationalization.

This conversation took place while we were riding a tram—for free, as usual. As we got off at our streetcar stop, I added, "See, only a chump would pay for a ticket when you can ride for free."

The words were no sooner out of my mouth when I felt a tap on my shoulder. I turned and saw, standing behind us, a middle-aged couple who were holding something in their hands—police badges! We were informed of our crime, lectured, given a ticket and marched down to the local police station to pay the fine immediately for fear that we would flee the country without paying and become Interpol's most wanted financial fugitives.

During the short, two-block walk to the police station, I—being the slippery weasel I am—attempted to talk my way out of the fine by claiming that I didn't even know where one was supposed to buy a ticket for a tram ride. I didn't see the driver selling any tickets on the tram, and there was no conductor.

I immediately realized that this line of reasoning was not going to fly with the authorities. The police patiently explained that tram tickets could be purchased at any of the omnipresent tobacco kiosks located throughout the city. The most embarrassing aspect of this affair, to me, was that, after traveling in Europe for 20 years, I didn't have a clue as to where to buy a tram ticket! One might say I got my money's worth out of European transportation, especially seeing as I had not paid one cent for a city ride in 20 years.

Evidently all those years in Catholic schools and all those religion units and catechism studies had not rubbed off on me as well as the nuns might have hoped. I can only say I must have been absent the day the good nuns taught the Seventh Commandment. "Thou shall not steal" is not a particularly difficult Commandment to understand or figure out—even on a budget! Somehow, however, living in America (and despite being a very poor man), I had developed a "corporate conscience"—at least when it came to paying for a streetcar ride!

Looking back at this episode, after all these years, even yours truly can clearly see that there was a moral lapse here—but who cares? I'm still going to heaven because I'm Catholic! The nuns will back me on this one. No one's perfect! So I missed one Commandment! Ha! I still have nine out of ten pretty well covered. Well, I'm also a little shaky on the Sixth one ("Thou shall not commit adultery"), due to my prolonged bachelor days, but you Protestants, even if you somehow cover 10 out of 10 of the Commandments, you will not be seeing Jesus or strumming your harp. The sign up at the gates of Catholic heaven says "Catholics Only!" So, with only one major breach—the Seventh Commandment—and a number of lapses on number Six, I'm in—and you're out.

Well, this unexpected interruption did not take that long, maybe 20 minutes, and the cost was not much, about two dollars. Monica and I headed back out onto the streets of Warsaw. Again we needed a tram to transport us, and I did something I had never done in 20 years; I bought a ticket—actually two: one for each of us. And I have to admit it felt good and moral—except in my wallet. I would say I felt saintly, almost angelic upon this historic occasion—me spending money.

It will be hard for the reader to believe what happened next during this moral euphoria. God placed a golden halo over my head! I am not making this up; I have witnesses. Well, actually, no one else could see it, but it was there in all its radiant beauty. I was in such union with God that I could be assured of entry into heaven even if I was a Protestant!

So Monica, me, and the halo jumped on the next tram to our destination. I had my two tickets in hand but was baffled as to what to do with them. After all, I'm the guy who had been riding trams and streetcars for free for 20 years. There was no conductor, so I walked to the front of the tram to offer them to the driver, who seemed to be a grouch and wanted nothing to do with my tickets. Perplexed I walked back to where Monica was sitting and sat beside here with the two tickets clearly visible in front of me. Nothing happened.

Eventually we got off, all three of us: Monica, me, and the halo (by now a great glowing, yellow-gold color that clearly screamed to the world, "THIS IS THE MOST HONEST AND MORAL MAN ON EARTH—AND HE'S GOING TO HEAVEN BECAUSE HE IS A CATHOLIC!")

I had never felt so religious and morally upstanding in my entire life when I felt a tap on my shoulder. I turned to face two Polish police officers with badges out and one writing my second ticket of the day. Clearly what I needed in Poland was not a halo but a "Get out of Jail Free" card.

Monica and I explained that we had tickets and showed them to the police. What the hell! Did they think I was some cheap, cheating, conniving tightwad who would try to weasel out of paying for a tram fare? The police responded that I had not validated the ticket. After 20 years of riding for free, I had no idea what this man was talking about. Worse yet, it must have also occurred to Someone Else that all these years of cheating were not in keeping with the Good Book, for the halo was now growing dim and fading away, almost as if I was starting to turn into a Protestant.

The two police officers actually waited for the next tram to stop, grabbed my two tickets and validated them in a little gizmo on the tram just so I could see how it was done, if I had been an honest person. So that's how you do it!

Even worse than the fact that I now would have to buy two more tickets, we were marched back down to the police station that we had just left for the same crime. We entered the police station among old police friends; it was almost like family. Actually not. The police behind their desks, seeing us being marched in a second time for the same offense seemed less than pleased with us.

I tried to explain to the Polish police that, after 20 years of willful crime, especially cheating on every single tram on the European continent, I had just recently—about 20 minutes ago—changed my evil ways and was now an honest fare-paying citizen. Unfortunately, they weren't buying it. They were not only angry, but, in American rather than in Polish, I would say they were pissed off!

The tension and loud voices on both sides was escalating by the minute. My greatest fear was not jail, a big fine, or even the police working me over, but Monica. At this point, I was afraid she was going to think that I was the biggest idiot on Earth. Everybody—especially me—had been telling her that I was a travel expert who had been all over the world, and here I couldn't get her on a tram without being detained, arrested, and fined twice in one day! This had to be some sort of world record! (Actually, me getting arrested twice in one day had actually happened once before—in the U.S.S.R. but that is another story for another day. See below.)

Now the most shocking and unexpected event occurred. My wife, Monica, the most calm, cool, laid-back, human being in the world, went on the warpath. Surprisingly, I was not the victim of her wrath. She took on the whole police force! Where did this come from? I have no idea, but even I took cover, and I'm usually not afraid of anything or anybody. She told everybody in that police station what she thought of them and what she thought of the way they had treated us—and, boy, it wasn't pretty. She lambasted the entire crew up one side and down the other. She was still going strong when they released us with no fine, I suspect, to just end the verbal beating they were being subjected to.

Once out on the street, she continued venting about how mean and rotten the officials seemed to be toward nice, honest American folks who just wanted to visit their country. I did my best not to remind her that she was walking with the biggest tram-fare crook in Europe. Worse yet, the halo was nowhere to be found.

Being detained, arrested, and marched down to the police station twice in one day was an inauspicious start to our Poland trip. However, the rest of our time there was wonderful, especially the time we spent in Krakow, one of the most cultural and intellectual cities on the continent. (It probably helped that we avoided tram travel as much as possible.)

Next stop: Russia

Russia and Photography

We arrived in Russia, a country I had already been to twice before, when it was communist and called the U.S.S.R. or the Soviet Union. At the time, I had been on organized tours operated by tour companies, which was pretty much the only way you could do it back then. Now, with the fall of communism and the Soviet government in 1991, and the advent of what looked like the birth of democracy and capitalism in this country, I assumed things would be a bit better.

In the old Soviet Union, I had been detained by police twice—once even within the safety of a tour group. Both times the issue dealt with my photography. I was a social-studies teacher attempting to document the country, its government, and its economy. At the same time, I did my best to follow their authoritarian rules and not get locked up. Nevertheless, the first time, I was detained, along with my entire tour group, for taking pictures of a top-secret area—a fruit market! Yes, it's laughable now and makes for a good story, but at the time it was not quite so funny. The whole tour group, me included, found itself in an Orwellian situation where no one in authority in this totalitarian and repressive system of government wanted to back down or look weak.

A few fat, mean- spirited Russian women working the fruit-market stalls had evidently taken umbrage at our market-place photography. As citizens of a country where liberty, freedom, democracy, personal choice, or dignity did not exist, these women displayed a Salem Witch Trial mentality, replete with loud accusations. The entire situation was reminiscent of experiences I have had and continue to have in Africa when it comes to picture-taking. In Africa, a near riot can sometimes ensue over my photography. Supposedly the people are protesting the invasion of their personal space or voicing concerns that the photographer is making money at their expense. That's bullshit!

The apologists and the overly politically correct may try to rationalize it any way they can, but the simple fact is that people in these situations are just ignorant, mean-spirited jerks. I fully understand it, both in the old U.S.S.R. and many areas of Africa today. These people live in abject poverty. They have little or no control over most aspects of their lives. They are oppressed and repressed by their government, the police, soldiers, tax collectors, violent gangs, a corrupt bureaucracy, crooked politicians, non-existent government services, crime, and a stratospheric infant-mortality rate. When they see their one opportunity to vent their frustrations, they act with alacrity. I understand it. I even sympathize with it—but, if you are on the receiving end of their wrath, it is just stupid.

These Russian women, who normally were not allowed to say "boo" without risk of seeing the inside of a prison up close and personal or winning a free all-expenses-paid trip to the gulags of Siberia, now had an easy target—some Western (American) tourists. From birth, the proletariat in this country had been taught to hate the enemy—us. Riling

Longitude and Latitude, with Attitude

up the masses and rallying against us was prime-time entertainment and a venting process for them.

In the end, it cost us little, only a couple of hours, as one higher-ranking police officer after another turned up, only to be baffled about what to do with the screaming mini-mob of fat Russian witches who worked the market. Everyone seemed afraid to make a decision, lest it be the wrong decision.

Finally, after lieutenant, after captain, after ever higher-ranking officer all passed the buck, one officer with some real authority (or brains, or guts, or balls, or all of these) put an end to this little street theater. He basically told the fat Russian women to shut up, and they did, recognizing authority and bowing to it in a servile manner.

On one level it was a sad and horrible thing to me. As someone who had studied Russian history and was a history major, I felt that this scenario I had just witnessed was a very bad replay of the long and tragic story of this land. Here again the Russian peasant had bowed like a beaten dog to submit meekly to a higher authority. In any case, my group and I were allowed to move on.

How many people, when they travel, get detained or arrested *twice* in one day? (Hint: *Rufus*.) That same day, on my own this time, I was again detained by a police officer, again for taking photographs—this time in a Moscow city park. Here's how it happened:

Our day's activities had ended, and we had checked into our hotel. As usual, I was interested in getting the real skinny, not the Communist Party line that we were continuously fed on every single tour at every single sight. After checking in, I walked out the hotel's back door and went exploring on my own. I wandered around Moscow for hours with no map or idea where I was, just a desire to see life as the Soviet people were really living it. To be honest, I did not make any great discoveries.

At one point I saw a small park where newlyweds were having their picture taken. Previously, I had snapped a lot of photos of newly married couples making the traditional visit to the World War II monuments in the city. During communist times, a crucial element of every wedding after the marriage ceremony at city hall (very few wedding were religious) was for the bride and groom, sometimes with the best man and maid of honor, to go to a World War II monument or memorial that every city, town, and village had, so that the wedding party could pay its respects and the bride could lay her wedding bouquet at the foot of the memorial. This was a tradition dating back to the end of World War II.

Few people, especially Americans, realize that, in World War II, the Soviets (Russians) suffered 20 million deaths—more fatalities than any other nation during the conflict, including Germany. It has been estimated that nearly every single Soviet (Russian) family lost at least one family member in the war. Many families lost many more. That fact should explain this solemn part of the wedding ceremony.

It *doesn't* explain why anyone would object to me photographing such a scene. But, after I took a few shots of the wedding parties, thinking nothing of it, and was about to leave the park, a policeman rushed over to me and, affecting a very commanding attitude, demanded in a very gruff voice to see my passport.

I showed it to him.

That made him glower and fume and fuss all the more because my papers were in order. Still, he did his best to intimidate me.

I did not feel threatened; I merely felt I was in the presence of a rude jerk. He continued to harass me, and the situation was pretty much at a standstill. Finally, I just turned and walked away. Many might think this move was pretty audacious on my part, but I was pretty convinced that this police officer was not only a jerk and not too bright but a bit out of his league, so I got away with it. (Good thing he didn't know how dangerous I was—that I was a repeat offender—or things might have gone worse.)

There you have it: Rufus arrested in Russia, twice in one day. (Okay—maybe not "arrested" per se; just harassed by the authorities. But it makes for an arresting story, doesn't it?)

John Steinbeck Is My Co-Pilot, or How Not to Fall out of an Airplane

My former 7th-grade student, Ian, mentioned earlier, was very helpful during this part of our journey. Ian was working for a big American telecommunication company that was revamping and recreating the old and out-of-date former Soviet communication lines, transforming them into the new telephone system that Russia needed to become a modern country on par with the West.

He provided us with a car and driver, and we spent part of a weekend at a dacha out in the countryside that he had use of. Ian's greatest contribution was helping me to secure plane tickets to Turkmenistan. Turkmenistan at that time in history was impossible to get into. There just seemed no way to get a flight into this new country that had once been a part of the old communist U.S.S.R. Ian, using all his connections, snagged the next-to-impossible air tickets to Turkmenistan.

Longitude and Latitude, with Attitude

Monica was a bit cautious about this one. The name alone went beyond exotic and her comfort level. Weird or scary would better describe her thoughts. When she asked Ian if he had ever been to Turkmenistan, his answer was no. Asked why not, Ian replied that neither his company nor his life insurance would cover his use of the old and unsafe Aeroflot (Soviet) planes that made the journey to Turkmenistan.

Hmm...so maybe Ian wasn't as helpful as he could have been. In other words, I could have killed him! My wife is not the most comfortable flyer to begin with, and this certainly didn't help matters.

Monica's concerns and worries started to become more vocal. I had to spend a good amount of time trying to convince my wife that everything would be okay. I even had assurances for her from the great novelist John Steinbeck—well, not personally or directly, since I never met the man, and he had died in 1968. However, Steinbeck had written in his 1948 book, *A Russian Journal*, that—although Russian Aeroflot planes were really junky-looking—despite their appearance, they somehow safely delivered their passengers to their destination. Now, this was back when my wife still liked me and trusted me, so, very hesitantly, she was still on board (so to speak).

We arrived at the Moscow airport in the early afternoon on a very hot summer day, when the temperature was probably in the high 80s. Monica always prefers the temps, indoors or out, to be somewhere below zero. So, right off the bat, she was not comfortable and—just to make matters worse—somehow the hot weather in Moscow was *my* fault.

As we waited to board our plane, it became very obvious that we would be the only two non-Turkmen on the plane. Nobody at our gate looked like us! All the Turkmen passengers were dressed in exotic outfits that included Persian slippers, magnificent turbans, very long beards, high black riding boots, and billowing pants. It's funny how two people viewing or witnessing the exact same sight interpret it so differently. I'm standing there thinking, "*Cool!*" Monica on the other hand goes, "Oh my God! Are we safe with these people?"

We boarded the Aeroflot plane, which, by the way, was a propeller plane of good size—and age. The interior of the plane was a total wreck! It looked like a bomb had gone off inside it. Every single seat was broken; most had torn upholstery. The aisle carpeting was no longer screwed down but lumped up all over the floor. And there was this smell, permeating everything...

We found our seats and sat down—and sat and sat—for a very long time. All the while the heat from the unusually hot summer weather built up in the plane. Monica started to get queasy.

The Turkmen—all of them—broke out their long loaves of bread, salamis, and cheeses. Breaking bread, cutting salami, and tearing the pungent cheeses for their feast, the Turkmen families ate, dropping small bits of food as they did. And now I realized the source of the foul-smelling and ripe odor that had hit us upon entering the plane. The many morsels of salami and cheese that were never picked up or cleaned up by the airline cleaning crews (if they *had* airline cleaning crews) were causing the near-choking stink.

Again the difference of opinion regarding the same object: Monica, "I can't believe these primitive people are eating that disgusting garbage! I'm going to puke!" Me: "It looks pretty good! I was hoping someone would offer us some of that cheese." Monica gave me a disgusted look, as if I had just said I would like to have sex with an animal. (But, hey!— that salami didn't look too bad, either!)

Monica has this habit when things go bad or get uncomfortable: she closes her eyes and hopes and waits for the best. That's what she was now doing before takeoff—that is, if we were ever going *to* take off. I now wish she had kept to that plan, but, no, she opened her eyes—and then she noticed it.

She had already noticed (it was unavoidable, given the state of the plane) that two teams had evidently been playing with live hand grenades inside the plane—with catastrophic results to the interior design of the plane. What she had *not* noticed, at least not until now, were the large, gaping holes in the floor, sides, and top of the plane. At first she couldn't believe it. *No way!* No way in this modern world could a large commercial airline fly lots of passengers in huge planes with holes the size of softballs throughout the plane.

Daylight could clearly be seen entering the plane through the many holes, large and small. There was a hole about the size of a large grapefruit next to Monica's window seat. In the aisle seat, I kept her engaged in conversation so that she would not turn back toward the window and notice the hole.

She continued to scrutinize the rest of the plane, noticing more and more holes throughout. I was not only busy trying to keep her looking at me and away from the large hole by her window but also doing my best to conceal a huge hole below my legs. The hole below my right foot was about the size of cereal box or hard-cover book (maybe entitled *How Not to Fall out of an Airplane*).

Making intense eye contact with Monica so that she would stay focused on me, I discreetly placed my right foot over the hole, attempting to cover as much of it as I possibly could. Unfortunately my foot was not nearly wide enough to accomplish this. I was having the most intense conversation I had ever had with this woman for only one reason—to save my ass.

I am happy to report that things were going well. Despite the stress and the palpable fear my wife was experiencing, she was enjoying a newfound sort of intimacy in conversation, which, up until now, we had never had. Unfortunately, she had married a man who was overjoyed to eat her wonderfully prepared meals, have sex with her, provide a second income, and do the laundry but was not into conversation, talking, or even listening. Up to now, about 85% of our conversations had been me saying, "Yes," "No," or "Not now."

Exactly *what* to say to keep this conversation going—in what now felt like 100-degree heat, with putrid-smelling, rotten cheese, rancid salami, and the BO of a desert people who seldom have the water or means to bathe—was difficult, to say the least. I gave it my best, but evidently I am not half as interesting as I like to think I am because I lost my audience.

However—a miracle! Suddenly, over the intercom, the Aeroflot stewardess, who was wearing a parachute, asked passengers to put their seatbelt on.

By the way, I made the parachute part up, but my wife, Monica, who has been in psychotherapy for Post Traumatic Stress Disorder ever since this flight, insists that she *did* see a parachute on the stewardess. We argue about it every time the issue comes up, and she insists there was a parachute involved. The one thing we both agree on, though, is that none of the seat belts worked—and that's when Monica started crying.

I tried cheering her up by suggesting that we tie the broken seat belts around us, as the wily Turkmen were doing, but she was having none of it. Again Rufus to the rescue like a knight in shining armor; I re-explained how safe Russian Aeroflot planes are. I again quoted John Steinbeck's observations of and experiences on these wonderful flying machines when, through her tears, Monica—who never swears and does not even use "hell" or "damn"—said, "Fuck Steinbeck!"

Well! Didn't she realize Steinbeck was a Pulitzer Prize winner, a *Nobel Prize* winner—and to talk about a man of letters as she just did was unthinkable? Didn't she remember that I have a minor in literature?

As she continued to weep, I explained to her the greatness of Steinbeck and how he was a great traveler like me. I went on to recount his war-time experiences in Spain during the Spanish civil war. (I would later be told that it was Ernest Hemmingway who served in the Spanish civil war, not John Steinbeck. The only conclusion I can come up with as to why I would make such a mistake is that it must have been one of those many days back in college when I skipped class and played pool and drank beer before lunch and then into the night.) I was attempting only to distract her, but things were definitely sliding south, and I guess you could say the honeymoon was officially over.

Despite her somewhat negative attitude, Monica was desperate enough to ask, "Should we really tie the seat belts around us?" I wanted to put a positive face on all this and show how confident I was in the mechanical engineering of Aeroflot, so I said not to bother. Unfortunately, in an effort to put a bold face of optimism on this situation, I was a bit theatrical in saying it, and somehow I must have put a bit of pressure on the floor. The next thing I knew, my right foot had broken through the hole in the floor, and now my foot and leg, up to about the shin, were dangling out under the plane. Passengers in the terminal could look out and see a large Aeroflot plane with a foot and lower leg swaying back and forth outside the bottom of the plane.

I dexterously pulled my leg back up and into the plane, being careful not to cut myself on the rusty metal. Monica, seeing this bizarre sight of my lower limb dangling from a plane, put her head down into her lap, not only crying but sobbing, "We're never going to make this one. We're going to die!"

Well, we didn't die; we survived quite well. And, as we got off the plane with Monica a little shaky and clinging a bit to me, I tried not to be an "I told you so" type. I also tried to avoid mentioning that we would be flying that same plane back to Moscow the next day.

Turkmenistan, Taxi Rides, and Hostile Hostelry

As it turns out, we were far from being out of the woods in this travel experience. We spent the day walking around the more colorful areas of the capital of Turkmenistan—me taking in the color, history, and culture and Monica attempting to recover from her recent nervous breakdown caused by the flight getting here. Ashgabat (or Ashgabad, as it was then known) provided an interesting array of Turkmen people in colorful outfits that often included Persian slippers.

When we had finished touring early that evening, I was again able to show off my travel experience and expertise by hailing a taxi and conveying to the driver where we wanted to go, despite me not knowing a word in Turkmen and the driver not knowing a single word of English.

We got into the taxi; the driver took off—and in a very few minutes we were outside the city limits. In fact we were out in a desert, the Karakum Desert to be exact.

A few minutes passed; now we were not only further into this desert, but night had descended, and it was very dark. (I looked out the back window and couldn't see the lights of the city anymore.) I didn't have any idea where in the hell we were or where we were going!

Monica finally asked, in all innocence, "Where is this hotel, and why is it so far out?" She directed the question to both the driver and me. The driver didn't answer. No surprise there; he didn't speak English, but he didn't even acknowledge hearing the question.

That's when I became alarmed. One of the oldest tricks in the annals of travel crime is for a taxi driver to take his passengers to a secluded spot (alley, forest, back road, or, in this case, 'way in the hell out in the desert), a pre-arranged spot where his awaiting accomplices rob the passengers at gunpoint or knifepoint. Monica, totally unaware of such a scheme, was sitting next to me quite content, although impatient to get to the hotel. I was sweating bullets. This was not looking good at all! I became very vigilant, attempting to scan the landscape in the darkness for any sign of a setup.

I was in a real pickle. If I were by myself, as I usually was, I at least had two options in a situation such as this. I could fight or run, and I am not afraid or too proud to do either. Whichever one works is my mode of survival. Now, however, I was responsible for someone else. Monica is not a runner or athlete, so running was out of the question. (Although I *am* a runner, I certainly wasn't going to run off and leave my wife with a pack of thieves who might not stop at robbery but go on to rape or murder or both.)

Putting up resistance, even if I care to get all macho about it, also didn't seem to be a very good plan. I could come out on the losing end of a fight. And let's face it: if there were three or four others waiting for us—no matter how tough I might want to think I am—I think everyone realizes who was *not* going to finish on top. If they were armed, there was absolutely no doubt how things would turn out. Putting up resistance would probably only make matters worse.

These thoughts preoccupied me as—without ever seeing the headlights of another car in either direction—we continued driving and driving into a desert that seemed to get darker and darker and more ominous as we proceeded.

When Monica asked the driver how much further it was to the hotel, the driver was silent and didn't answer. Very strange—very suspicious—behavior for a cabbie. In my experience, taxi drivers, from one end of the world to the other, usually can't shut up. Not knowing a word of your language doesn't deter their conversation or chattering an iota. (Of course, now that they've all acquired cell phones and can talk with their buddies or bookies or whomever, they still chatter—only not to their passengers.)

At this point in our journey, I could only hope that the worst that would happen was that they would relieve us of some American Express Traveler's Cheques and our cash. Just when I thought it couldn't get any worse, the driver (who by now must have taken us 800 million miles out in the middle of the desert) made an abrupt right hand turn onto a little gravel road that had absolutely nothing on it. Oh shit! It was a not-too-bumpy road that appeared to be leading us nowhere except into further darkness.

That's when Monica, now surprised, became a bit alarmed, though she remained (thankfully) clueless about what was going through my mind. Before we became sitting ducks or spineless victims, I was just about ready to take charge of things by grabbing the driver around the neck, tossing him out of his vehicle, and commandeering the taxi back to civilization—if I could even figure out how to get back!

I was on the verge of doing something—anything—rather than being a gutless victim who does nothing, when the taxi pulled up in front of a dark building that materialized out of nowhere. My adrenalin was pumped up to the point where I was ready to explode, ready to take on not only a gang but an army of thieves, when I heard Monica say, "This looks like a nice hotel!" I completely deflated with relief. The driver turned to us to collect his fare, but I was still in such a hyper-vigilant mode that I almost attacked him before I figured out what he was doing.

I exhaled loudly a few times as I got out of the taxi and noticed the hotel seemed to be closed—no lights were on. I refused to pay the demanding taxi driver until I sorted this all out. Although I was quite relieved that my wife and I were not going to be robbed, beaten, raped, or killed by thieves, I didn't really want to sleep outside the door of a closed or out-of-business hotel.

We knocked a few times with no results, and the taxi driver was more loudly demanding his money. If he only realized how pumped up I was, he might well have kept his big mouth shut. I had been through 'way too much in the last 60 or 90 minutes and was ready to pound someone.

Finally, a very old and frail woman answered the door. She didn't seem too eager to welcome us into her hotel. In fact, she tried to get us to leave. But that wasn't going to happen. I had a reservation for this hotel, and I was not about to start driving around in this desert looking for another. We were staying there for the night, one way or the other. Her Turkmen, our English conversation was going nowhere when she put her hands up in a waiting gesture and walked into a back room.

She returned a few minutes later with a small, frail, old man who appeared to be her husband. His hair was in a swirly mess from the sleep we assuredly had awakened him from. He did speak English, though. I had my printed reservation form for this hotel, and I presented it to him. Barely glancing at it, he very rudely tossed it back at me as though I was some underling or serf. This was a bad mistake on his part. I don't take treatment like this from anybody—especially an ugly, little, scrawny, bad-haired twerp like this guy. But, before beating the hell out of this arrogant little bastard, I figured I might as well try to be polite and diplomatic for my wife's sake. The goal was to get a decent room for my wife, who at that moment was quite worried about that very fact. At first, he just said there were no rooms and he couldn't honor the hotel reservation.

I tried negotiating. Then I asked for consideration for my wife, but that too did not move him. In desperation, I suggested we would settle for the cement floor of some hallway, closet, or maintenance room. The answer continued to be no.

At some point during these proceedings, I had paid off the very impatient and increasingly angry taxi driver and he was long gone. So I didn't even have an escape or backup option. We were in the middle of a huge desert at what appeared to be the only damn hotel this side of Mars, and the owner would not honor my hotel reservation or give us a room. My wife, Monica, was concerned, upset, and nervous.

Okay, it was hardball now. If this guy wanted to see or deal with Super Prick, he was now going to get his wish fulfilled. I put my face very close to this little shit's and said, "You son of bitch! You are going to find a room or some place for my wife, or I am going to beat the hell out of you so bad you won't ever walk again!" He was visibly shaken because he could tell I meant it—and I did mean it. A little surprise though: even though I could tell he was frightened and was visibly looking for a way to hide or run, he still shook his head no. This guy didn't realize who he was dealing with. I guess he didn't realize how low I would sink and what I would do—not for myself but for my wife.

I am not proud of what I said or did next, but—as God is my witness—I would do it again, no matter how bad I might look. I said, "If you don't get some sort of room for my wife, I'm going to, right here and now, beat the hell out of your wife!"

I started toward both of them, and he was now trembling. He put his hands up to stop me, pleading that he was under orders from the government and that he had no say in it, and he would be in terrible trouble with the police and the government. As he related his tale of woe, it appeared that the Prime Minister of Turkey and other high-ranking Turkish officials were making an unexpected trip to Turkmenistan, and they were to lodge in this hotel. The entire Turkish entourage was expected the next morning, so no rooms were to be rented out. Those were his orders from the authoritarian police state of which he was a citizen.

We continued arguing and debating this issue for a time, with this poor man being sandwiched between an irate, violent, and perhaps mentally unstable American who was going to beat the hell out of him and his wife and his own government that would figuratively (if not literally) kill him for screwing up a diplomatic visit from Turkey.

Monica asked if she could just get a few hours' sleep in a bed or room somewhere, at which point he told us that the Turkish delegation was arriving a bit before noon. In light of this new revelation, I bargained, "Fine! Get us into my confirmed room, and we guarantee we will be out very early in the morning."

The little man said, "You must be out of the room no later than 8 a.m.!"

Well, that was no problem at all. I had thought he was going to come up with some ridiculously early hour like 4 a.m. or earlier. All this arguing and stress and all we needed to do was be out of the room by eight!

We got into our room, which was actually a huge suite and very nice. Evidently Ian's secretary, who had made the plane and hotel reservations, must have thought I was a rich American or making as much as Ian. Perhaps, based on her experience, all Americans were wealthy. So we not only had a room but a palace—at least in sheer size. With nerves still on edge over "there is no room at the inn," me threatening to beat the hell out of two little, old, frail senior citizens, and the living nightmare of a potential highway robbery, it was a miracle we got any sleep, but sleep we did—and it was a good sleep to boot.

The next morning I was up first. I got out of bed and walked out onto our balcony. A balcony! It was the first time in my life I had ever had a balcony. I can assure you that none of the places where I have slept—the park benches, all-night-train seats, city parks, or the back seat of my car—ever had a balcony. Outside our window were the incredible and beautiful yellow/gold sands of the Karakum Desert. The swirls of the sand formed geometric patterns of golden yellow across the low dunes. The balcony and the view made the entire eventful trip worthwhile.

The beautiful Karakum Desert in Turkmenistan from our hotel window. We suffered that flight in a rickety, holey Aeroflat plane; took a scary ride out into a vast emptiness, fearful we were about to be robbed and killed—or worse; and then endured an altercation with the hotel proprietor and his wife, all for this. Even in black and white, you can see the view was worth it.

Did I happen to mention that our return flight from Turkmenistan back to Russia was uneventful and that we did not crash and die? Save for a few dirty looks from Monica, not a single negative incident occurred.

I'm "in" with My In-Laws Because, Luckily, Ladies Need to Use the Bathroom a Lot

If you were to be at a party or barbeque and heard this happily married couple recounting their trip to Turkmenistan, you would hear one member of the marriage (the one who did not do so well in picking out a mate) describe it as a horrific, terrible, scary, and life-threatening experience. On the other hand, if you bothered to hear the other side of that story from the charming, good-looking guy who is the other partner in this marriage, he would say it was a fabulous experience in an exotic land that few have ever visited.

Now, the way I was looking at it, at the time, was this way: We had now been to three countries, and I had succeeded in getting us ticketed, arrested, and detained twice; had put our lives in jeopardy twice, flying the most unsafe airline and plane on earth; had endured a late-night robbery scare out in a desert; had been refused entry to the only hotel for nine-billion miles around; and had threatened to beat up two old, feeble pensioners—one being a little old granny half my size! I hate to brag, but that's quite an accomplishment—and we still had more countries to visit! Now you know why that woman I married loves me so much!

Unfortunately, I composed the preceding summary *before* we left Russia, which technically meant something could still go wrong. This may shock you beyond belief after having read how smoothly our trip was proceeding, being led by perhaps the most talented and experienced traveler in America (that, of course, would be me), but we did indeed endure one more incident. It was not the most serious incident of the trip but another screw-up that certainly could have been pinned on me. But, again, because I'm Catholic, God stepped in and saved me from another potential tragedy.

What I mean by this statement is that God, who is a Catholic, did not use his divine power to stop or alleviate this serious incident but did something far better and more miraculous. He made sure Monica did not find out about it. Now, to make sure Monica did not find out about this serious incident, it did take some subterfuge and lying on my part, but God allows you to do that if you are Catholic. Some may make the claim that I just got lucky, but that simply is not true. This was a case of divine intervention: my wife never found out because she was busy at the time going to the bathroom.

In God's supreme wisdom, women were created in such a manner that they have to go to the bathroom all the time. This started back with Eve. Because women constantly have to go to the bathroom all the time, this gives normal men more "alone time" to scratch themselves in private places and, better yet, attain something that can never be had when your wife is around: silence.

So, on the last leg of our Russian journey, which was playing out in St. Petersburg, Monica announced to our driver that she needed a

Longitude and Latitude, with Attitude

bathroom—which he was able to locate pretty quickly without an accident, at least on Monica's part.

Thus far, things had gone along pretty well here in St. Petersburg. We had not been arrested, imprisoned, or made any kamikaze flights. My travel agent back at Greatways Travel in Grosse Pointe, Michigan, had again, unfortunately, failed to follow my implicit instructions to travel as cheaply as humanly possible. We were being chauffeured around in a brand-new black Mercedes. It was immaculately clean, inside and out. I would occasionally break out in a cold sweat whenever I thought of what this was costing me. The driver was very professional and not only dressed better than me—no surprise there; everybody dresses better than me—but was one of the best-dressed men I had ever seen at any formal gathering. He wore a very expensive tailor-made suit with a starched, button-down, white shirt and a colorful tie. His black leather shoes were polished to a mirror-like sheen. The only peculiar aspect of his attire was a very long, full-leather trench coat. He was something of a contrast not only to all the other Russians on the street in their rougher-looking clothing, but to me, dressed in a pair of faded jeans, a t-shirt, a 15-year-old frayed and stained jacket, and running shoes.

While Monica was off doing her business, both the driver and I stood outside the Mercedes, biding our time and engaging in small talk. It started to mist a bit, and the driver went to his trunk and provided two black umbrellas. These were not the cheap-ass umbrellas I buy at Kmart or the dollar store. These umbrellas had some weight and heft to them. But it was not the umbrellas that had my attention. When the driver opened the trunk to retrieve the umbrellas, which he did quickly, I couldn't help but notice that he had a stash of weapons of some quantity in the trunk. In fact, if the Nazis had chosen to return for a rematch, Russia might well defeat them using just my driver and his arsenal located within the trunk of his Mercedes.

A wiser, more discreet person might well have let this incident go without calling attention to it, but I have a tendency when traveling with people who carry bazookas and machine guns in their trunks to ask questions, and that is just what I did. "What's with the weapons in the trunk? Are you expecting World War III this week?" I asked jokingly.

The driver gave a short laugh and then very seriously said, "It's for protection from the Mafia." I had no idea how tough or efficient the Russian Mafia was, but one thing was for certain: they better not count on this guy running out of weapons or ammo. As I continued to engage him in conversation, I couldn't help but notice that he continually scanned the surroundings. He said Russia, after the fall of communism, was now a rough and violent place, but he was sure nobody was ever going to get him.

I made some comment like, "You never know!"—at which point, he faced me, put each of his hands on a lapel of that full-leather trench coat and briefly opened it up. On the inside of that long coat, running down both sides, were four weapons. On the top-left side, he had an Uzi with a long clip of rounds protruding from the chamber and, below that, he carried an automatic pistol. On the right side, he had two more automatic pistols loaded with long clips.

He closed his coat and gave me a short, tight smile as if to say, "Anyone taking me on will have a fight on their hands."

Monica finally returned, and I decided to let this incident slide without comment to her. Prior to our leaving for this trip, her side of the family—the Polish side— was sick with worry and concern about me taking her to Russia. (If I had bothered to mention to them that Turkmenistan was on the itinerary, they would have murdered me on the spot.) I had continually informed them that Russia was safe. Going even further, I explained that, being a social-studies teacher and world traveler, I was probably more informed and knowledgeable about this than they, so they should back off with their unreasonable fears. I never really did convince any of them of my viewpoint. And now here I was standing with, and being chauffeured by, the Russian equivalent of Rambo and Billy the Kid wrapped up into one.

There is something to be said for knowing when to keep your mouth closed and just letting things pass by without comment. There is even more to be said for being dishonest and untruthful—especially to your wife. For years now, I have had the ultimate joy of showing up at family functions—the Polish side—with my loyal wife always reminding her family and relatives what a wonderful man she married, an assertion accompanied by a reminder of how they got it all wrong about the safety of the Russia trip and how her brilliant, well-traveled, and, I might say, cosmopolitan husband (I just made up that "cosmopolitan" part because it sounds so good) got it all right! I just stand there among the family, trying not to be a big show-off and very modestly accepting the family's "I guess you were right on that one, Rufus." My only concern now is that, when this book hits the stands, my approval ratings in the polls among the family—the Polish side anyway—may take a dive. No problem! I am still relatively safe with the Irish side of the family—though, even there, since my mom passed away, things are a little shaky with my two siblings, who often debate where in the hell the family got me.

The bottom line is that, although things had not gone smoothly in the first three places we had visited (Poland, Turkmenistan, and Russia), Monica was only aware that the first two had been a problem. My batting average, as far as she was concerned, was .333—not too shabby. But *I* knew I had struck out. For me, it was now three failures in a row. (We had also spent a full day in Belarus, but we were in and out so fast that it didn't even feel like an "at bat"—more like a walk, which doesn't count in your statistics. See below.) But I am a man of incredible strength and endurance and love a challenge. Friends and family interpret that last sentence a bit differently and say I am a reckless idiot who is too foolhardy to ever be fearful or cautious. Take your pick as to who is correct in their appraisal of my personality, but I say these other people just don't have any sense of adventure!

For example (at the risk of ruining the surprise), you should know that, from Russia on, our trip never got better, and we descended into what my negative wife likes to refer to as "problems" but what I call "adventures." (See above.) You be the judge. We have four more countries to go.

Boring Belarus
—and Then a(n Unpleasant) Surprise

Belarus: Perhaps the most boring tourist destination on earth. The entire country looks as though it has been swallowed up by huge white apartment complexes—unfortunately Soviet style and quality. We walked from one endless apartment complex to another—all white; apparently no other color or hue had been allowed in Soviet times.

Our guide, pointing in the direction of one of these monotonous hulks, said, "There was an American living here in this apartment complex. You may have heard of him, but he is not so famous." I was expecting to hear about some obscure American poet or violinist—the Russians were really into that sort of thing—as she pointed out the exact apartment. Our guide stammered a bit trying to recollect the name and finally said, "Lee Harvey Oswald." Now that got our attention. Lee Harvey Oswald—the assassin of President John F Kennedy, one of our most beloved presidents, the martyred president,—and a good Irishman to boot!

"Not so famous" indeed. That's because *infamous* is the word.

Rufus McGaugh

Macedonia:
Mountains for Lodging and Dying On

Macedonia. We are talking about the brand-new (1991) country of Macedonia. We are not talking about the great ancient Macedonia of Alexander the Great who conquered most of the known world. In other words, we are talking about the imposter—the fake Macedonia, but try and convince the UN of that. The fake Macedonia has the UN seat. The real Macedonia is now part of Greece. Alexander the Great is probably rolling in his grave over this but can't do anything about it because, after all, he is dead, and has been for some time. But I know Al, and, *if* he were alive, Al would definitely kick some ass over this usurpation of territory and name. Just the same, we went there and had some good times.

Despite a few (how should I put this?) "problems" (I guess that's the word I'm looking for), great adventures, which I truly love, were there for the taking. This was 1995, and, although I had only somewhat recently learned how to use a computer, I was getting more and more skillful and competent with it. At least that's how I saw it. I had yet to use a computer for trip-planning purposes. I was using a very competent travel agent for flights and hotels, so there was little or nothing I needed to do myself. However—for some strange reason that I now forget after all these years—my travel agent was not able to book a hotel in Macedonia. So I was informed that I would have to do it—and, believe it or not, I did! I might well have been the most lame and inexperienced human using a computer and the internet back then (probably still am), but I navigated about and—*shazam!*—I had a hotel room!

The only other business that needed to be taken care of was some sort of tour throughout this small country. Nothing there. So I then looked into rental cars. Nothing there. Finally, I looked into a car and driver. There was something there but not at prices I would ever pay. So I decided that, once we got there, I would wing it.

When we flew into Macedonia and arrived at the capital with the funny-sounding name of Skopje (*scope-ski*), things started to unravel a bit. Monica inquired about the hotel. She did this with a sense of fear, desperation, and anxiety. After all, I didn't exactly have a great track record in the hotel department, or the aircraft department, or tram department, or the . . . All right, all right, I get the picture. I had been a miserable failure up to this point, but now modern technology by way of the computer and the internet was going to bail me out and make me the shining star of the travel industry I knew I was destined to become.

Upon arrival, we did have a *city* tour arranged, and we spent the remaining daylight hours touring the very pretty and very historic capital, Skopje. This land had once been part of the Ottoman Turkish Empire, so there were many Turkish baths, mosques, and forts to visit. When the tour ended, our driver announced he would drive us to our hotel.

Again it was truly amazing to see the two very different expressions on the faces of the cast of characters. I was beaming with excitement and joy, boasting of my new computer skills and how I had bagged a truly great lodge. With supreme confidence I was bragging about the deal I had snagged while other suckers squandered their money. Monica, on the other hand, had an expression of dread and foreboding. The fear of what rat hole she would end up in that night was palpable. Boy! Some people are just never satisfied and never learn to let their guard down and trust someone—especially a travel expert like me!

I reached into my travel security pouch and produced my hotel reservation form with a flourish, all the while reassuring all the naysayers, pessimists, critics, and skeptics—meaning Monica—that not only did I know what I was doing but, as a newly certified computer genius, I had pulled up pictures of the hotel/lodge, and—you are never going to believe this in a million years—it wasn't a total dump! Monica, at this news, was totally dumbstruck. A decent hotel was totally out of character for me. So off we went to what I described as the Taj Mahal of lodges.

We drove and drove, and then drove some more, and continued driving, kept driving, continued to keep driving, and proceeded to drive some more. But eventually we got there!

The lodge stood at the top of a mountain. Up close, looking at it from the outside, we could see that it was not the Taj Mahal of hotels or lodges, but it wasn't bad. In fact it was a step or two up (actually a full staircase up) from what we usually stayed in, so there was no second-guessing or complaining (on that score, anyway) from a very relieved Monica.

In all fairness, I feel duty bound to mention one minor inconvenience of our new home (which you may have discerned from the previous paragraph), and that was distance. Yes, the computer images of the lodge were true and accurate and not misleading, but those images did not show or mention that this little lodge was far, very far, from the city center. In fact, I was not sure, after that lengthy drive, if we were even in Macedonia—or Europe— any longer. A certain, very sarcastic person was even bold enough to ask if we were still on the same planet. I try to never let negative people with their continual and never-ending second-guessing get to me. So I just ignored my wife and all her slights and insults that as usual led to comments about my intelligence. Using my tour maps and Google distance charts, I was able to show her that we were indeed on the same planet, though I reckoned we were approximately 899 billion miles from even the nearest ancient Neanderthal cave.

Let it be said that, after all the failures on this trip, I needed the equivalent of travel Viagra to get things up and going again at this point. I am not exactly sure what my wife was thinking. Actually I was afraid that a list of words might have been passing through her mind—words like "idiot," "fool," "divorce," "moron," etc. While I was standing on the mountain's peak—I think it was called Mt. Everest—peering into the horizon, trying to determine if we were still in Europe or perhaps on some other continent, Monica had walked into the lodge, to check it out. (Why can't that woman just once trust me and my judgment? One of the greatest problems in our marriage has been the lack of trust a certain someone has for a very dependable and reliable husband.) She came back smiling! She informed me that it was a nice lodge and, even better, there was a restaurant here, so she wouldn't starve—for at least this part of the trip! Thus, for the second time, as when she reamed out the Polish police for arresting us—I was off the hook. And so, folks, you are witness to a true love story. If my wife does not end up in a filthy dungeon and has at least a morsel to eat (not three meals—let's not get carried away in this romance), she is ready to renew the wedding vows.

I had dodged the bullet on that one and would partially dodge the bullet on the next adventure. The next morning, we had scheduled another half-day tour of Skopje. The driver picked us up at the hotel after we had had our complimentary breakfast. Monica is usually a very light eater but hunkered down to get vast quantities of food into her, knowing that, since she was traveling with me, this would probably be the only meal of the day—and, as it turned out, she was correct.

In a few hours we had finished our city tour and were let off in the middle of the city. Monica asked, "What now?"

I said, "We are going to drive to Lake Ohrid, which is the border of Macedonia and Albania."

"You told me earlier that there are no car rentals or tours and that the car-and-driver rates were too expensive; how are we going to get there?" Monica asked (with a bit too much suspicion for my taste).

I said, "This is where the suckers are separated from the travel genius like me. Only a fool would pay the prices I saw on the internet for a car and driver. I'll just go out on the street and find someone on my own, for half the price. You will shortly see why everyone is in awe of my travel skills."

Longitude and Latitude, with Attitude

I took Monica to a coffee shop and told her I would be back shortly—and I was! I had a car! I had a driver! And I had a great deal to boot! "Let's go! Time's a-wasting!"

Monica was suspicious, but she was game for the travel experience. I had finally redeemed myself. The old Rufus was back, swaggering and wheeling and dealing in the one field I know best, travel. We got into the car— not, of course, before a critical look-over by my wife, but it passed her skeptical inspection. And off we went through beautiful mountainous countryside broken now and then by small valleys of green and bright yellow with crops looking very abundant on this sunny day.

About two hours into the trip as the mountains became higher and steeper and the curves becoming sharper and tighter, the driver started having problems with his brakes. The more he used his brakes, the more they played out and had less and less stopping power. No problem. This is very typical of cars in poor countries; they never have good brakes. Nothing to worry about. The car was a stick-shift, and the driver now used his lower gears to slow the car down as we drove through the winding mountains. He also slowed his speed significantly, so, all and all, we were still doing okay. That is—everybody but a certain somebody in the back seat, who seemed to have somehow in just the last few minutes received a Harvard degree in auto engineering.

This newly minted professor of engineering, residing like a monarch in the back seat, claimed driving a car with no brakes through the mountains was dangerous. What in the hell did she know about cars? Obviously nothing. Yes, you, the reader, can see and agree with the driver and me that slowing down, pumping the brakes excessively, and down-shifting whenever things get a little too dicey and it looks like you are going over a cliff are all you need for a safe journey. For Christ's sake, it's not worth having a heart attack like a certain hysterical person in the back seat was having!

Monica wanted to turn back. "*Are you crazy?*" I responded. Besides we were only an hour, maybe an hour and half from our destination, and I wanted to see what some described as one of the most charming lakes in the world, Lake Ohrid.

As it turned out, Lake Ohrid was not all that great, or worth dying over, but, of course, I didn't know that at the time. So on we went—and we got to Lake Ohrid—and it was all right, I guess.

Lake Ohrid in Macedonia. A body of water not worth dying over. But I didn't know that until I got there. You never do, do you?

After a little visit and a little photography, it was time to head back. Now Monica was bitching that she didn't want to drive back, at least not in the car we came in with no brakes. Well good luck trying to find another car in Macedonia in 1995—especially one with brakes! I don't know if this is true or reliable, but years later I was told that having brakes on a car in Macedonia was optional and they did not become standard until 2010.

This is the one thing I hate about marriage and putting up with another person: *First Monica complains and bitches about getting to Lake Ohrid, and, now that she finally gets her way and we are going back, she is still bitching and complaining over a stupid thing like the car having no brakes.* It wasn't as if the driver and I hadn't bothered to explain to her a hundred times that, yes, brakes were nice, but a lot of men like us were fully capable of driving sharp mountain roads with no brakes. It's called "gearing down with the stick shift," but, of course, this was beyond any woman's knowledge in auto mechanics.

So, despite an awful lot of irrational fear on Monica's part, we began our journey back to Skopje. Despite all the complaining from "Little Miss Skeptic" in the back seat, we were doing fine. There was one little issue, however, on the horizon, and that was darkness and its impending arrival—like in a few minutes. We were driving reasonably slowly. When we were going down mountains, the driver expertly downshifted

Longitude and Latitude, with Attitude

to slow us to a speed that would not cause us to go hurtling off the steep mountain roads to certain death in the valley below. Going downhill also involved the driver constantly pumping the brake pedal—which did little or nothing to slow the car.

We were proceeding with caution and making our way slowly but surely to Skopje when we started careening down a very steep decline. The car continued to gain speed at an alarming rate despite everything the driver, now desperate and in near panic, did to slow the car. The curves of the mountain were now steep and tight. We swerved to the right, then to the left, back to the right, and immediately to the left, all the time the car gaining speed and the driver losing control. Our bodies swayed in whichever direction the driver swerved to. Racing straight down on the last curve, we were out of control. We were now so desperate that the driver and I had the same thought and then proceeded to act on it. We both, without saying a word, opened our doors and dragged one foot in an attempt to stop a speeding, out-of-control car. Did two dragging feet do the trick? I have no idea if that desperate action really made a difference, but we did survive without going over a mountain—barely.

Interlude: Requiem for a Shoe

Perhaps the most embarrassing and humiliating aspect of this story is the epilogue to it. And perhaps I might be the only person on earth to sink to such a low level and feel no shame whatsoever.

I had been a big-time runner ever since I had joined the Marines in 1968. For years, cheap Kmart running shoes were all I needed. Friends, and even strangers, had warned me and advised me for many years to part with a few extra bucks and buy some decent shoes. They warned that running in Kmart shoes would destroy my knees, my shins, and various other body parts. Finally succumbing to good common sense, even if it hurt my wallet, I bought my first pair of good running shoes. For the life of me I can't remember which brand—New Balance, Adidas, or Nike—but it was a name brand with good ratings from the running crowd.

I hadn't owned this first pair of really good running shoes for very long when I had to use them as a very unconventional braking system on a jalopy in the mountains of Macedonia. My left shoe was like new. My right shoe was so worn away it was translucent. Not only could you see daylight through the sole and heel of my brand-new shoes but you could also make out the design woven into my socks if you happened to look at them from the bottom. I now also walked with a limp whenever wearing these shoes, due to their unevenness. I was heartbroken. Somehow I got through the trip—with a limp and one destroyed shoe.

But it doesn't end there. One of my many character flaws (at one time I did not feel that I had that many, but then I got married) is the inability to spend any of my hard-earned money without suffering acute pain over it. I'm not talking just dollars but quarters, dimes, and nickels. I had planned for these shoes to last me a decade or more. Now I know what you are thinking. Running shoes are usually good for a year, but you would be surprised at how long a very frugal person can make them last. (I'll give you a hint: multiply the norm by ten.) If this catastrophic accident had happened when the shoes were, let's say, four years old, that would have been very bad. At five or six years old, that would have been sad. Because they were brand new, that was a real hit and psychological trauma for me.

So, when I got home, I wrote a letter to the manufacturer, telling my story and explaining my dilemma: having only one good shoe when I of course have two feet. Did the manufacturer happen to have a right shoe, size eight, lying about in the factory, that perhaps I could have for free? Or, if payment was needed, perhaps I could send a token fee to cover shipping costs? After all, how many one-legged or one-footed runners are there? It's not like the manufacturer could really sell a single shoe, if it happened to have one, and I would be forever appreciative if they sent it to me!

About six weeks later I received a letter from the manufacturer telling me they had never received a letter quite like mine. (There you go! If that doesn't prove my exceptionalism and uniqueness, nothing will!) But, no, unfortunately they did not have a size-eight right shoe to give me or sell me. I was screwed.

In the past when I have told this story, people—actually good friends—have looked me straight in the eyes and said something like, "Are you actually that damn cheap that you tried to buy a single shoe? I can't imagine anyone sinking to such a pathetic level, trying to buy just one shoe!" Well, when they put it like that, I guess they have a point.

Back to Our Regularly Scheduled Adventures...

Now for those of you who have been following this sad tale (or, as I like to describe it, our merry misadventures), you may have hoped to see my wife dump the incompetent loser she was traveling with, fly home on the first flight to be had, and immediately file for divorce. No way! My wife, Monica, deep down, knows she won the lottery when she snagged me! How she squares that with the fact that she is an otherwise very intelligent woman is the only inconsistent and unexplained part of our union. But loyalty is her virtue, and, if this doesn't explain why she married the clod she did, it might well explain why she stays with him.

It was only after this last incident of the run-away death trap we had just escaped that she started to notice and recite what she called "a litany of near-death experiences" in non-flyable planes, cars with no brakes in the mountains, two arrests by the police on the same day, and a terrifying night-time odyssey in the deserts of Turkmenistan—and we still had a week to go!

I, on the other hand, looked upon these last seven days as great news, thrilling to the thought of more adventures. So far, except for what I consider to be the usual small bumps in the road, the trip had proceeded flawlessly. Monica, on the other hand, asked me if it were possible to change our plans a bit and fly home—today. Some people just have no sense of adventure!

I took my new bride in hand and explained that we would never be able to change our flights and, even if we could, it would probably cost a fortune. But I sealed the deal with this famous axiom: "Look, Monica, everyone knows that all the problems in a trip come in the beginning. Every tour book and every travel writer has written about and testified to this fact—and we have just finished the beginning of the trip, so no more problems! We have pretty much worked out all the kinks and issues for this trip. Just sit back and enjoy the rest of what is going to be a completely enjoyable and flawless trip of wonder and pleasure."

To be completely honest with you, I don't have any idea why I say things like this, but sometimes words just come out of my mouth. I have no idea where the above came from or why I said it. I think it comes from a medical condition known as having lots of personality—and enthusiasm. But who gives a shit?—she bought into it despite the lack of logic behind it. I was again master of this ship, or at least this trip. So now I redoubled my efforts to make this the coolest trip anyone at any time has ever made. As far as I was concerned, it already was, but a certain somebody let slip she did have some reservations despite being led by the coolest guy to ever travel.

Slovenia, the Hidden Gem of Europe

One of the strategies I used to dispel all this negativity was to really build up our next destination which was the country of Slovenia, about which I knew absolutely nothing, except that it wasn't Slovakia—or Siberia, I thought. Although I have to admit I kept getting the last two mixed up. Or was it the first two? Can't remember now, but it doesn't matter because I was doing what I do best—whipping up excitement and enthusiasm for what I called "the hidden gem of Europe." Who would not want to visit a country with such a title? Truth be told, I had just made that title up, but I was certain Slovenia would live up to the sobriquet I had just crowned it with.

So we caught our flight from Macedonia to Slovenia, and everything appeared to be going smoothly when Monica asked me what there was to see or do in Slovenia. I immediately replied, "To be honest with you, I'm really not sure. It's a brand-new country." It was created in 1991. "I've never been there, and don't know anything about it."

A pause and then, "So why are we going there?" she asked.

"Because I have never been there" was my instant response.

A slightly longer pause and then, "So you have never been to Slovenia; you can't tell me anything about it; you can't tell me if there's anything there worth seeing or doing; you can't even spell or pronounce its capital—and yet we are now going there for some reason?"

Hey, I'll admit I am not very good speller and admittedly not a very good pronouncer at all, (and some might even be mean and say a not very good tour guide), but I always get us there, and we *always* muddle through it, having lots of fun along the way! Besides, who in the hell could spell or pronounce some weird-ass city like Ljubljana!

After admitting that she was correct on all counts, I thought and hoped this demeaning ridicule would come to an end so that we could get revved up for the new impending adventure that awaited us. Alas, this was not to be. After a very long pause, I heard, "So explain to me again why we are going to this place."

"Place"? That reeked of insulting sarcasm! Here I'm taking this woman to the greatest site in Europe, Slovenia—including its unpronounceable capital, Ljubljana, at no extra charge—and she has the audacity to second-guess me. After I have successfully escorted her from one top tourist destination to the next, in flawless fashion, she has the nerve to second-guess my decisions. Some people just don't appreciate what they have!

I patiently explained to this spoiled aristocrat that we were going to Slovenia because it was on the "list."

"What 'list'?" she asked. I could hear the cruel sarcasm.

"The list of all the countries I haven't been to," I answered.

A very, very, long pause, and then—like Mount Vesuvius erupting, because she could no longer take it—she dropped the "F" bomb. (That made it the second time within one trip!) "Are you trying to tell me the only reason we are going to Slovenia is because you've never been to this fucking country?"

Well! Let me speak on behalf of every single Slovenian—and there aren't a whole lot of them: our feelings have really been hurt by this tirade and emotional outburst. There might not be a lot of us—and I am including myself within this persecuted minority, just for solidarity's sake, even though I am Irish—but we don't deserve such an unwarranted insult!

Here we were, heading for the greatest country on Earth, and some obscure American woman was hurling insulting disparagements at my very favorite country in the world.

So we did what most married couples have done from time immemorial in a situation like this—namely, we sat there in icy silence, refusing to speak to each other.

I am sure by now that the reader has already taken my side in this ridiculous argument and can clearly see who the unreasonable half is and who is just dead wrong in what truly was going to be an amazing adventure that we would cherish for years to come. And (just to show you how big I am) the smarter one, the more worldly one, the nicer, calmer one in this marriage—me—even attempted a little cheer-up conversation but was met with stony silence.

In any case we did land and arrive in Slovenia, and the one single thing that I had, that just possibly might bail my ass out of an already tense situation, was a hotel voucher. With this, I was already counting our arrival in the greatest country in Europe—all 7,000 square miles of it—a great success. No searching for a hotel manager. No sleeping in the street or in a bus station or on a park bench out in the rain, worrying about thieves or bad guys, as we had in the past. We had a home for two nights bought and paid for.

Spoiler alert: a certain dissatisfied, malcontent gadfly was not happy. Jesus Christ! What now? Well, it seems that the hotel, once we arrived and were settled in our room, was very typical of any of the communist or post-communist countries. This meant that the sleeping arrangements were always set up (even for married couples providing a certified wedding license or marriage certificate) brother-sister style—and Monica always had a real problem with that. Whereas I didn't give a damn about it at all. Hey, we're traveling and having great adventures; don't worry about the small stuff. Not true for Monica. In her book, when you are married, husband and wife sleep together: with sex or without sex, you sleep together.

This was actually one of the more appealing qualities about my wife—she always wanted to sleep with me. I had not gotten married until I was 44, and I can assure you that, during that time, there were hundreds—no thousands—of women who did not want to sleep with me. So this was quite appealing, a woman demanding sleeping rights with me. Now, like every other single, red-blooded male God has ever put on Earth, I wanted, was willing to have, and hoped for sex three or four times a day. The fact that I was capable of sex about once a week—and that was stretching things a bit—did not deter me (like every other normal guy) from talking a good game about wanting sex five or six times a day.

As long as I am on everybody's favorite subject (sex), did you ever notice that the term "sleeping together" has completely different definitions depending on whether you are male or female? The female definition of "sleeping together" is "falling asleep." The male definition is "getting laid."

I finally convinced "Little Miss Libido" to quit complaining about the sleeping arrangements and get moving so we could hit the streets and see this weird-sounding city of Ljubljana. Monica, the most pleasant human being on earth, now in a somewhat foul mood over recent setbacks and failures, caused by a certain someone who was included on this trip, followed my lead down the now darkened city streets of Ljubljana.

Let me reword that a bit. These were not *streets* but pitch-black, can't-see-your-hand-two-inches-in-front-of-your-face *alleys*, with the most uneven, hard-granite stone-laid streets in Europe. Talk about a mugger's paradise—this was it. In the Marines, I had spent a year in Nam going on night ambushes deep in enemy territory, with no light, with darkness that was solid black, so I had a certain balance and awareness in such situations. Just the same, it was really dark, and one moved more by feel than sight.

We both heard faint music in the distance and were perplexed as to its origin or meaning, but continued onward. At one point Monica wanted to turn back, and I was in partial agreement, but wanderlust, curiosity, or stubbornness led me on. Then suddenly we emerged from the darkness into a surreal very bright light.

Without getting into hyperbole or exaggeration, let me just say that we stood transfixed, staring at what appeared to be a fairy-tale land of architecturally amazing snow-white buildings of marble, limestone, and granite. The fact that a major European music festival was presently taking place within the confines of the city made it all that more magical.

The light, the architecture, and music led us further into the city center that now revealed a number of what appeared to be small white-marble bridges spanning the Ljubljanica River. Every step brought us closer to the music of world-class orchestras at every square in the city. Two weeks of mishaps and travel problems were swept away by this charming fantasy world.

Again the difference in perceptions. Through brilliance or just dumb luck I had pulled off a magnificent coup. My quest to go everywhere and see everything had truly paid off beyond belief in this enchanted land. Monica was now actually starting to think that Rufus really did, after all, know what he was doing. Later we actually found our brother-sister hotel without a problem. I can't remember if we had sex that night—but, even better, I had bailed my ass out and had my rep back!

The next morning it was really more of the same—a very nice and wonderful same! Ljubljana is a very small capital city, easily done on foot, and we had probably seen everything the night before. In daylight, though, there were very colorful markets, and we could better see and appreciate the water of the river and the medieval architecture. We ate at outside cafes and on a lark went to the McDonald's, not for the food but for a beer and a glass of wine, something not ever possible in the U.S.

Ljubljana, Slovenia, one of the loveliest, most beautiful cities in Europe.

The Albania of My Existence

As I have already mentioned, in every city, in every country, we had been warned—actually scared straight— about our plans to visit Albania. Every single person, and there were many, warned that we would be cheated, robbed, and assaulted and my wife would be raped. (Maybe I would be, too!) European people warned us—some even pleaded with us—not to go. Others predicted a trip to Albania would be a crime-filled nightmare. The Albanians were the scum of the Earth, criminals, thieves, murderers—lawless, uncivilized, backward peasants who traveled in violent gangs—the list of epithets went on and on.

Now, I am (take your pick) reckless/fearless/stupid/brave/insane/bold—or a combination thereof. I am ready to go anywhere, any time, but I am not about to put anyone else in danger or jeopardy. I had taken vows in matrimony to do all kinds of things for this woman, but getting her killed, raped, or needlessly exposed to disease was not part of the bargain. So, on our last night in Slovenia (or Slovakia, or Siberia, or wherever in the hell we were—I told you I got them mixed up), as Monica slept, I spent half the night pacing, thinking, and debating whether we should fly to Albania in the morning or bail out and go home. At about three in the morning, I took the position that pretty much everybody in Europe was—how can I put this politely, without offending anyone?—full of shit when it came to the Albanians.

This position represented quite a leap of faith because I had never met any Albanians or been to their country. I had vast experience in my own country with racism, especially when it came to African-Americans. I was the son of a Tennessee farmer who was a segregationist and racist. I was raised and schooled in the all-white neighborhoods of lower-middle-class blue-collar workers, so I knew racism, and I knew it well. The talk in Europe of Albanians was identical to the talk in America about African-Americans, and it was based on a lot of misconceptions, stereotypes, fear, and ignorance, so I bet my bottom dollar they were all wrong and I was right. This conclusion was not based on knowledge, research, or personal experience but on a gut feeling. I have to admit, at the time, it was a very shaky conviction. President Andrew Jackson once said, "One man with courage is a majority" and that's what I was going on, a defiance of the norm.

The next morning Monica asked if I had made a final decision about our plans, and I said, "We're going to Albania" with assurance and conviction, sure and convinced that I was doing the right thing and the safe thing. We flew into the capital of Albania, Tirana, and were greeted at the airport by what appeared to be a full-blown riot. I'll explain this in

Longitude and Latitude, with Attitude

a moment, but let me give you a little background on what once was a very strange little country—the North Korea of its day!

In 1995, when we arrived in Albania, this country was at the very bottom rung of poverty in Europe. It was ranked as the poorest, most isolated, and socially backward nation of Europe. The credit for this all goes to Enver Hoxha, who ruled this small communist country from 1944 until 1985, when he did his country—actually the world—a big favor and died. Hoxha was the Kim Jong-un of his day, and his day lasted 40 years. From decade to decade, Enver Hoxha never disappointed the editors of *News of the Weird*.

He began his Kim-Jon-un-like odyssey of the surreal in 1946 by overthrowing the only Moslem king in Europe, the king of Albania, King Zog (gotta love the name!). All the way back in 1953, and onward, Hoxha was always good for pushing any event to the limits of excess. When the great tyrant and mass murderer Joseph Stalin of the Soviet Union died that year, Hoxha literally had his entire nation kneel and recite a 2,000-word pledge of "eternal fidelity" to their "beloved father" (Stalin).

In the next decade, the sixties, when the U.S. and the West were facing off with the U.S.S.R. (Russia) in a Cold War and nearly getting into a nuclear war over the Cuban Missile Crisis, Hoxha was breaking off relations with the Soviet Union (Russia) because it was not communist enough! Hoxha was having none of that liberal "peaceful coexistence" stuff with the West that was being advocated by the soft wussies of communist Russia.

By the seventies Hoxha had dumped communist China for the same reason and decided to go it alone: Albania versus the world. This resulted in a number of bizarre steps that included the cult of personality with him bearing titles such as "Supreme Comrade" and "Great Teacher." (I tried that last one with my 7th-grade students, but they revolted and I was nearly overthrown in a classroom coup.) The Albanians were told that Enver Hoxha was a genius in everything. They bought it. I tell my wife Monica the same, but she tells me I am full of it, so I guess the Polish are not as incredulous or as trusting as the Albanians (although, in my defense, I am still holding on to my title of Family Dictator—just barely, with lots of dissent from *three* of them now: Monica and our two boys).

As Hoxha's mind deteriorated and his rule became more authoritarian, thousands and thousands of Albanians were arrested, imprisoned, and tortured due to his paranoia. Standing sentinel to the outside enemies Hoxha feared were over 750,000 thick concrete bunkers facing out. The enormous sum of money to build something of this magnitude in such a poor country boggles the mind.

A Digression to the Former Yugoslavia (and Albania, Sort of), for Birdwatching

And now, as I so often do, I must digress a bit to take you on a winding path of related stories that all tie in. The first will be very surprising to the reader. Albania, at one time, was probably the most "forbidden" country on earth. Due to its isolation and Hoxha's paranoia, nobody got in and nobody got out. Travel visas were impossible, and border guards kept the country sealed—and yet, in the 1980s, I got in— kind of!

I had been on a tour of Russia and Eastern Europe when I became good friends with an older retiree from California by the name of Bert. He had worked in the oil industry and had traveled a bit throughout the world, but now in retirement he wanted to see a lot more of the world, as a lot of us want to do. He was a very intelligent guy who really knew his history. His biggest passion in life, though, was birding. And, like many birders and Audubon members, he had his list of birds that he had seen or spotted and a much, much longer list of birds throughout the world that he hoped to see. One day while we were in the old Yugoslavia, Bert approached me and made an offer. The tour we were on was very good, but a bit slow moving. His plan was to rent a car and tour behind the tour bus but to break off sometimes to go birding. He would pay for everything if I helped out by doing the bulk of the driving and map reading and remained a patient, good sport about his time peering through binoculars following little birdies through the forest.

I offered to split the cost, but Bert would have none of it. He had planned to rent a car beforehand, before meeting me, so he now felt he had the better part of the deal, getting both help with the driving *and* companionship. (Probably he had taken notice of my clothes and the way I dressed, plus he may have also observed me skipping meals to save money, which would surely have convinced him there was to be little or no money to be had from Rufus.)

So off we went—on a bird adventure.

For the next few days, Bert tried to draw me into birding and make a new convert, but I had to gently let him down and dash his hopes. "Bert, I know you love your birds and you have that humongous list of hundreds and hundreds of birds that you want to see and check off, but, for me, there are really only two kinds of birds: big birds and little birds."

Longitude and Latitude, with Attitude

I am not sure if Bert was disgusted with me or exasperated with me, but he let it go with a laugh.

In any case, on one of our days exploring and birding, me driving and Bert with his binoculars, we looked at our map and saw that we were on the road to Albania—the forbidden land! I said, "Bert, let's give it a shot and see if we can get into Albania."

"Sounds dangerous and reckless to me, but, if that's what you want to do, do it. I've lived a long life, and getting shot at the Albanian border might just be the way to go," he said with a laugh.

Now, there's a traveling companion for you! Not like little "Miss Scaredy Cat" with whom I was now traveling but a bold man ready to die for a good cause—getting into Albania. Bert kept saying it was never going to happen, but he was up for the sure-to-be adventure.

Just before we got to the border, in a more serious tone Bert asked if I had any sort of plan. "Yep" was the single word I answered with, and Bert was fine with that.

As we approached the Albanian border we could see what looked like six Albanian soldiers with rifles. We passed a number of signs in numerous languages telling us to turn around and that there was no entry into Albania. Signs like these are for wussies! "Push the limits a bit, and you often get great results" is my motto. So on we went. I just kept proceeding, slowly. I stuck my arm out the rolled-down window of—yes, you guessed it—a Yugo, and was waving and smiling at the guards but not stopping. The guards were actually smiling and seemed like good guys, not totalitarian robots as I later witnessed in North Korea. There was a wide, bright-yellow line painted on the asphalt road by the guard post that said "STOP!" but I just kept rolling by, slowly and then stopped over the yellow line and into Albania.

For just a brief second or two the guards dropped their smiles and became very serious, unshouldering their rifles. In that brief second, I was already backing the junky little Yugo up and smiling and babbling on with nice "hello's" and "how are you's," which immediately brought the smiles back.

Once we had backed up over the thick yellow line and back into Yugoslavia, I continued the banter and asked as innocently as a little child, "What, can't we go into Albania, the greatest country in the world?"—which brought even bigger smiles from the soldiers. All six of the soldiers crowded around the Yugo in a very friendly manner—much to my relief. They were all joking and bantering—in Albanian. Only one soldier seemed to have any English vocabulary, and he appeared to be the friendliest guy in the world, but—no (and he turned to his comrades for affirmation), no, we couldn't enter Albania. I don't think I have ever been blown off or rejected in such a friendly fashion in my entire life.

As you can clearly see, I was willing to go to any lengths to get into a new country—especially those countries you were supposed to stay out of, such as Albania. Driving my rental car past six armed soldiers so that I could say I had been in Albania, all of ten feet of it, seemed like an acceptable risk to me—Bert not so much, although, as we backed up, I did hear Bert mutter, "This turned out OK despite just about scaring the shit out of me, Rufus."

As we turned the car to head back into Yugoslavia, our six new friends all smiled and waved and said a bunch of somethings in Albanian. And now Bert was one happy man. After all was said and done, and we were out of range of rifle fire, Bert was enjoying our recent brush with danger as quite an exploit. Every now and then, throughout the day, he would chuckle while we were traversing the back mountain roads of Yugoslavia in search of birds to add to his growing list. Every episode of chuckling was accompanied with a hearty, "Boy! That was one hell of an adventure back there, Rufus!"

Bert couldn't be more pleased with himself. A number of times he mentioned how he couldn't wait to tell his friends and family back home about the adventure we had just been through. I always had to remind him that the best part was that we not only knocked off another country—but it was *Albania*! That would always set Bert off chuckling even louder. He was so happy he was beaming.

That night, after meeting back up with our group, Bert was having a grand time recounting our adventure to one person, couple, or group after another. This went on for a few days until every member of our tour bus had heard the story.

A Postscript to the Digression: Lost Passport

One small postscript to all this that I did feel very bad about. The next day, late in the afternoon, as Bert and I were roaming around the mountains and back villages in small solitary valleys, he noticed he did not have his passport. After some thought, he figured out what must have happened, and it was not good.

That morning, a policeman had ticketed me for driving through a green light. Strange, I know. The traffic light was not red, not amber, or even getting close to amber. The light was green and remained so for many seconds after I was pulled over. This fact, however, was not going to deter the police officer from giving me a ticket. Bert and I protested, but eventually decided it was a waste of time, and the puny five-dollar fine—paid on the spot, receipt included—would not break the bank. Besides it gave us a good laugh about getting a ticket for going through a green light and a great story for years later.

This explains the missing passport. The police officer wanted to see both our passports when he pulled us over, and Bert for some reason had not put his away but held on to it when we pulled away. Later, he would remember getting out of the car and fumbling with his binoculars to spot another rare bird. He had put his passport on the roof of the car momentarily—and then forgot about it, until now. Retrieving it would be impossible. We were now hours away from a spot in the back mountains that we would never find again. This was a problem.

The saddest part was how badly this situation affected Bert. He was a happy-go-lucky guy, probably in his early eighties, and very intelligent, but now he was very down and depressed and losing confidence in himself by the minute. I did what I could to cheer him up and tried to demonstrate a sense of confidence that we would work it all out and that he shouldn't worry, but Bert was hit hard and pretty beaten up by this situation.

To be honest, I was thinking to myself that this was a pretty serious problem and that Bert might be in a serious fix, and I am sure that was exactly what Bert was thinking at that very moment. As it turned out, it wasn't too awfully bad. In fact, looking back, after all these years, it was really not that bad at all—though that's easy to say now. We got to our hotel and re-joined our group, and then Bert and I corralled the tour leader and explained our—Bert's—dilemma.

As Bert poured out his story and problem, the entire group fell silent. Like me, everyone in there felt this was a serious problem and might only get worse. I think every American is taught or at least feels his or her U.S. passport is a sacred document like the Declaration of Independence or the U.S. Constitution. The only difference is that *you* are the one responsible for your passport. We were in a communist country during the Cold War, and nobody seemed to have any idea what sort of trouble or issue a lost passport might cause.

Chris, the tour guide, to his credit, knew exactly what to do and pulled it off like a military operation. First, he told Bert to cheer up and that they would work it all out. Then, at an earlier-than-usual dinner that night with the whole group present, Chris laid out his plan and asked the group for our support. Everybody was in favor of the plan before they even heard it, because everyone on the trip was basically a nice person who wanted to help, and everybody really liked Bert and wanted to do whatever they could to get him out of this jam.

The plan was that Bert and Chris would immediately take off and drive in the rental car all the way to Belgrade, the capital of Yugoslavia, to the U.S. Embassy and get Bert a new passport. The next day, after getting Bert his new passport, they would head back, and, if things went well, meet all of us at the next hotel the next night. Everybody was all for it and wished Bert good luck and much encouragement.

Up to this point, I was giving our fearless tour leader, Chris, A+'s for leadership. Then suddenly I started to have some serious doubts. For, before leaving with Bert, Chris announced that, in his absence, he was appointing Rufus—me—as temporary leader of the whole busload of travelers. Was this man out of his mind? If you have been reading this book, you surely realized long ago that, through fate or some sense of bad luck, every single day of my travel life somehow ends up in a disaster, adventure, or life-threatening experience. People love to hear about my adventures, but that doesn't necessarily mean that they want to go through those adventures with me. They just like to hear about them. (That's why you're reading this book and not accompanying me on my next trip.)

Even more surprising than Chris's decision to promote me to tour leader was the group's universal acceptance of their fate under my leadership. *These people*, I thought, *are even crazier than Chris!*

As things turned out, everything went perfectly. Chris and Bert made it to the U.S. Embassy, got Bert a brand-new American passport (the U.S. Embassy issued him one in a very professional and efficient manner in very little time), and had a nice but very long drive back, missing dinner but being reunited with all of us the next morning to continue the tour. For our part, the entire busload of tourists, while Bert and Chris were on their mission, under my charismatic leadership, had an absolutely wonderful time. I fulfilled all my duties in an exemplary manner by sitting in the first seat at the front of the bus and answering all questions from our large group with an "I'm not sure" or "I don't know." There is just no substitute for real leadership, as I always say.

Another Digression: The First Lengths I Went To

Years earlier, while serving in the Marines in Vietnam, I pulled another such stunt. At that time, I had very few countries under my belt, but just the same I wanted to travel and add countries to my list.

Longitude and Latitude, with Attitude

When I enlisted in the Marines in 1968, my list of countries was pretty small. It fact it was pretty much *one*—the United States—and that was it. I had a long way to go to see all of the world back in those days. I had walked over the Ambassador Bridge from where I lived in Detroit into Windsor, Canada, but that was only 7,000 feet in distance from the U.S., so it didn't exactly feel like a foreign country. I had spent a few hours with a couple of high-school friends walking around downtown Windsor, but it was really no different than Detroit, just smaller.

While stationed at Camp Pendleton in California, I did take a bus to Tijuana, Mexico. Even as a naïve 20-year-old who had really never been anywhere, I suspected that Tijuana might not be typical of the entire Mexican nation. (It's not.)

After I finished my infantry training at Camp Pendleton and we shipped out to Nam, our plane did make a re-fueling stop on Wake Island in the Pacific. Wake Island is not of course a country; in fact, it is a U.S. territory, so I didn't feel I had accomplished much in my two-hour stopover there. We also stopped for one day on the island of Okinawa, but, again, at the time it was a U.S. possession, so not much of a feeling of accomplishment in the travel department. (Perhaps, with my lust for travel, I should have joined the Navy. But how does that old song go? "He joined the Navy to see the world. / And what did he see, and what did he see? He saw the sea.")

So, if you don't count two overseas islands that were owned and possessed by the U.S., and walking a couple of hundred feet over our border into Windsor, Canada, at one end, and Tijuana, Mexico at the other end of our country, I had been nowhere!

I did finally arrive in South Vietnam, and that was a somewhere, but a hellhole of a somewhere. Even after spending a tour of duty there for nearly a year, I really saw little of the country. My first three or four months were in a tiny isolated area of the Que Son Valley that consisted of nothing but stinking rice paddies, little villages, and tiny hamlets. My last six months were up in the Que Son Mountains, where there was nothing but mountains (back-breaking to scale and to hump up and down) and impenetrable jungle.

Here is my very condensed memory of one year in Vietnam during the war in the 5th Marines as a grunt machine-gunner (for a more expansive memory, see the first two chapters of this book): filth, the heat, monsoons, leeches, blood suckers, malaria, immersion foot, yellow fever, dengue fever, pneumonia, sores, jungles, mountains, booby traps, punji sticks, night ambushes, search-and-destroy missions, rocket attacks, patrols, incoming, friendly fire, lob bombs, napalm, razor wire, C-rations, the wounded, the sick, the dead, the maimed, artillery support, "guns up," body counts, medevac's, hospitals, typhoons, air support, my M60, claymore mines, land mines, frags, fraggings, snakes, centipedes, scorpions, rock apes, malarial mosquitoes, flies, cockroaches, rats, swamps, bomb craters, stagnant water, perspiration, body odor, dysentery, diarrhea, coughs, Cobras, gunships, murder, death, fear, cruelty, payback, poverty, hunger, rapes, torture, guerillas, Viet Cong, Charlie, NVA, amputations, fighting holes, bunkers, night watch, point, tail-end-Charlie, Tet, A-gunner, AK47s, RPGs, jungle canopy, tanks, causalities, being overrun, South China Sea, B52s, sucking chest wounds, bayonets, jungle knives, fire fights, battles, chaplains, the bush, body bags, base camp, flak jacket, fire bases, LZs, M16s, Recon, sappers, shit burning, lifers, the "World," Operations, missiles, air support, carpet bombing, artillery, free-fire zones, drugs, black market, Khe Sanh, hot landing zones, killer teams, howitzers, Phantoms, body parts, Purple Heart, million-dollar wounds, smoke grenades, the Arizona, the Phu Nans, the DMZ, air strikes, and atrocities.

In any case, in those rare moments when we Marines were somewhat inactive, such as sitting in a fighting hole, half filled with stagnant and malarial water with weapons pointing out for defense of our position, we had an opportunity to talk. Those conversations were often far ranging and many times pretty impractical. We were 18, 19, and 20 or so, and the one single common element that coursed its way through every discussion was the future. The future involved such topics as jobs, food, school, girls, beer, cars, and travel, all to be done as civilians.

It will surprise no one that even then I had a keen interest in travel and spoke of it often. The other Marines, when they heard my plans about traveling the world, would either smile indulgently, trying to disguise their friendly skepticism, or would outright say I was nuts, or full of it, or both. (After over 40 years of receiving post cards from countries all over the world, most of these guys have cried "Uncle" and have graciously conceded that I was one of the few who went out and did what I said I would do: see the world.) Just the same, they would listen to all my wild talk about seeing the pyramids and the Great Wall of China because it was good talk and there was nothing else to do in any case.

As mentioned earlier, I already had my "list" of countries, which was pretty pathetic—consisting only of the U.S., Wake Island, Okinawa, South Vietnam, Canada, and Mexico. The first four were places every one of these Marines had been to. The other two—Canada and Mexico (especially since I was honest about only having been to Windsor and Tijuana)—didn't impress any of my fellow Marines in the least. In fact, most gave me no credit at all for the last two.

Longitude and Latitude, with Attitude

A little past the middle of my tour of duty, I would go to Thailand for my R & R, so there was one more real country on a list that was not very long. Then, towards the end of my tour of duty, the 5th Marines were called upon to execute a POW rescue mission on the border of South Vietnam and Laos. I was to be one of the machine gunners. Our landing spot and staging area was within the shadow of Khe Sahn, the heroic and near mythical site of the Marines standoff against the North Vietnamese Army in 1968. That year, 6,000 Marines fought off over 30,000 hard-core North Vietnamese Army troops in one of the most spectacular battles of the entire war. For 77 days, Marines at this isolated mountain base resisted everything the communists could hurl at them. This was a battle that ranged from vicious hand-to-hand combat to massive B52 bombings. This was the Iwo Jima of our war, and the Marines, outnumbered five to one, stood their ground and held fast. In 1968, I was just out of high school but I surely knew all about this epic battle.

Here I was in 1971 on patrol as a Marine machine gunner, patrolling the outside of the famous Khe Sahn. It was now a ghost of a base. Deserted—no one there—but very eerie and spooky in its ruins and total silence. To me, a person who would become a history and social-studies teacher just two years later, it was like walking the grounds of Gettysburg or Normandy Beach shortly after those famous battles. It was probably the coolest thing I did in Nam.

The next day I was on patrol again. As usual, my gun team (Marines have a three-man machine-gun team) was toward the back of the patrol being led by the other grunts (infantry riflemen). True to form and strategy, we were strung out over a pretty good distance, each man keeping a wide distance between him and the man in front of him and behind him. This formation ensured that, if a booby trap was set off, only one man would be wounded or killed rather than many.

We had been patrolling for miles through light forest and jungle when the grunt in front of me turned and let me catch up to him. He knew me—and my constant talk of travel and my list of countries—well. With a smile he said, "The point (the first man in a patrol, usually with the map and compass) said to pass it back: '30 meters to our left is Laos.'" The patrol had stopped moving, and most of the Marines were looking back—at me—smiling, because they all knew what I was going to do.

And, sure enough, if you had been there that day, you would have seen a full patrol of Marine grunts taking a short halt, all laughing (silently) as their machine gunner immediately started off to the left,

Rufus McGaugh

going about 30 or 40 meters (just to be safe) to set foot in a new country to put on the "list." Then the patrol started back up. Today, if I were to show you my list of the 251 countries and lands I have visited, you would see Laos as number 8, right after the U.S., Canada, Mexico, Wake Island, Okinawa, Vietnam, and Thailand.

There is a sad postscript to the above amusing story. We rescued no American POWs. There was a mix-up or screw-up of map coordinates, and we were off target a bit, and the noise of the choppers and our landing had given notice to the enemy to escape—with any POWs they may have had.

Now Let's Get Back to Our Story in Albania

As mentioned earlier, when my wife and I landed in Albania, we had a full-blown riot on our hands—at least that's what Monica was calling it. Let me explain. We disembarked from our plane into a huge crowd of people, all men, and all very excited and yelling. As far as I was concerned: situation normal. This was typical crowd behavior in many Third-World countries, so I didn't give it a second thought. My wife, however, thought we had descended into a huge outdoor insane asylum.

I wish she would have said something. Unfortunately, whenever we get into a bad situation where it looks like we are going to die, Monica has the awful habit of going into terror-filled silence. I wish she would break that habit.

Being the take-charge guy I am and having lots of experiences in similar situations, I handed off the luggage to Monica and begin bargaining for a ride into the capital, Tirana. Now, the way it works, especially if you are a sharp guy like me, is you gotta negotiate and bargain—and I'm pretty good at it, mostly because I don't have the money to do anything else.

I was negotiating away with the taxi drivers, oblivious of the fact that my wife was surrounded by what looked like hundreds (to this day Monica insists that she was surrounded by thousands) of screaming, yelling, angry, Albanian criminals. At this point Monica had given up any attempt to save her virtue and was now only hoping her life would be spared.

I had finally cut the best deal in Christendom for a taxi ride into the city and was making my way back to Monica. When she finally spotted me approaching, she looked at me for the first time in two weeks as if she still actually liked me. Desperation and a near lynching will sometimes do that to people. She was scared and not talking too coherently but I heard a stream of vocabulary that included "kill," "rape," "mob," "gang," "murders," and a few other incoherent words.

As you will see throughout the Albanian part of our trip, I was the cool, calm, and rational guy who had a way with words. I simply said to Monica, "They're taxi drivers."

She looked at me as if I were a Martian from Jupiter and in an incredulous voice asked, "What?"

I repeated, "They're taxi drivers," as though that would explain everything.

Now, Monica doesn't get angry often, and—on those rare occasions that she does (usually when traveling with me; I refer you to the Polish tram incident above)—she's never loud like me and never violent (well, except for that Polish tram incident), but this time…well, it wasn't very pretty what she said. For the third time on this trip, she let loose with the "F bomb": "I don't fucking care what they are; they're going to kill us!" (Just between you and me, I think Monica has a problem with her swearing and obscene language. I don't think it's very lady like.)

It isn't that I'm stubborn or a man of limited vocabulary; I'm more of a guy of few words. So when I said for the third time, "They're taxi drivers" in an attempt to explain away the angry mob we were surrounded by, her anger—and a temper I had been unaware of until then—became focused on the buffoon standing in front of her, singing the same refrain, "They're taxi drivers," over and over again.

To be frank with you, she didn't give a shit about what they did for a living; all she knew was that "They're trying to steal our luggage and grabbing me and trying to push me into a car!"

Well, of course. "They're taxi drivers" I almost said again but then thought better of it due to her foul mood—and the terrible language she was now prone to using!

I gave her a quick explanation of taxi driving in the Third World. It's a very competitive business—dog-eat-dog for survival in these poor countries. Taxi drivers throughout the world are pretty aggressive—if they can get away with it. All these poor men were trying to do was grab our luggage—not steal it—only so they could get it in their taxi and thus earn a fare from a paying customer.

Upon hearing this, Monica was fine with it. I have to admit, she recovers from trauma remarkably quickly. Better yet, she doesn't hold a grudge. There were no hard feelings about what I had inadvertently put her through. In fact she even stopped looking at me as if she wanted to kill me. I'm telling ya, ours is a marriage made in heaven—or at least in Albania.

There was one little issue that was lurking about in terms of the taxi driver I had chosen. I had negotiated too well. I had beaten this poor taxi driver down to a price that I think he realized, the more he thought about it, would yield him precious little or probably nothing out of the deal. He was not in a very good mood now. My plan was to pay him more or tip very well if he kept to his part of the bargain by delivering us safely to our hotel. I had done this before. I'm tight with my money, and I want a good deal, but I don't want to do it on the backs of the poor—people with far less money than me. All over the world, I bargain right down to the last penny just so I don't look like a chump or a sucker. Then I pay more or tip very well so that a poor man can feed his family or send his kids to school.

The taxi driver walked us over to his taxi, which was an older black Mercedes but very clean and very well maintained. All the taxis were Mercedes. In fact, all the cars in Albania appeared to be Mercedes. The word on the street was that the diaspora of Albanians throughout Europe were stealing Mercedes left and right and then making a mad dash back to Albania to become—you guessed it—taxi drivers. From what Monica and I could see, it appears every single Albanian in Albania owned six or seven Mercedes.

We finally got on the road to Tirana, a road not in very good shape, so we were traveling pretty slowly with a driver who was not very happy about the fare he had just settled for. It was hard to ignore or miss.

But nobody of Albanian extraction on that road was very happy—or behaving well. Both Monica and I looked at each other in near disbelief. What we were witnessing, and quite often, were Albanian men, of all ages, acting like the middle-schoolers I taught. By that, I mean they were into adolescent macho posturing. Albanian men of any age would deliberately walk in front of a moving car (a car moving very slowly because of the bad roads) and then glare at the driver as if to say, "Are you going to do anything about it?" It was really silly and childish. In the ten miles or so to get into Tirana, we witnessed a number of fist fights and near fights. Our driver was in a rotten mood to begin with, but these guys stepping out in front of his taxi and then giving him a challenging glare were causing him to do a slow burn.

At last we arrived in Tirana, which is not huge by any means. In fact, one can easily walk the city from one end to the other. As it turned out, we were just about to our hotel and the end of our ride when an older man, about 50, gray haired, stocky, and tough looking, surrounded by his entourage of 12 or 15 younger men, deliberately stepped in front of our driver's taxi. Maybe our driver had had enough. Who knows?

Instead of braking, our driver continued on and bumped the man. *Are you crazy?* I thought from the back seat. This guy must never have heard of General George Armstrong Custer or what happened to him at the Little Big Horn after he bumped Sitting Bull. Nor what happened to a small group of Texans hopelessly outnumbered by an army of Mexicans in a little place called the Alamo. But I bet the dozen or so guys in front of our taxi had—because they were acting a whole lot like those Mexicans, running over to the driver's side in a very Alamo-like way. I was tempted to give the driver a brilliant and inspiring lecture about the heroes of the Alamo but had a feeling he might not be in the mood for a history lesson.

So the fight began. Despite the 15-to-1 odds, the driver did have one advantage: it certainly was not brains or common sense, or even self-survival—it was the fact that it is very hard to beat the hell out of guy if you have to punch through a small open window, even if there are 15 or so of you. (Maybe *especially* if there are 15 of you because there's no room for everyone to fit in order to hit.)

To his credit the driver was gutsy, maybe even brave—more likely stupid or insane. I like to think of myself as a fighter and someone who doesn't take any shit from anyone. However, when you're facing 15 pissed-off Albanians, that might be just the time to talk and perhaps work things out—or run like hell. Running like a wimpy coward is not my thing. Then again, I do enjoy living, so, in this case, I would have been tempted to suggest to the driver to do just that. Unfortunately I was a bit late in getting my exit strategy verbalized to the driver because the gang now had him out of the car and was giving him a total-ass whuppin'.

Monica and I remained in the back seat, and she was hysterical. Now, at this point, if any further proof were needed as to what a cool guy I am or how collected I am under stress or pressure, let me recount the calming ability I possess. I simply put my hand on Monica's knee and said, "Monica, don't worry. They're mad at him, not us." She was not amused.

Well, the gang finally did leave. They didn't threaten us or accost us at all. In fact, I'm not sure if they even noticed that we were in the taxi, so intent were they upon their mayhem. We weren't exactly sure where the driver was. We had lost eye contact with him, at some point, and not because he had run away. Like George Custer and the Alamo heroes, he stuck it out to the end. I suspected he was on the ground because that was one hell of an ass-kicking he had just undergone. You just don't see an ass-kicking like that every day—even in Albania! I didn't want to embarrass the guy by peeking out the window; he was already having a bad day. So we waited a few minutes, and nothing seemed to be happening—and we did have to get to our hotel—so I got out of the car, walked around it, and there he was!

He was on the ground, and he didn't look too good, but I helped him up, and now he looked even worse, but he was functioning and able to drive. He had a number of bruises and cuts, and it looked as if his one eye was going to develop into a real shiner. His speech was slurred, not only from his deeply cut lip, but because he appeared to have fewer teeth now than when we had begun the trip. He did get us to the hotel, but he wasn't talking too well, though I'm not sure I would know bad Albanian from good, well-spoken Albanian anyway. I had planned on giving him a good tip, but now I added to it because he was going to need to see a doctor or go to the hospital. (Here was a guy who should definitely make a change of sport. Instead of fighting and wrestling, if I were him, I would go into track, cross-country running, or jogging—especially if I happened to live in Albania.)

Our hotel was all Stalinist in style and architecture, meaning the exterior was grand and over the top, while the interior was dumpy, cramped, old fashioned (not in a good way), and dingy. Our room was a tiny little dump of a hovel. However, after the harrowing mob scene with the taxi drivers, and then the brutal attack on our cabbie by a gang of ruffians, Monica would have been satisfied with a pup tent out in a field. So there were no complaints on her part. (And this pretty much sums up my strategy for being recognized as what I modestly call "the Best Husband in the World": Put 'em through hell getting there—and then there's never even a peep of complaint about the hotel or the room. Every guy reading this has now declared me a genius!)

As usual, "Little Miss 'I'm Hungry'" had to eat.

I don't know where this eating all the time comes from because Monica is not at all like this at home. When we travel, she thinks it's a vacation, and I'm always correcting her and telling her it's not a vacation; it's a trip. We've been through it a million times: she asks the same dumb question—in a very snotty and sarcastic way, I might add—"What's the difference between a vacation and a trip?" And I remind her, "A vacation is where you go someplace and do nothing but eat all the time. On a trip, you don't eat; there's too much to see and do." Geez! Some people just never get it!

Then she gets all into her "logic" with me. For instance, in this case "Little Miss Smarty-pants" couldn't refrain from reminding me that the 7:00 a.m. flight we took to get here meant that we had to leave Slovenia before we could get our complimentary breakfast at the hotel, that the flight had served no food, not even coffee, and that, as usual, I had us skipping lunch because there was so much to see and do. Then we attended the riot at the Albanian airport. From there it was a prize fight involving our driver and 15 hoodlums. The hotel was a disaster, and our room was a dump. (Oops. So maybe my strategy didn't work out as well as I'd hoped; better save the "Best Husband in the World" label for later.)

At this point her voice was getting louder and shriller—I would say almost emotional. In a near shriek, she concluded, "It's almost 7:30 p.m., and I haven't had a fucking thing to eat all day!"

Well! I was certainly taken aback by her obscene language, dropping (for the fourth time, if you're counting) the "F bomb" again—a record for any of our trips. I certainly don't approve of language such as this, even if I use it *all* the time. I happen to firmly believe in a double standard when it comes to such things and especially the "F bomb." In fact, everything in our marriage is a double standard, and that's why it's rock solid. I get all the "do's" and Monica gets all the "don't's."

Well, it looked like somebody was hungry. That last statement alone demonstrates what an observant and intuitive person I am. But, no! "Little Miss Anorexic Ethiopia" never gives me credit for anything! So now Monica was on a mission for food, and that usually meant a restaurant—and unfortunately I have always found restaurants to be very expensive. Time and again I've tried explaining to the most stubborn woman in the world that there are alternatives to restaurants. The first is simply to skip meals. You save money, and you never gain weight.

"Little Miss Stubborn," as you have already seen, was having none of that. And, for those of you who have been talking behind my back about the state of our marriage, this is proof positive once and for all as to who is the stubborn one and who is the more flexible one. I think I am a very strong and willful person, but, when this woman gets on a kick, it is just simply easier to back down and let her have her way.

On the way to the hotel restaurant, I had gently suggested we not waste precious daylight by eating but by taking a short walk around the city to check out the sights. That innocent suggestion was met with a scornful glare. In fact, as I stared into Monica's face and focused on the pupils of her eyes, the word "murder" seemed to appear there—and I swear I am not exaggerating or making this up!

Attempting to be magnanimous, I agreed to eat. We were given seats at a table on the hotel's huge outside terrace. It was a beautiful night, although the beauty was ruined a bit by the constant refrain of "This is a hell of a late hour to be eating" by a certain somebody. Our waiter was a small, skinny man dressed in what looked like a waiter's tuxedo. He immediately took on the role of waiter, wine steward, body guard, confidante, and lifelong friend. He couldn't do enough for us, and he did everything with a flourish!

After "Little Miss 'I Must Be Pampered All the Time'" was seated, we were handed menus—with a flourish, of course. The menu offered a good selection to choose from, but we had read and been warned about the quality and purity of water, drinks, and food in Albania, so we were a bit cautious in our ordering. Monica was going for steak, which led me in the same direction. I asked the waiter, standing behind me, if the steak was a good choice and he very enthusiastically assured me through language, nods, and smiles that it was—although, as he continued to praise the quality and choice of the restaurant's steaks, he was reaching over my shoulder and pointedly indicating the "Spaghetti Bolognese" on the menu.

"So the spaghetti bolognese is also very good?" I asked. Our waiter assured us that it was.

Monica then spoke up and said, "I think I'll have the steak." The waiter rushed over to her side of the table and, standing behind her, lavishly praised the steak even as his arm reached over her shoulder and his finger very distinctly landed on "Spaghetti Bolognese" on the menu.

This action threw Monica off a bit, and she started to question the waiter when I cut her off and made what turned out be a very wise decision, albeit after many warnings. "Monica, I think the man is trying to tell us something."

She looked at me quizzically. "What?" she asked.

"He wants us to order the spaghetti and not the steak. I think he has made that very clear, and we have been very slow at taking him up on it."

"Why would he want us to order spaghetti and not a steak?" she asked.

"I'm not sure, but I will tell you this: when a waiter tells me *not* to order something, I am going to take his advice and not gamble," I replied.

So we skipped the steak and had a great spaghetti meal with good wine, all served by the best and friendliest waiter on the planet. Even better, we didn't die of food poisoning from a steak.

*****

The next day was all about adventure. As I mentioned earlier, at the time (1995), Albania was one of the most reclusive countries on Earth. It truly was the North Korea of Europe. We spent the early morning exploring the area in and around the capital, Tirana. Centered in Tirana was the Mausoleum of Enver Hoxha, a giant modern pyramid constructed of glass and concrete. We were told many stories about this building. It was supposed to be Hoxha's final resting place—a tomb to rival Lenin's lying in state in Red Square in Moscow. Others said it was a museum—a museum, unfortunately with nothing in it (typical, I hate to say, of Albania, at least at that time). Still others said it was a conference center. Today there is talk of tearing it down and building a new Parliament building on the site.

Tirana, the capital of Albania with what was supposed to be the tomb of its long-ruling dictator. Enver Hoxha ruled Albania from 1941 to 1985. His erratic and strange behavior made him the Kim Jong-un of his day.

As we ventured out further, we visited fortresses, castles, walled cities, and very pretty narrow mountain valleys. There were some Roman ruins, including a small coliseum in pretty good condition. Churches stood side by side with Moslem mosques. Unhappily, our visit took a dive at the end, when it seems we had accidentally saved the worst for last.

It wasn't hard to miss the concrete bunkers; after all, there were 750,000 of them built to last for an eternity. It's hard to fathom the enormous amount of money that must have been sucked out of the economy of this small, impoverished country for their construction. Even worse, we discovered a number of poor families attempting to live in these horrible things. The room within the bunkers was closet-like, with dirt floors covered in mud and green mold. The lack of heat, water, and electricity made living there even more ludicrous. It is heart breaking to see anyone, anywhere, living in such poverty.

Then we caught a ride to Durres to what is considered to be one of the best beaches on the Adriatic Sea. It was filthy and completely covered in litter, plastic bottles, and outright garbage and sewage. (Today I read travel reviews of how pretty and clean it is, but, back then, Durres was a wreck.)

If you happened to be at a party or barbeque with Monica and me at any time after we completed this trip, and if the subject of travel came up and we shared our experiences with you and perhaps the other guests, you would have come away thinking that we had made separate trips to opposite ends of the Earth. "Little Miss 'Everything Has to Be Perfect for a Fun Trip'" would regale you with stories of near-death experiences and various other terrifying incidents that I personally feel are a bit exaggerated. Listening to my (more authentic) version of the trip, you would learn how I personally and expertly led us with military-like precision without a single hitch.

To demonstrate the utter decay and deterioration of Western civilization, most people hearing our travelogue accept the snake-oil propaganda of "Little Miss 'I'm Victimized by This Brute'" rather than my more rational and factual version. People, especially the women, start throwing around words like "crazy," "over the top," "insane," "out of control," and "domineering" to describe me. At the same time, everyone seems to be competing in an effort to place a halo over my wife's head and skipping the Vatican beatification process in order to confer immediate sainthood on her simply because she accompanied me on a trip. Hey! I'm not that bad! Not to brag, but I *am* the guiding force and leader on these trips, the one who always gets us out of sticky or bad situations. Admittedly I'm the one who gets us *into* these sticky situations in the first place, but, as my friend and writing colleague, William, recently said (1598) "All's well that ends well."

It's really no different at home. Whenever the boys say "Dad said this" or "Dad said that," their mother "Little Miss 'I Know How to Raise the Boys Much Better Than You'" counters with, "Well, you know how your father is." What's that supposed to mean? I'm a pretty normal guy who pays his taxes, votes, and is a productive citizen. Well, I used to be a productive citizen—then I retired, and now I don't do much of anything except teach a little, travel a lot, drink beer, and write some silly stories. I even served my country for two years as a Marine and spent a year in Vietnam going through all kinds of shit and getting shot up. It's really hard to be modest here, but we probably wouldn't have won that war without me. I know exactly what you're thinking—and you're dead wrong. I personally own a t-shirt with a big ol' map of South Vietnam on it. (The hell with North Vietnam. There's nothing up there but commies, anyway.) And in big bold letters above that map, it says, "We were winning when I was there."

So there you have it. I hate to brag, but the Viet Cong were terrified of me and could barely sleep at night just thinking that I was anywhere near. Even when my school district invites me back to teach about the Vietnam War, I give all the teachers a heads up and warn them, "When I teach it, we always win." (Nowadays, we have the entire scientific community of psychologists and psychiatrists telling us that Post Traumatic Stress Disorder is a problem or a bad thing when, actually, being delusional is a beautiful thing. Just ask me.)

To get to the end of this part of the story, I took you on a wandering journey and told you a wandering tale, just the way we Irish like to do it. I am sure at various points in this book, some readers may have asked, "Is he ever going to tell us about his trip to Albania?" I am also sure some readers wondered how a story about Albania ended up taking us to Canada, Mexico, Wake Island, Okinawa, and the Vietnam War. Well, now you know. (I hate to brag, but I have a talent for doing stuff like that. It was not accidental; it was natural. It's the way I talk—and I have had to talk to some rough customers over the years—to wit: rebellious middle-schoolers.) Like any writer, I want to entertain the reader and hold his interest. I hope I have accomplished that mission.

Rufus McGaugh

Three Quick Takes on Three Obscure African Countries

[Note: Although I've taken many trips to Africa, the trip described below, made in 2011 or 2012, was the first I took after my so-called-retirement. I say "so-called" because, as I was writing this account (late February 2015), I was once again working not only at Brownell Middle School but also at Parcells and Pierce Middle Schools, Grosse Pointe South High School, and Maire Elementary School as a substitute teacher. Jeez! I was busier in "retirement" than I had been when I was employed full-time!]

Somaliland-ing and Taking Off

I made this particular trip to Africa so I could go to an odd assortment of obscure African countries that are seldom visited by anyone. In this day of easy and mass transportation, it was amazing how difficult it was to get there. I touched down on four continents and made 17 flights to visit only three countries in Africa.

The first was Somaliland, a breakaway region of Somalia. Somalia, at the time, was perhaps the most violent place on Earth, with urban warfare taking place in the capital of Mogadishu. For almost two decades, Mogadishu had been the scene of horrific urban warfare and violence, and there was no sign of a let-up. Somaliland was the exact opposite: very peaceful. The people wore exotic, colorful clothing; the desert had a stark beauty to it. In Somaliland, I saw some of the oldest and best Neolithic cave art.

Vibrantly dressed Somali women in Somaliland, the northern break-away region of Somalia.

Longitude and Latitude, with Attitude

Vibrantly dressed Somali.

Vibrantly dressed Somali, face fully veiled.

My Somalialand body guard as I toured Las Gell where some of the earliest cave paintings exist in Africa. (See the wall behind him.)

An open-air bank in Somalialand—no building, no walls, no roof, no vault. "Your money is safe with us!"

[132]

Life is not all colorful costumes and cave paintings in Somalialand, as you can see in this photo showing the slums and poverty of Hargeisa, Somaliland.

After promising friends and family on a stack of bibles that I was going nowhere near Mogadishu, one can imagine my surprise when we made an unannounced and unplanned stop *in* Mogadishu. The few Somalis disembarking were told to do so quickly, and the rest of us were warned not to stand in the doorway of the plane and risk making ourselves a target. Despite these dire warnings, nothing happened. To be honest, the whole thing was pretty anti-climatic.

The Tuscany of Africa (But You'll Never Know It)

Many of my friends feel that my quest or goal to see every country can be silly and not worth the time, hassle, and expense—especially if there isn't much to see or do at a particular destination. I agree, to a point—but, nine times out of ten, the experience is very rewarding.

An example of just such a rewarding experience would be my trip to the little central-African country of Burundi. Most people have never heard of it, and, even looking at a good map of Africa, one can barely see it; it is so small. Spending an extra $1,500 to $2,000 to go there seemed a bit pricey even to me.

Longitude and Latitude, with Attitude

Well, Burundi turned out to be the big surprise and worth every penny. It was absolutely beautiful and breathtaking!—so much so that it inspired me to write an article that I hope to see published, entitled, "Burundi: the Tuscany of Africa." (So far, that article remains unpublished—I blame the Italians who don't want Tuscany upstaged or who fear it'll be labeled the "Burundi of Europe." You'll just have to settle for what little I have written about Burundi in this book.)

I spent my last night in Burundi at a little mom-and-pop hotel (which looked like a 1950s American motel) on Lake Tanganyika. Lake Tanganyika is a huge lake with a sandy shore. It's like an ocean with no waves. I had a good dinner and two cold beers while I watched a perfect African sunset.

The Time I Had in Chad

The third and last country I visited was Chad, which many people describe as bizarre or surreal. I have never heard or read of *any*one going there. My favorite story about Chad appeared in the *New York Times* in the early 1980s. Chad—which is a huge country, three times the size of California—had only a single traffic light in the entire country (in the capital), and it had not worked since 1967! One of my goals was to see that traffic light, which I did (I think): I have good news and bad news about this issue. The good news is that there are now a number of traffic lights in Chad. The bad news is that most of them do not work. However, the broken traffic lights don't seem to matter in any case because, based on my observations, in Chad the rule of thumb seems to be that green means go, amber means go, and red means go!

Young, turbaned boy working as a cattle herder near Lake Chad in the country of Chad.

[134]

My guide in Chad was a 61-year-old Italian who runs the only travel agency in the country. When I asked if I was the first American to venture into Chad, the man broke my heart and robbed me of all bragging rights by saying no. I was the fifth American in 20 years.

I have to give this guy credit for getting me deep in the bush, where I am not sure anyone has been before. We traveled by boat down the Chari River and into Lake Chad and then upstream into little tributaries and swamps and visited some of the most isolated villages I have ever seen. I spent my last night in Chad at a nice river camp watching a pink/purple sunset on the river and then had a decent steak and a few cold beers. Eighteen hours later in unreal time (I was gaining time flying home), I reunited with my family at Detroit's Metro Airport.

Nomads near Lake Chad.

Longitude and Latitude, with Attitude

Hotel check-in, my first day in Kurdistan, Iraq. Note the "no weapons" sign to my right. (So I had to surrender my rocket launcher, pistol, rifle, and machine gun before getting my room key.)

One of my three Kurdistani bodyguards. He got to keep his weapons. Of course, he didn't have a rocket launcher (I don't think).

Rufus McGaugh

Kurdistan—No Joke (Though It Ends with One)

The 2012 trip I took to Kurdistan, Iraq, was one of the most fascinating trips I have ever been on. The wealth of history, archeology, religion, and geographic features was phenomenal. When *National Geographic* named this trip one of the ten best trips of 2011, its only error was in not naming it the number-one trip, period.

For starters, I flew in to the city of Erbil, one of the oldest continually inhabited cities in the world. It dates back to at least the 23rd century BC!

This land is the land of religion. After the Muslim conquest, small pockets of Christians fled to the mountains, where they established two incredibly beautiful Orthodox monasteries that still exist today, surrounded by small villages of their believers. Both monasteries possess and use a lost Christian ceremony that is very similar to an exorcism. A steel chain and collar are attached to a wall, and a person is chained to the wall while the monks perform the ceremony to rid the person of the devil. Even more amazing is that these people and their monks still speak and write in Aramaic—the language spoken by Jesus Christ!

In this same area some people practice the little-known religion of the Yazidi faith. These people in the very northern reaches of the mountains of northern Iraq believe in reincarnation and that the Creator appointed seven archangels to rule over earth. The religion has numerous taboos (I had to take my shoes off in the temple area, never let my feet touch the floor posts of a doorway and not touch the carved black snakes coming from below the earth up the sides of their temples). The Yazidi store hundreds of huge ancient vessels that hold olive oil, which they burn all night so there is never a time without light.

I was allowed to participate in one of their ceremonies in which you throw a rock at separate holes in the ground to reveal whether you will be reincarnated or will go to heaven or hell. I don't want to give away what the result of this endeavor was for me, but let it be said that—when I die—I won't be coming back, and I will need some sort of portable air conditioning.

Longitude and Latitude, with Attitude

The tomb of a thirteenth-century prophet in a Yazidi temple. Devout Yazidis drape the prophet's tomb with brightly colored pieces of silk and colorful fabric to honor him. (Note that not a piece of material has "Kmart" on it; obviously I didn't drape any fabric on it—not even a "Lufus shirt.")

The Yazidi religion is ancient—perhaps the oldest religion on Earth (even older than Zoroastrianism, often regarded as the world's oldest surviving religion)—and the only faith in the Middle East whose followers believe in reincarnation.

Not far from this was the site of one of the most important battles ever fought in human history, Gaugamela, where Alexander the Great defeated Darius and his Persian army in 331 BC.

In this land, there are still ancient Jewish cities, and in one I saw the tomb of the Old Testament prophet Nahum covered in an elaborate green death shroud, almost buried by the ruined synagogue that housed it.

I stood in the mountains and looked down at the green fields of the plains of Nineveh and the valley of Mesopotamia.

I saw all kinds of ancient bridges, arches, and statues. Nobody, including the archaeologists, has a clue as to who built them.

In one museum I saw actual clay tablets written in cuneiform in the time of King Hammurabi of Babylonia, the great law giver. Right next to these were still older clay tablets in cuneiform that went back to the time of Gilgamesh—who, up until very recently, was thought to be only a mythological, not a historical, figure. Then there were rooms of artifacts from the Sumerians, whose civilization is considered to be the first on Earth.

The trip included Oriental bazaars (spread over labyrinthine paths and alleys, where vendors sold everything one would need to exist)—not to mention a visit to one of Saddam Hussein's many palaces, which, like a lot of them, came complete with prison cells and torture chambers. These places, now converted into museums, often hire victims who survived to tell their story, and you can't imagine the tales of brutality and depravity that I heard.

But it gets worse! From there we went to the town of Halabjah, famous for the poison-gas attack on it ordered by Saddam Hussein. First it was napalmed and then gassed (with a type of mustard gas), and, as grotesque as it may be, the Kurds wanted the world to see this horrific act. Nearly every single victim was photographed when people re-entered the town. It was ghastly.

Just when you thought it was impossible to see much more history or archeology, or at least anything more ancient, we drove close to the Turkish border to see a huge cave high up in the mountains that an American archaeologist discovered in 1961. After digging inside, he found a large Neanderthal burial with 36 bodies. But, more than that, what he discovered at the site has changed our outlook on Neanderthals. A few were buried with flowers, showing that the surviving Neanderthals experienced sorrow at the loss of their loved ones. Even more amazing was the discovery of a disabled Neanderthal who was cared for by the group for many years before his/her death, demonstrating compassion, which, prior to this discovery, most social scientists felt to be a uniquely human trait or quality.

Besides all this, I saw Assyrian forts and citadels, scenery throughout the whole trip that would make you think you were in the mountains of Colorado or the canyon lands of Utah, and green farm land that looked like something you would be more likely to find in Nebraska or Montana.

Waterfalls in Iraq? Yes, and beautiful.

The Kurds themselves are a non-Arabic ethnic group in this area of the world. They are a friendly and proud people. The men are clean shaven but sport dark mustaches. They wear a distinctive turban and loose, baggy pants that deliberately sag in the middle, along with a very wide belt of cloth around their waist.

Usually I have to be quite sneaky and surreptitious about getting "people shots" in these exotic areas, but not in Kurdistan, Iraq. When they would catch me taking a picture, they would bring out their kids, then their wife, and, in a few cases, walk a toothless granny out to pose for a picture.

Kurdish man in a coffee shop. Note the distinctive turban and wide sash, convenient for sheathing a large dagger, like the one in the photo.

Kurdish man, member of the Yazidi religion.

A pair of Kurdish men with distinctive turbans and dark mustaches.

Older Kurdish man.   *Man selling honey from his car.*

    Because I had such a fun time, I feel it only fitting that I should end this section with a modern Kurdish joke that the Kurds love to tell, and it says something about the Kurdish people in that they have no problem poking fun at themselves.

    Two Kurdish men from different cities take their wives shopping at the very crowded bazaar, and, before you know it, both men end up separated from their spouses, unable to find their wives. The Kurd from Erbil, which is a very conservative place, notices the other man looking around.

    The other man introduces himself—he's from Sulaymaniyah, which is a very liberal city.

    The pair quickly decides to start looking for their wives together, figuring that it would be a more beneficial, methodical approach to the problem. So the conservative man says, "We will need to know what each other's wife looks like so we can find both of them. My wife dresses very modestly and conservatively. She is attired in all black, covered from head to foot, and is wearing a veil. Now tell me about your wife so I know what to look for."

    The man from the more liberal Suleimanyah says, "Well, my wife dresses very Western. She never wears a head covering: she just had her hair done and dyed blond at a beauty salon. She's wearing a very short mini skirt that goes half-way up her thighs and a blouse with a plunging neckline, and—"

Longitude and Latitude, with Attitude

The conservative man immediately interrupts him and says, "Let's stop wasting time and start looking for *your* wife."

Sulaynaniyah, Kurdistan, Iraq. One of Saddam Hussein's many palaces that included torture chambers. It is now an open-air museum and play area for kids.

Some Enchanted Islands: the South Pacific, Rufus Style

In 2013-14, while everyone in Michigan was freezing in one of its worst-ever winters in recorded history (dubbed the "Polar Vortex"), I made two separate trips to a number of beautiful South Pacific islands. This caused me to be very happy and everybody in the state of Michigan to hate Rufus.

Wallis and Futuna

The first destination on this trip was the tiny, practically unknown island group of Wallis and Futuna, which few people have ever heard of and fewer still have ever visited. These small, beautiful islands are a French Overseas Possession.

From the minute I arrived, I confirmed that Wallis's reputation for beauty was not exaggerated. I found it to be one of the most attractive islands in the South Pacific. I also confirmed that its reputation for being even more expensive than French Tahiti and Bora Bora was well deserved. To illustrate both points: I stayed at a very small French hotel, high up on a hill, with a marvelous view of the ocean (I could see a number of tiny, pretty islands within close view), a great pool, good meals, and a quantity of beer, all of which cost me about $420 for two-and-a-half days. The air conditioning unfortunately was next to useless, and—because I was coming from our polar vortex to the opposite extreme—the very warm and very, very humid weather took some getting used to.

How humid was it? I'm glad you asked. I did a lot of walking and took a lot of pictures, and, when I came back to the hotel, I looked like I had been caught in a rain storm or had fallen into the ocean—it was that humid. Wallis' climate is most conducive to staying in the pool or sitting in the shade drinking beer—Foster's (of Australia) in this case.

These trips often—unfortunately—indicate to me my debauchery or at least my lack of moral restraint. By that, I mean it's always a little sobering (so to speak) to see that my bar bill exceeds my food bill. I blame it on the heat and the adage, "Don't drink the water."

My next stop: New Caledonia, another French Overseas Possession.

Longitude and Latitude, with Attitude

Trouble in Paradise!

Well, for my flight to New Caledonia, I left about 15 minutes earlier than the hotel staff suggested, saw the plane sitting right next to the little shack they call a terminal, walked in to check in, and heard my plane take off! I asked an airline worker what was going on, and she asked, "Didn't you hear that the flight was taking off an hour early today?" As a matter of fact, I had not! The airline had kept that minor bit of information from me.

I took a drive down to the airline office, and, after a long wait—three-and-a-half hours—I was told that *maybe* I could get on the flight two days from now, or maybe not; maybe it would be the flight next week or the week after that—or whenever; who knows?

Now, I am not one to panic, but, first, I had eight more flights, six hotels, four drivers, and three tours lined up (and paid for) in four different countries, and the likelihood of me accomplishing any of that was not looking good. Second, as pretty and beautiful as Wallis and Futuna were, they were a nice place to visit, but I didn't want to *live* there: I did have hopes of rejoining my family at some point before I passed on to the great beyond.

It took another three hours for me and the entire hotel staff to get my netbook connected to Wi-Fi and then countless emails to my travel agent in California to see what he could do. Via Skype, I left messages, stating that I was in deep doo-doo, on three different phones (including the travel agency's emergency number) and got no answer. Because I was on the other side of the International Date Line, I forgot that it was Sunday back in the States. (Being on the other side of the International Date Line is a problem: I can barely function in the present, let alone the future.)

Wallis & Futuna. Two beautiful French islands of Melanesia that no one's ever heard of. Without warning, my plane left an hour early, stranding me in this very lonely paradise in the middle of the Pacific.

[144]

To cut to the chase, my travel agent did eventually receive my emergency call and raised hell with the airline about a stranded client in Wallis and Futuna, and my wife, Monica, emailed the airline, too, telling them that, yes, she eventually wanted me back home—but, if it took a few months, that was fine with her. (I promised she would pay for that line when I got back—*if* I got back!)

Ultimately, I hoped to see everyone again, in the next few weeks, months, years, or decades it would take to get out of an odd little place called Wallis and Futuna.

To add insult to injury, it seemed that even God hated me. Here I was in paradise, and suddenly it started raining so hard that I couldn't see the palm trees 20 feet away.

New Caledonia

When I finally arrived in New Caledonia, I found it, too, to be very beautiful but very different from Wallis and Futuna. The early explorers who first laid eyes on this beautiful spot named it after the Caledonia in Scotland, with which they were familiar. Its green countryside, rolling hills, wide plains, and small mountains do bear a strong resemblance to old Caledonia.

The weather was a great improvement over Wallis and Futuna. Although I was looking forward to escaping the polar vortex back home and I enjoy warm and hot weather, the humidity along with the heat made Wallis and Futuna difficult at times. The weather in New Caledonia was more like California winter weather—very mild, pretty warm during the day and then cooling off in the evening (75 degrees at 7:00 p.m.). Another big difference: whereas Wallis and Futuna is almost your stereotypical South Pacific island paradise, Noumea, the capital of New Caledonia, is more of a mini Paris (or, due to its warm weather, a mini Marseilles) with a distinctly Mediterranean flavor. (In case you don't know, New Caledonia—despite its British name—is a French possession, hence the French comparisons.)

Typical of France or anything France owns or occupies, nothing in New Caledonia was cheap. I found the cheapest outdoor café in town—no surprise there, considering my survival instincts and innate cheapness—but, even so, the beer was $10.50. The restaurant a few doors down had pizzas for $25. You can imagine the psychological dilemma poor Rufus' brain was suffering from: would I continue to hold onto my well-earned reputation as the cheapest human being and tightest tightwad on Earth, or would I go through self-imposed Betty Ford Clinic alcoholic withdrawal? Both choices were equally painful. Which would win out? (I will give you a hint: I say let's drink to my success!)

The next day, I had a ticket for the "hop-on, hop-off" cultural adventure ride through Noumea. The bus continuously circles through the city—and it is a big city—and you get on and off at will. (I find this weird—not the on-and-off part but the big-city part. All these islands in this part of the South Pacific have between 7,000 and 20,000 inhabitants, total, living in thatch-roofed huts and not really doing all that well economically. But Noumea is like a real city, and a European one at that. Very strange, very odd!)

I wondered if New Caledonia had any adventures in store for me—adventures that I could regale the folks back home about (though, actually, I was hoping there would be *no* adventures because, if you've been reading this far—and paying attention—all my adventures are usually bad, causing me no amount of trouble and all kinds of problems.)

New Caledonia, Day 2

Oops! I forgot to mention two incidents from Day One in New Caledonia (probably because both of them occurred before I even got there). The first was that Air Calin, in an attempt to make up for its screw-up, promoted me to business class to compensate me for the grievous inconvenience it had put poor ol' Rufus through. Such a perq would have worked better if it had happened on one of my 11- or 13-hour flights rather than an hour-and-a-half flight, but you take what you can get. White tablecloth, white napkin, real silverware, better food than what the schmucks in the back of the plane are eating (one of whom, by the way, under normal circumstances, is usually Rufus). Bottom line: the food still sucks.

The other incident involved the older French gentleman sitting next to me on the trip. He had a huge laptop and spent the entire flight watching porn. He spoke perfect English and at one point asked if I cared to share the screen and also watch. I didn't want to seem ungrateful, so my response was, "Thanks, but I never do porn before breakfast."

In any case, Day 2 in New Caledonia turned out pretty well. The weather was pretty close to perfect, again very similar to California's. As I explored the city of Noumea, my first impression was reinforced. It really was like being in Marseilles, France. The people (both the French and the native Polynesians [Kanaks]) are into their water sports and beach activities. I am not sure I have been anywhere in the world, including Rio de Janeiro, where I have seen more yachts and boats in the water.

On my "hop-on, hop-off" pass, I did the Aquarium and three museums, all first class and first rate. The museums were small but very good. The Aquarium, too, was not the largest I have ever seen, but it was the best.

That night, I made either a bargain with the devil or a Solomon-like decision. You be the judge. I try to be as frugal as I can, and I don't believe that I should be living high off the hog when I travel. Thus, the night before, in this very expensive area of the world, I managed to eat and have a beer for $20. So again I attempted to stay in that price range, which meant going back to the cheapest place in New Caledonia where I had eaten the night before. A small hamburger was $9.50, and a beer was $10.50. Since I wanted keep my food purchase to right around $20, the menu choice was quite simple: I had two beers for dinner.

Vanuatu

After two good days in Noumea, New Caledonia, with weather that was nice and warm rather than hot and humid, I began my journey to Vanuatu, the first real independent country of the trip.

Things did not start off too well. I showed up quite early at the airport, where the airline agent told me there was a "problem" about me boarding the airplane. I assured her that there was **NO PROBLEM** and that, one way or the other I was getting on the plane. She turned my ticket over to a manager; he disappeared, and I waited. And waited.

Finally, I turned to the agent and said, "If I don't have a boarding pass in ten minutes, I'm moving back to the head of the line, right in front of your desk, and I'm not moving. You can call the police or gendarmes or the army if you want."

A few minutes later I had my boarding pass.

Why the airlines do this kind of thing and put people through this ordeal is beyond me. What was this "problem," anyway? When I got on the plane, there were 20 empty seats! The airlines must just enjoy messing with people and making them miserable.

When I got to Vanuatu, I found things there to be very organized and efficient for a poor Third-World country. The people were some of the friendliest and sweetest I have ever met anywhere in the world.

Longitude and Latitude, with Attitude

There are over 800 languages on these 82 islands. All the natives speak three languages: English and French (because, from the 1800s, Britain and France shared the governing of these islands) and Pidgin English. Pidgin English, spoken in one form or another throughout the world, is basically English peppered with the local language or dialect; the natives keep some of their own words intact and sometimes use both languages to make a word, getting very creative when it comes to spelling and pronunciation. (A great example is the "Lufus shirts" I bought in Hong Kong years ago; see my chapter on the "Hong Kong Tailor.") I loved the attitude of the Vanuatu natives about Pidgin English. They call it "mixed-up English."

A native of Vanuatu in traditional dress. The Vanuatuans are the friendliest and sweetest people that I have encountered in the South Pacific.

My driver told me the roads were built by the Americans during WWII. I believe it! They don't feel as if they've been repaired since 1945. We crossed the longest bridge in the country; it took exactly 1.4 seconds. The bridge was about 35- or 40-feet long. Form a mental image of the shortest freeway overpass you have ever been on in America, divide by four, and you'll have a pretty good idea of the longest bridge in Vanuatu.

Vanuatu has a lot of WWII artifacts. The strangest was something right out of *Planet of the Apes* or some lost civilization: During the war, Seabee bulldozers formed mounds of dirt into a huge above-ground "U S A" so that American pilots high in the air could tell that Vanuatu was an American-held island rather than one of the nearby Japanese-held islands. The enormous *U* could still clearly be seen.

The Americans would use Vanuatu as a base for their assault on the relatively nearby Solomon Islands. And for me personally this is where history comes full circle. The First Marine Division would fight one of the most horrific and bloodiest battles of WWII on the island of

Guadalcanal in the Solomon Islands. I was in the First Marine Division in Nam. The insignia for the First Marine Division, then as now, is the number one, inscribed with a single word that runs down its length: Guadalcanal. The First Marine Division in Nam would take more casualties in that war than any other unit in the Marines or the army. And I became one of many of those casualties when I was wounded in the Que Son Valley in December of 1970 (See "Shot Up in the Que Son Valley," above).

Solomon Islands. Artifacts from WWII.

The Solomon Islands, Reggae Rufus, and Traumatized for Life

So I arrived in the Solomon Islands, which turned out to be the shabbiest place of the entire trip. The people were very friendly and nice as on the other islands, but the Solomons were pretty dumpy. I saw some great WWII sites and artifacts and stood on Bloody Ridge where the Marines fought a memorable (and memorably bloody) battle with the Japanese.

The oddest aspects of my trip, however, though not really having anything to do with travel, were two of the most unusual and bizarre occurrences that have ever happened to me.

The hotel I was staying at evidently was hosting on their hotel grounds "the Musical Event of the Century" (at least by Solomon Island standards). My hotel was a zoo, as thousands of mostly young Solomon Islanders packed the grounds for this once-in-a-life time event. At one point during the night, having nothing else better to do, I wandered down to the concert, following the very loud music and amazing light show. I walked right past security despite not having one of the $350 admission tickets, and what a sight!

I have never been to any sort of big concert, so this one was a revelation to me: three or four thousand young Solomon Islanders packed like sardines in the concert area, all in a state of ecstasy, their sleek black bodies (Melanesians have dark black skin) dancing and gyrating as they sang, drank, kissed, fondled, petted, and hugged. The young gals had their lips, hips, and hands all over anyone and everyone. In fact, just walking and trying to make my way up to the stage, I accidentally had sex with three different women.

Now, if you want to imagine one of the strangest sights you can think of, picture an older white man (Rufus), clueless as usual, who knows nothing of music, does not have one iota of rhythm in his body, befuddled by the overt sexual energy and music bombarding him, discovering that he has just entered a "Shaggy" concert. I had no idea who "Shaggy" was. I still don't know who in the hell "Shaggy" is even after spending nearly two hours at his concert. But he sings, and he is actually pretty good. He talks a lot about Jamaica, drugs, and sex.

But this story gets just a little bit stranger. I figured, as long as I was at the concert, I might as well try to work my way up to the front and see if I could destroy what little there was left of my hearing. Believe it or not, I did get all the way up to the front, but there was a solid mass of security in blue uniforms and yellow jerseys stopping anyone not sporting a laminated VIP card around the neck from going any further. I kept moving forward anyway, trying to get to the VIP area when one of the guards said, "Stop. Who are you?" I said," I'm Rufus," and he allowed me in. It's all in a name, folks—either that, or someone has been impersonating me over here.

Of course, maybe they let me into the VIP area because nothing of consequence was going on in there, anyway. My time spent in the VIP area was a bit anticlimactic. It wasn't much different from being anywhere else on the concert floor—just louder.

Go on YouTube and pull up a video of Shaggy's tour in the Solomon Islands. Among the young, all-black crowd of concertgoers, you will see an older white man—the only one at the event with a Medicare card in his wallet, I can assure you—walking about very confused and bewildered, with a true Forest Gump expression on his face.

The second incident gets better or worse, depending on how you look at it. The high point of my last day of touring was supposed to be a trip to a traditional village that has done little to move into modern ways. So we drove to this little village some distance away off a little dirt road and entered it. A few people and kids came out to check out who the stranger was or what he wanted. They were all dressed like everyone else I had seen in this country—shorts, t shirts, dresses—when, out of nowhere, appeared the two biggest, fattest women I have ever seen in my life, wearing *no* clothes! Well, actually, after I took a better look, I could see that they both sported short grass skirts—but that was it. They both had huge, enormous breasts, which had probably caused me to miss the short skirts. They came out to offer me coconuts. (No jokes here, please! Everyone reading this is supposed to be a mature adult.)

Solomon Islands. The two women I had a beer with. Also the largest breasts I had ever seen on human beings.

My first reaction, by impulse and instinct, was to "get the shot." I learned long ago that, with photography, when an opportunity comes along, you shoot first and think about it later. So I started taking some shots of these women when my brain finally kicked in. I began thinking, "I've been from one end of this island to the other, and everyone is wearing clothes. Why are these two very fat women running around naked? Could the Solomon Islands have a law requiring the two fattest women on the island not to wear clothes?" That didn't seem likely. "Or could it have something to do with the fact that I'm a tourist who just arrived in a tour bus, and they—like everyone else in this country—are poor natives who have very little and will do anything to earn a living?"

Once I figured it out, I stopped taking pictures and felt like a chump. I asked my driver/guide if there was anything I could give the women to help them out. I was expecting them to ask for some money, so I started taking out a few singles (notice I didn't say fives, tens, or twenties—Rufus is always a big-time spender!). Instead they said they would like a bottle of beer each. Now, these were my kind of people!!!

What next? We needed to find a bar, of course. Here we were in the middle of nowhere, but, by God, there was a bar. So the four of us—me, the driver, and the two women—ambled down to what they called a bar, anyway. It was a long 1x6 plank of unfinished wood resting on two tree stumps. I asked for four beers, and the "bartender," wearing a pair of shorts and no shirt or sandals, reached into an ice chest that had no ice but did contain a total of five beers. He gave one to each of us.

So there we were at the bar, in this order: the driver, one of the women, me, and the other woman, sipping warm beers under the coconut trees. It was very tranquil and serene, and the driver and I leaned on the bar to make ourselves more comfortable when the two women lifted up their huge breasts and placed *them* on the bar. From that point on, I stared straight ahead and gazed at the ocean because looking to the left or right meant looking at the four largest breasts I have ever seen, which (call me crazy) made me very uncomfortable.

I am not sure whether this tranquil scene is equal to the South Pacific stories of Robert Louis Stevenson or belongs in the *National Enquirer*, but it was my "as-the-sun-sinks-slowly-into-the-west" fond farewell to this trip to the South Pacific.

Rufus McGaugh

I Walk the Straight and *Nauru* (with a Half-Dozen Digressions Along the Way)

Getting There and a Political Demonstration in Australia

April 2015: Just getting to Nauru, this obscure, unknown, little island country out in the middle of nowhere in the South Pacific, is something of an ordeal unless you happen to love sitting on planes or lingering about at airport terminals due to layovers. My journey went thus:

- one-hour drive to the airport
- three-hour wait for my flight from Detroit
- five-hour flight to Los Angeles
- five-hour layover in Los Angeles
- 13-hour flight to Auckland, New Zealand (Don't despair or get impatient; we are now pretty much at the half way point!)
- two-hour layover in Auckland
- three-hour flight to Brisbane, Australia
- 15-hour layover in Brisbane
- seven-hour flight to Nauru

And there you go; it was as easy as that! I don't recall if, after those 54 hours—what with the lack of sleep and jet lag—I had any sanity left (but, on the other hand, I didn't have a whole lot of sanity to begin with). The good news is that I earned enough frequent flyer miles on this trip to go to the moon and any four planets I chose.

During the Brisbane layover, I decided that, although I had a hotel room at the airport to use that day and early evening before my 1:00 a.m. flight, I should probably check out Brisbane, an Australian city I had never been to. I had 15 hours, and it seemed senseless to sit in a hotel room.

I have pretty much lost all interest in cities. They are all starting to look alike. To me, the only cities worth visiting are the old European cities with their history, sights, architecture, museums, and vibrant "livability": wonderful public transportation, outside cafes, green parks, and pedestrian malls. (Major streets are closed to automobiles: humans only allowed). There was some of that in Brisbane.

Brisbane has a fantastic public-transportation system, with lots and lots of buses that go to every area and to every neighborhood. Wherever I was, it took only minutes for a clean, modern bus to arrive. And, each time, the friendly driver patiently answered all my redundant questions.

The bus system is complemented by a number of very thorough air-conditioned trains that snake all through the city, leaving even the downtown area relatively free of auto traffic and thus making it easier to walk around. For instance, if one wanted to walk from pub to pub to indulge in one delicious ice-cold Foster's beer after another, and one was very hot, tired, jet lagged, and thirsty, one could do so!

Deciding that drinking beer in one pub after another was doing absolutely nothing to make me knowledgeable about the city of Brisbane or adding to my travel experiences, I begrudgingly surrendered my bar stool and went back to exploring the city. (This exploration was abbreviated because there were just too many interesting pubs to check out.) I'll make the description of Brisbane short because I just spotted another interesting pub I would like to check out.

Brisbane is a nice, clean version of Chicago, with skyscrapers, nice, well-manicured single-family homes (few apartments), and a number of really beautiful public and government buildings made of various stones and granites that go all the way back to the convict days. (Australia was founded and developed by Britain as a penal colony for convicts. A very large number of the convicts were Irish. Knowing the shady past of past and current members of my family, I was expecting to discover more McGaughs over here than in Ireland.) The wide Brisbane River snakes through the city, adding to the atmosphere. I covered the whole downtown of the city on foot, making mental notes of interesting pubs to come back to and then ambled down to the tip of a peninsula, where Brisbane has its very large and beautiful botanical gardens along the river. Not surprisingly, I quickly became bored walking around the city once I had seen its highlights, so I decided to take the train back instead of the buses.

As I was walking to the train station, I came across a huge political demonstration, and it proved to be just too much temptation for Rufus. Anyone who knows me well knows my love of travel, beer, and politics. In fact, I'm perhaps best described by that old joke: "I've spent 90% of all the money I've ever earned on travel, beer, and women. The other 10% I just wasted." (That must be the "politics" part.)

So I wandered over and discovered that the demonstration was a rally of white supremacists. Their Victims of the Week were Moslems, specifically the Moslem practice of Sharia law (Islamic religious law).

The white supremacists were venting their anger and fury about Australia someday being ruled by Sharia, which I found strange. How many Moslems could there possibly be in Australia? As it turns out, not many.

The furor reminded me of these little towns in, of all places, Tennessee, which are constantly petitioning their state legislature to protect them from living under Sharia when there isn't a Moslem within a hundred miles of them.

The Australian white supremacists were skinheads, and many wore Nazi insignias and were jackbooted. Between them and a much larger group of counter-demonstrators was a cordon of police officers to keep the two sides apart. The counter-demonstrators were dressed even weirder than the white supremacists and had pink, orange, and purple Mohawks and more rings through their noses and lips than can be found in the entire inventory of a jewelry store. Of course, with the way I dress, I was able to mingle with and cross between the two groups with no problem or suspicion.

Remembrance of Demonstrations Past...

I don't think you'll be startled if I mention that this demonstration was not the first time I was involved in a political event in a foreign country. In the 1980s I was traveling with a group through Russia and Eastern Europe, which was about the only way you could travel to communist countries back then. We had left the communist Soviet Union and had entered Poland.

Poland was a wreck of a country during communist times, and the Polish psyche was at the breaking point after having lived for almost 50 years under two brutal and repressive regimes, first Nazi Germany and then the communist U.S.S.R. Not only were the Poles living as a conquered nation under the rule and bayonet of the Soviet Union, but they were forced to try to function under a communist political and economic system that had devastated their country. They had had enough! Despite being outnumbered and outgunned, the Poles put up a stiff and heroic resistance to the Soviet Union through what was called the Solidarity Movement. It started with the shipyard-workers union and spread to the nation as a whole.

Now, on the day I arrived in the Polish capital of Warsaw, we had gone through an all-night train ride from the U.S.S.R. and then spent all day touring the sights of Warsaw. We had a few hours before we were to meet up for dinner, so everyone could make their own decision about how to use their free time. I decided to go off exploring alone, to see what I could on my own without a communist guide giving the official spiel.

I started wandering around Warsaw, and it wasn't long before I stumbled upon a Solidarity Movement demonstration at a Catholic church. Standing before a stone cross outside the church, hundreds of Poles had dropped bouquets of flowers on the ground to form another cross. In a peaceful protest, the Polish people were using their Catholic faith as a protest against their communist and atheist conqueror, the Soviet Union. They were singing religious hymns quietly in unison in a very peaceful manner when suddenly the riot police made their appearance.

Warsaw Poland, 1983. A Solidarity Union protest by the Polish people against their life under a communist government forced upon them by the U.S.S.R. (Russia). The flowers are being laid on the ground so as to form a cross, a sign of the Polish people's deeply held Catholic faith. Armed soldiers in riot gear eventually showed up and violently broke up this peaceful demonstration. Like everyone else, I had to run for my life.

The riot police stood in formation at the end of the street, looking very ominous in their riot gear and helmets, each carrying both a club and a rifle. The people at the church became visibly nervous.

Suddenly, without warning or provocation, the police charged, running toward the crowd with weapons out. Everyone scattered, including me—my backpack flapping up and down on my back as I barreled away, holding my camera close, like a halfback protecting a football. I knew my camera would definitely make me a target, but, back then, I was a serious runner, so I was not concerned about outrunning police loaded down with heavy gear and weapons. I also had the presence of mind not to run into one of the many cul-de-sacs or dead-end streets where I would be trapped with no doubt fatal results for my camera (and maybe me, too).

The police were brutal and vicious, hitting and striking people for no reason other than their own fury. I personally saw a number of elderly women who had fallen behind being beaten and viciously clubbed about the head by the police.

I eventually made it back to my hotel—and just in time for dinner. One member of the group asked what people had done with their free time. Some replied they had rested or did some reading, but most said they had caught 40 winks. When asked what I did, I relayed the above story about the demonstration, which caused one member to say, "When given free time, most of us nap; Rufus starts a riot."

The Other Foreign Political Story

The other foreign political story is how I single handedly, with my gifted administrative and negotiating skills, ended a major labor dispute and strike on the island of Guadeloupe—and you know how I *never* exaggerate!

In 1999, my wife, Monica, my son Eric (about four then), and I made a spring-break trip to the French Caribbean island of Guadeloupe. Most people going on vacation, especially to an exotic place such as Guadeloupe will dress nicely, perhaps with a couple of new outfits. That's most people. You can only imagine what Rufus looks like on these excursions after hurriedly grabbing only what's on the closet floor back home for his stunning attire. On this trip I had an especially hideous, old black t-shirt which came complete with a number of holes in it that I somehow had not noticed until Monica pointed them out and then, for further humiliation, started to count (it turned out to be a fairly large number).

To her horror or amusement (I seldom can tell the difference), she noticed it was a shirt I had bought to support the striking newspaper workers at the *Detroit News* and *Free Press*. It had a huge, poorly drawn, ugly rat on the front to illustrate the fact that the newspapers were using scab workers (rats) to break the strike. I wore it all the time, not so much because the strike was a long one but just to piss off all the capitalists in

Longitude and Latitude, with Attitude

Grosse Pointe when I walked around the two shopping centers known as the Hill and the Village wearing it. Hey, if we didn't win the strike, I at least annoyed a lot of rich people in Grosse Pointe.

So here I was, a thousand or more miles away from the strike, wearing a shirt that my wife repeated over and over again had more holes than material. My take obviously was a bit different. The message was still there on the front, so I was still able to annoy people. So maybe I failed in the fashion department but succeeded in the political department. I was fine with that.

On our third day in Guadeloupe, the three of us went out for a morning walk, and, as we returned to our hotel, we found that it was in the midst of a major strike by its workers. They were sullen and angry, especially with anybody crossing their picket line, including hotel guests—which meant us.

Now I was in a pickle as to the proper course of action. As a strong union supporter (one who was even wearing a union shirt at the time), what was I to do? I really didn't want to cross a union picket line, but I was hundreds and hundreds of miles from home without a whole lot of extra money on me to go to another hotel. I hate to bare my soul here and make a true confession, but, on the moral compass, there is only one thing more precious to me than union solidarity, and that is my money—and beer. And with money I can buy beer.

And now it was decision time—to live up to my ethics and morals as a union supporter or to walk into that hotel demonstrating that, deep down, I am one lying, hypocritical, two-faced, self-serving, looking-out-only-for-himself, self-centered rat. I decided on the latter and walked into the hotel.

Well, not really. I was saved in a sense. As I stood there in what could only be described as an epic moral dilemma in the life of Rufus (do the right thing and support the union or be a despicable hypocrite and loser and walk in), the striking workers noticed my strike-supporting t-shirt (different strike in a different country, but, hey, it worked!) and cheered me and my family into the hotel with "*Viva* whatever." So I was safe, meaning I didn't have to sacrifice or compromise any of my precious political beliefs and be a hypocrite; even better, I didn't have to spend any of my precious money that I love even more than my first born—sorry: that last part was the Republican coming out of me).

Scenic Guadeloupe

Before I get back the island nation of Nauru, I thought that I might add one more incident that occurred on the French island of Guadeloupe. Besides single handily ending a bitter labor dispute and strike on the island, I also had one of my most wonderful and voyeuristic experiences.

I am a bit hesitant to disclose this story and my actions because most female readers might be tempted to assume that Rufus is a perverted, sex-starved, voyeuristic sicko. All I have to say is that anyone who makes that preposterous and unwarranted assumption would be absolutely correct.

There are only two things on earth that tempt me to stray from the exceptionally moral life I have lived, and that is beer and women—especially when they have no clothes on. As I have mentioned, this Caribbean island of Guadeloupe is a French island and comes with all the French ways and customs, which includes French beach fashion, which means the women wear no tops and many go a step further and wear no bottoms.

Being a social-studies guy, I immediately treated this phenomenon as an academic puzzle, wisely concluding that France is such an impoverished country that poor French families were forced to send their daughters far away to toil and sweat on the hot sandy beaches of Guadeloupe. Why all the daughters of poor French peasants were delectable, stunning beauties and so well-endowed physically was something I left to the scientists and nutritionists to figure out. (I was a social-studies guy, remember?) I had my own agenda.

Permit me to demonstrate to you what a wonderful and fantastic husband and father I am (okay, maybe a crummy husband and a pretty lame father): each morning, I would take Eric out for play time to give Monica a break. And where did little toddler Eric want to go? To the beach—with his father's strong approval. While Eric played, I took in the beautiful scenery—if you get my drift.

The best part was that Eric couldn't even squeal on me to his mother. Being only four, he was clueless that the French women were topless and some were outright nude (a fact not lost on his dad.) It turned out to be a wonderful trip. Monica got lots of rest, Eric had lots of play time, and Rufus saw lots of scenery.

A Brief History of Nauru, Its Rise and Fall

So back to the main story. Here I was back in the South Pacific, on the island of Nauru—perhaps the least known and most obscure island country in the world. Nauru's nearest neighbor is the island country of Kiribati, which is another place that virtually nobody has ever heard of—and, yes, I've been there, too.

Nauru has the second smallest population in the world. Only Vatican City (which I don't even count as a real country) is smaller.

What makes Nauru such an oddity is not how little it is (a measly eight square miles and yet an independent country), nor its ridiculously small population (about 9,000 souls on a good day when everyone is home), but the fact that the entire island is made up of bird guano, aka bird do-do, aka bird crap. This has led to all kinds of clever names for the island—most of them not very flattering—such as "Bird-Shit Island."

When the price of guano (bird droppings for fertilizing crops) was at a high in the 1970s, Nauru became one of the richest countries in the world in terms of per-capita income. It actually rivaled Dubai (with all its oil money) as one of the richest places on earth. Everyone was technically a millionaire, and this on an island whose people once lived on coconuts and fish. The Nauruans had their own national airline that often left visitors stranded for weeks on Nauru because chiefs and politicians would commandeer planes for family and friends to go on shopping sprees to Hong Kong and Singapore for a week or two.

Originally they planned on mining their island and home right out of existence. They were going to dig and mine every last ounce of guano (phosphate) until the island was no more. Large tracts of property had been bought in Australia, and the plan was to move the entire population of Nauru over to their purchased property in Australia when their island finally disappeared. Then the bottom fell out, figuratively. The price of phosphates (guano) went south—and the Nauruans had little left in any case. Terrible management of their money resulted in the banks confiscating all the planes in the national airline and basic bankruptcy for the island country of Nauru.

In 2016, the CIA WorldFact book ranked the island country of Nauru's economic GDP (Gross Domestic Product) 194 out of 195 countries in the world, making it one of the poorest places on the planet—below even that of Ethiopia! Of course I had to see this place!

Nauru has tried a number of schemes to get back in the game: off-shore gambling, off-shore banking, money laundering, and even a prison-for-hire to the Australians. Today the unemployment rate sits at 90 percent. The country imports everything, including its water! They apparently are still a very dysfunctional society. (For example, Nauruns are the fattest people in the world. Ninety-seven percent of men and 93 percent of women are overweight or obese. As a result, Nauru has the world's highest level of type 2 diabetes.)

> *"Travel is fatal to prejudice, bigotry, and narrow-mindedness"*
> – Mark Twain

Nauru, the Reality of Being on the Island

The topography of Nauru is a little like an inverted cereal bowl. From the air (at least, from the brief half-minute view I got from an aisle seat before we landed), it looks somewhat flat, though there is definitely some elevation. On the ground, the elevation is most pronounced when you're driving to the top of the island because you notice the continual uphill drive. Obviously, I found that out later.

Flying into Nauru and looking out the plane window leads one to think—at least from the air—that Nauru may not be quite as bad as it sometimes is made out to be. After a seven-hour flight through the night from Brisbane, Australia, Nauru appeared to be lush and very green with no environmental damage to be seen. Based on the drive from the airport to the Menen Hotel (which, back in its flush days of cash, had been a five-star hotel), Nauru appeared to be typical of most of the Pacific islands I have been to, raggedy and seedy rather than abject in its poverty.

Main entrance to my hotel in Nauru—probably one of the worst (of the many bad) hotels I have stayed at during my travels. Nauru itself might well be the best example of a failed Third World nation in or out of the Pacific.

Longitude and Latitude, with Attitude

The Menen Hotel is now a wreck, though the workers miraculously keep this dilapidated monstrosity working and clean. It looks just like Detroit's ghettoized Central Railroad Station but is somehow still working and functioning. At the check-in desk, an army of ants was marching its way from the floor up my leg under cover of my pants and exiting through the sleeve of my shirt to then show off their maneuvers on the hotel check-in desk. Very impressive.

Even later, when I composed this very sentence on my netbook in my room (yes, this place did have electricity most of the time but no Wi-Fi), the ants were crawling up my leg and across the keyboard and screen. With this chaotic army skittering across my lit screen in every random direction, I'm surprised I didn't come home cross-eyed from the experience.

While checking in at the Reception desk, I inquired about a pool and, much to my surprise, learned there *was* a pool—still more or less in operating order. The bad news was that I was not allowed to use it.

"Excuse me," I said. "I'm not allowed to use it?"

Again the answer was "No."

Well, that was pretty clear but a bit baffling. "Why can't I use the pool?" I inquired, *seeing that I am paying $150 a night for this dump*, I thought but didn't voice aloud.

"It's for the people."

Hmm. This explanation sounded very Marxist, especially coming from the desk clerk, Comrade Lenin. As it turned out, keeping me out of the pool was not some evil communist plot but a product of the failed economy. What was once a huge and beautiful resort/hotel was now basically a slum tenement made up primarily of poor, unemployed people. (This is not the time to start making smart-aleck cracks about how I must have fit in perfectly.) Only a few rooms on the bottom floor were for rent as hotel rooms for the rare odd duck like me who shows up from out of nowhere. The rest was one huge, decaying slum tenement with all the traditional trappings—peeling paint, rotten wood, leaky pipes, broken windows and doors, holes in the roof, sagging beams, and a sporadic flow of water.

Bottom line: the pool is for the local people only.

Entertaining myself that day by the pool—not *in* it; I wasn't allowed—I decided it might very well be a blessing that I was barred from it. It was very small and built of primitive concrete and remained empty of water six days a week. Then, on Sunday they rummaged up a huge, long hose about 200 yards long and stretched it to the ocean. They pumped water into the pool, and the ghetto kids used it for most of the day. ...I didn't want to get beat up by the ghetto kids, anyway.

On this island in this miserable economy, you could get a blow job for $8.00—that's a blow job, the drink, not the sex act (although I suspect the sex act could be had cheaper due to the poverty). I sampled neither, preferring beer to the former and fidelity to my marriage vows to the latter.

The entrance to the hotel was flanked by some of the ugliest pre-fab housing I have ever seen. From what I could tell, this was where Australian ex-pats stayed, to help Nauru out, during their temporary tours of duty. They looked like metal shipping containers stacked on top of each other, and each row had such charming names as "Toms Cabin" and "Den's Place," demonstrating that Den was a much smarter kid and better student than Tom because he knew how to use a possessive apostrophe. (This is the only bone that I am tossing out to the English Department.)

I went to my room, which was not too bad once I forcibly evicted a few cockroaches and lizards. The ants I gave up on. I grabbed my backpack and camera and went off to explore the island. It was a long hot walk with little shade, but I did find two WWII Japanese concrete bunkers. Like all the Japanese bunkers I have seen in the Pacific region, they were built to last and take a pounding. The concrete is incredibly thick, and they will probably survive longer than the pyramids.

As usual, by the time I got back to my room, I was beyond sweaty. I was drenched, soaked through and through. The humidity on these islands is unbelievable.

I got into the shower—only to discover there was no water, so that caused a trip to what they call "Reception," which means two people lying on the floor sleeping. After disturbing their slumbers, I was only then notified that there was a "water schedule": each day, based on some arbitrary schedule, water is available a total of 13 hours out of every 24.

So, as you can see I continue to indulge myself with nothing but the best in creature comforts and luxury when I travel. It would have been nice if they had informed me of this before I set off on a blazing-hot two-hour walk; now I had an hour and a half to wait for water and a shower. And, when the water came—you'll never believe this in a million years!—there was no hot water. And, as hard as it is to believe in such luxurious accommodations, the one towel was threadbare and had so many holes in it that it could have been confused for one of my shirts.

There was a kernel of good news in all this, and that is the restaurant, which I feared would have sky-high prices. It was a Chinese restaurant run by Chinese right from China, featuring my least favorite food in the world, Chinese. But it was cheap, had beer, and the food was actually good.

The Worst Hotel in the World (Naturally, Rufus Stayed There)

For those of you reading this, no doubt you are thinking that my accommodations on Nauru were about as poor and rank as they could get. You could not be further from the truth. Of the many, many, many horrible hotels I have stayed in, let me tell you about the worst. (Due to time and space I will not go into the—let us say—unusual spots I have laid my body down to sleep which at one time or another would include park benches, cow pastures, a zoo [South Bend, Indiana], outhouses, work sheds, my car, trains, doorways of shops and stores, train stations, floors of airports, decks of ferries, and vacant buildings.)

When I would tell this story to my 7th-graders, I would preface it by telling them that, often, when people are at a party, barbeque, or some social function, the subject of travel comes up, and, in many cases, people start swapping horror stories, including stories about the worse hotel they had ever stayed in. I used to tell the kids, "Whenever I have been in a situation like that, where people are competing for whose hotel story was worst, my story has beat everyone else's, hands down. And—I don't want to sound arrogant—but nobody's story is every going to top mine." You be the judge.

Back somewhere in the 1980s, I made a major trip to South America through an American Express tour that pretty much covered all the major countries and attractions. However, they did skip a number of countries because—let's see if I can say this nicely—they sucked, big time. So, when the tour ended in Rio de Janerio, Brazil, I independently took off on my own to such hot spots as Paraguay and Guinea that nobody in their right mind, in South America or out, ever goes to for any reason. For the most part, they were hot, impoverished, disgusting hell holes, but, of course, I had to make my journey to them.

One of my destinations was French Guinea, famous for being the site of Devil's Island, the infamous gulag of the 1800s for the worst of the worst French criminals. French Guinea is located at the northern top of the South American continent. French Guinea is not a real country, being a French possession, but it was on the "Rufus List," so off I went.

I flew in and landed on what appeared to be a jungle runway and deboarded the plane to discover there was neither a terminal nor any buildings. There was a "structure" made of bamboo, leaves, and vines that served as Customs/Immigration.

I somehow got into the city of Cayenne and discovered there were just three hotels. Using my acute powers of observation, I discerned what appeared to be the worst-looking one, thus the cheapest one. The other two hotels looked to be somewhat kept up, but my future home seemed to be in need of a wrecking ball. It was the most unusual building in this poor, dilapidated colonial town because it was a skyscraper of some great height—I would say 30-35 stories high—in a community that seemed to have not one building taller than three floors. It was very tall, and, like most skyscrapers, narrow—its height being the predominant characteristic.

I walked into the lobby, where nothing seemed amiss or unusual (at least not when it came to your typical, run-of-the-mill, low-class hotel—the kind with which I was intimately familiar, having made a point of sleeping in such dives as this all over the world).

The price of the room was $26—sky high for a dump like this, but there seemed to be no other options, so out came an American Express twenty-dollar travelers' cheque and six dollars—five singles and four quarters that I had to rummage through my pockets to find. I was given my key, told I would be on the 29th floor, and took about four steps toward the elevator when the desk clerk declared, "The elevator just broke today and is not in use."

Let me digress here just a moment to share with you an amazing and unbelievable fact about me and broken elevators. I don't want to brag or exaggerate, but, in my travels—always in poverty and always staying in the pig sties of any nation I visit—I, more than any person on this planet, have checked into more hotels that seem to have a broken elevator. That isn't even the amazing part. The most astounding thing is that I have set the world record for staying at hotels with elevators that just broke that day—hundreds of them; no: thousands! What an unbelievable coincidence! None of these elevators broke two days or three days ago, nor a week or a month ago, but seemed to have disintegrated, broken, and fallen apart just as Rufus walked into the lobby. Some guys apparently have all the luck!

Back to the story. In this particular case, a broken elevator was indeed a problem. The temperature was in the high nineties heading toward a hundred and as humid as a sauna. I was tempted to demand my money back, but I knew I would never get it. In the poor Third-World countries of the world, once money has left your hands and is in the hands of a poor man, it is gone forever. This man, like all the poor I have encountered, would prefer death over returning or surrendering just the

Longitude and Latitude, with Attitude

four quarters I had given him. You can only imagine the scene for the full $26. Even with my lack of morals, I refrain from killing a man over money—even for my four precious American quarters.

So I headed for the stairwell—backpack on, $2 Shoppers' Fair sleeping bag (tied at the bottom of the pack with two old boot laces) flopping from side to side.

By the way, the old Shoppers' Fair at 8 Mile and Gratiot in Detroit was the Kmart of its time before there was a Kmart—no surprise that Rufus shopped here! Before the demise of Shoppers' Fair, before it went under and disappeared, it was able to make an innovation that stunned the scientific world: it invented and produced a cheap $2 sleeping bag that somehow made you colder when you got inside it than you had been before getting into it. In fact, I had written a letter to the company offering to be a spokesman and do magazine and television testimonials, stating that I had used their sleeping bag on my frequent backpacking and camping trips all over northern Michigan and had nearly frozen to death in it many times, but I never heard from them.

Twenty-nine floors and a whole lot of stairs later, I made it to my destination. I went to my room, inserted the key, opened the door and was beyond surprised or shocked.

First, let me say that, with the experiences I have had in life, I'm not the sort of person who is easily surprised or shocked. In fact I could go so far as to say I'm never shocked and seldom surprised, but the adage was just lost in this situation.

The first thing was the view. From 29 stories up, of course you would expect a magnificent view, but my view was on a whole unique level. It seems that my very tall skyscraper hotel had once had another tall building next to it—and they had shared a common wall as they sat side by side. Then, at some time unknown to me, the building attached with the common wall was razed and knocked down, leaving the skyscraper that was now home for me missing an entire wall (exterior and interior) from the top of the building to the ground. It was similar to living in a doll house, except I was 'way up there.

I couldn't believe it. I walked over to the edge, my hand grasping the wall to avoid an accidental 29-story plunge. I looked down as from a mountain top at the people walking the streets below, looking, of course, ant like. This was really bizarre, even by Rufus standards. But, hey! Look on the bright side; this place still had three good walls—and three out of four isn't bad!

Wait! It gets worse—or better, if you happen to be the reader! I don't think I have ever rolled or fallen out of bed in my life, but, due to the cloud I sometimes seem to travel under, I reckoned that, if ever it were to happen, tonight would be the night, especially given the placement of the bed so close to the yawning opening. So I placed my backpack down, leaning it against a wall, and went over to the bed.

That's when I noticed what a horrid mess it was. I had planned on moving it a bit away from its potential roll-out-of-bed suicide position near the missing wall. But, once at the bed site, I noticed that the mattress was, strangely, half on, half off the bed, and touching the floor, that the bed had not been made up, and, even worse, that the one white sheet on it was stained with dirt, lots of blood (was this a murder scene?), and what seemed like vomit, urine, and human waste.

I took the sheet off and threw it in a corner—the one with two walls—repositioned the filthy mattress squarely on the bed, and decided to put my sleeping bag on top, figuring it would provide a bit of a barrier between me and all the filth. With the sky-rocketing heat, I would not need to get into the bag, especially since—huge surprise here—the room had no air conditioning. Although I have to admit that, when you are missing an entire wall 29 floors up, you do get a pleasant breeze.

While I was taking stock of my surroundings, I couldn't help but notice the unusual floor. I had so many other issues with this room that I had not had the time to look into that until now. The floor was a deep, deep black, as black as an old-fashioned school blackboard—but soft and spongy. Why? Moving the bed away from its suicide position, uncovering a spot where one of the legs of the bed had stood forever, solved the mystery. At one point the room had been covered by bright red carpeting, but, over time, the filth and vermin had turned it jet black—think of a very badly burnt grilled-cheese sandwich, and you get the picture of the color and texture.

But it gets worse!

As bad as it was, I would only have to stay here a few hours because I had a very early flight the next morning—to another hell hole—so I set my alarm and was going to go to bed early. I had already walked the town of Cayenne and determined it was a crime-ridden, very unsafe place to be, plus I really didn't want to climb those stairs again. I was so broke (think paying part of your hotel bill with four quarters), with miles still to travel, so I decided to skip dinner to save money. (For years—as I may have already mentioned—people would ask, "How do you keep yourself in such good shape and at the same weight you were when you were in the Marines?" It's called starvation. Besides, traveling always gave me more pleasure than eating did.)

As I lay down on top of my wafer-thin sleeping bag on top of the filthy mattress, nature called. I got up from the bed and walked over to

Longitude and Latitude, with Attitude

the bathroom that I had not yet visited. I flicked the switch to the turn the light on, and—no surprise here—the bulb was burned out. It was cave-like dark and didn't smell too good, so I went to my backpack, found my ultra-light Eddie Bauer backpacking flashlight and went back to the bathroom.

Whoa! Not only was the light bulb not working but the toilet wasn't, either. That, however, had not stopped people from using it many, many times. This lonely, derelict toilet was filled from bottom to top with brown human feces. Even this had not stopped people from using it. Somehow people squatted over this and continued adding their human waste so that the toilet now looked like some huge, bizarre Dairy Queen ice-cream cone of chocolate human waste.

Now the reader may regard my next actions as craven or uncouth, but you gotta do what you gotta do. I can assure you from the bottom of my heart and what few ethics I have left that I had never, ever peed in a sink or even thought of peeing in a sink-until then. So I turned to the sink with my flashlight, and I had to stop in my tracks. Evidently, when just no more human waste could get into that broken toilet, people had come up with the same idea I had—but the difference was that I had to pee and they had other more serious issues (commonly called bowel movements) to deal with,. So the sink, under the beam of my flashlight, looked very much like the toilet: another brown Dairy Queen cone. This latest development was not helping me with my urination problem.

So I went down 29 floors to an alley, where the deed was done, and then back up 29 floors, now amounting to a total of three times I had made this exhausting journey—not counting the fourth time, when I would have to go down again to leave. The good news was the temperature had dropped from 97 degrees F to 93.

But it gets worse!

Back in my room, I lay down, sweaty—huge surprise: the shower didn't work—and attempted to get a little sleep. I had just started drifting off when I heard a noise. My first thought was that someone was trying to break into my room as this was a very dangerous, high-crime area where gangs paraded right out in the open.

Quickly forming plans for any fight or violence I might need to deal with, I quietly rose, and that's when I discovered what the true situation was. It was rats—big rats, big enough to saddle. They were getting into my backpack, where I must have left some airline food for future eating on my starvation food budget.

I ran toward my pack, flashlight in hand, and there must have been 40 huge rats gnawing at my backpack. My greatest concern was that the rats might damage my backpack; on Appalachian backpacking trips, using huts for sleepers in bear country, I had seen mice destroy such packs. The fenced-in huts protect backpackers from bear attack, but the inevitable crumbs from food attract the mice, who do tremendous damage to packs and sleeping bags in their effort to get to food.

So I shooed the rats away and found what food there was and threw it out by way of the missing wall, hoping I would be done with the rats.

It was not to be my lucky night. I walked back to my bed and lay down, and, within minutes, the rats were back at the backpack, so I threw one of my boots at them, and they skedaddled away.

They came back minutes later, so I threw the second boot at them, and again they retreated.

They came back again, and now I was out of boots, so I jumped up and chased them off. And so we repeated this scenario all night: throw boot one, and the rats retreat but then come back. Throw boot two with the same result. Finally get up and chase them off, pick both boots up, and start the whole process over again all night.

The rats never gave up, and I certainly did not get much sleep. I always used to tell my students, "Nobody is ever going to beat me when it comes to stories about the worst hotel they have stayed at unless they are murdered in their hotel room. In that case, they won't be around to tell the story."

"Not all those who wander are lost."
    – JRR Tolkien

Almost Everything You Never Wanted to Know about Nauru

As I walked out after breakfast one morning for a short walk down the beach, I couldn't help but notice what a beautiful island Nauru could be. It is very green and lush—a postcard tropical island with huge waves crashing onto the shore.

But there are so many obstacles preventing Nauru from ever being able to survive in a pleasant or prosperous way. First is the geographic issue of distance and isolation. Nauru is a long, long way from anywhere. Its closest neighbor of any size, Australia, is over seven hours away by air. Forget about Europe and America; it takes two days to fly to Nauru from either continent! Nauru is basically devoid of any natural resources now that the phosphate (bird poop) is gone. And finally the cultural psyche seems to be one of despair and depression (I was starting to join them in this). It's an impoverished island with few jobs and no resources—it has to import its drinking water from Singapore! The word or concept of hope did not seem to exist on Nauru.

I have to hand it to anybody still reading this recitation about a tiny, little dipshit island (no pun intended) that they probably never heard of before and that, now, after my encomiums, care even less about. The longer I stayed there, the more I started to feel like Robinson Crusoe or Tom Hanks in the movie *Castaway*. However, I did continue to learn more about this island while I was marooned there.

In one of the smallest, most isolated and homogeneous societies in the world (about 9,000 people), the Nauruans still ended up dividing themselves into 12 tribes. Some of the tribes have flashy names like the black-fish tribe and the dragon-fly tribe. Others don't show as much pizzazz (e.g., the eel tribe, the crab tribe). Some are just outright boring (e.g., the fish tribe). I would love to hear the history of the water-drinker tribe. What! Did they run out of beer? At least two of the tribes have loser written all over them, and that would be the flotsam-and-jetsam tribe and the louse tribe.

Politically, Nauru is divided into 14 districts, which would be equivalent to our states. A number of districts have but one single attraction within the entire district, such as a Chinese restaurant. One district had only a closed and out-of-business gas station to hype.

And, just in case you were curious, the head is sacred to the Naurans; you can only touch the head of a close family member. Good fun fact to know just in case you end up there someday.

Big News out of Tonga

But the big news in the neighborhood—and, by the neighborhood, I mean the immense area of Pacific islands, covering thousands and thousands of miles of ocean—was in the island nation of Tonga, which I visited the year before, in 2014. Tonga, as you may know, is the only monarchy among the Pacific island nations and is ruled by a king—a big king because these are the biggest people on earth. The Tongans are not necessarily fat but big and rotund. A recent Tongan king reportedly weighed 350 pounds, though everybody thought that was a lie because rumor had it that he was much closer to 400 pounds. Some Tongans claim that past kings weighed as much as 600 pounds, but that one is debatable.

In any case, there was a Tongan princess who was ready for marriage, and the bidding war for her had begun, with everything from cash to pigs being offered for her hand (and all the rest of her). The princess had no say about whom she got to marry. That was up to her father, King Tupou VI. The one major requirement was that she marry only royalty—which was a problem. Within the royal ranks, there were only eight single women and six single men—and they were all cousins!

It was quite a dilemma, especially since, according to an August 7, 2013, UK *Daily Telegraph* article, two princesses had already opted out of royal marriages: "Princess Salote Lupepau'u Tuita, sixth in line to the throne, is marrying a former rugby player, while her younger sister, Princess Frederica Tuita, who is tenth in line, is marrying the son of a businessman." Considering such female defiance in the royal house, you can (maybe) understand why pretty much all the Pacific was watching this soap opera the same way that many folks in the States follow the British royal family.

(I can assure you I am as uninterested in the British royal family as any person on Earth, but even I can't escape the non-stop news about Kate—whoever Kate is—and her new baby or her new washing machine or whatever it is that seems to interest so many people.)

This marriage story pushed the other big Tongan royal story to the back pages. As you probably know, the British royal family often makes the news for its affairs and divorces, for saying something extremely stupid or getting killed in a car accident. Well, the previous big news out of Tonga before this marriage crisis was that the brother of the aforementioned princess, Prince Ata, wanted to be baptized a Mormon—and in fact *was* baptized a Mormon, in Hawaii, even though his father, the king, tried to persuade him to postpone the ceremony, even going so far as to send in the army to stop it. (Well, okay, not the *army*; he sent his royal guards and the former Prime Minister of Tonga, who, apparently were unable to dissuade Prince Ata from becoming a member of the Church of Latter Day Saints. For all I know, Ata is now riding around on a bicycle in a nice suit, white shirt, and tie, spreading the Mormon word.)

Be Careful What You Wish Wouldn't Happen

As I continued meandering down the beach, I again noticed the huge amount of trash, litter, and garbage that carpeted the sand and shore. I *almost* started thinking something along the lines of "Gee, I would sure hate to somehow get stranded in this crummy place." But I didn't go

Longitude and Latitude, with Attitude

there; I would not allow myself to go there. And that is when I almost fell into my one and only superstition.

Superstition, luck, fate, mysteries, and the supernatural are all hogwash to me, yet one superstition has been branded into my psyche and, try as I might, I cannot dislodge it. My one and only superstition is to never, ever say out loud—or even think—of some event possibly occurring or happening that I desperately don't want to happen.

When we were first married, my wife, Monica, did not know of this superstition when she had planned a trip for us (before the kids) to Canada. She had told me weeks earlier that she was planning a cool trip for us, and, of course, I was all excited and all for it. Three weeks later, she announced we were going to Canada, and I had the first heart attack and nervous breakdown of my life.

"*CANADA!!!*" I reacted with my usual calm reasonableness. "God Almighty, no wonder it took you three weeks! It would take that much time and research to find the most monotonous and boring place on earth!"

After collecting myself and cooling down, I allowed myself (like a fool) to hope that Monica had plans that would make this insane idea palatable. Were we, at least, going to go to the very northern limits of Canada and perhaps use dog sleds to get into the Arctic Circle, I hoped?

No, unfortunately. Nothing like that was in the plans. It was the first time I contemplated divorce.

Well, I tried to be a good sport about it. I had been hoping she would have planned a canoe trip down the Congo or a mountain trek in the Himalayas, but, no, it was to be a flight into the Maritime Provinces and then a drive around to such exciting and thrilling places as Nova Scotia. Nova Scotia! I couldn't believe marriage had sunk me to this level!

In all fairness, we had a great time and, despite my cynicism, saw a lot of great scenery. Although I will never admit it to my wife—after all, one has to keep up one's appearances—it was a great trip. Better to let her think I was just being a good sport.

Actually I shouldn't have been such a great sport about it because the next year she planned a four-day trip to (are you ready for this?) Ottawa, Canada's capital—in the middle of winter, so that I would then be both bored and frozen. You can see for yourself this marriage was heading downhill real fast.

Getting back to my superstition, on the first of the trips to Canada, we had arranged for a car and driver for a very long and lengthy trip across Newfoundland. It was a pleasant and scenic ride and ended at the edge of the Earth, located somewhere in Canada. My goal that day was to take a short ferry ride over to the last two European possessions in the North American continent, the two little French islands of St. Pierre and Miquelon. (And, yes they are on my list of visited countries and lands.) No one lives on Miquelon—but France hangs onto to it for dear life! We went to St. Pierre, and it was like being in France, except we were less than one mile out in the Atlantic from Canada. We took the ferry back to Canada and waited for our ride back to our hotel.

Now, Canada is mostly a beautiful, neat, and well-kept country, but this little decrepit town at the edge of Newfoundland looked as though every ignorant hillbilly from the back hills of Appalachia and the swamps of Louisiana who were too ignorant to live among their own folks had moved and settled here. Calling this place the ugliest place in North America would be too complimentary.

That's when my wife Monica broke the rule. She stood in disbelief and disgust and uttered these fateful words, "I would sure hate to ever get stuck in this place."

I couldn't believe she did it. She had actually broken the rule (my only superstition): "Don't ever say out loud, or even think, your worst fear because it will become reality." (To be fair, I had never told her about this "rule.") I remember speaking very softly and saying, "I wish you had not said that," and then just let it go, hoping the issue would resolve itself before becoming a self-fulfilling prophecy.

The next thing we knew, every bus, taxi, and van departed from the parking lot, leaving us stranded. I shook my head in disgust and gave my wife a dirty look—because, obviously, she was the cause of all of this. We went into a little building—no, a shack—and explained our situation to the lady behind the counter. She immediately started working the phones—and I do have to say this about the Canadians: everyone (I mean *everyone*) jumped into action to help us out. The lady at the phone was off the clock and working on her own time. The company responsible for the mishap apologized profusely and immediately made arrangements to get us back to civilization.

The company had to pay for a private individual to drive us back to the hotel. The one and only person in the area with a car was not interested in driving through hours of darkness until he heard an American couple was stranded. He then interrupted his dinner and showed up within minutes.

The problem with irrational superstitions is that, just as in this case, they often re-enforce themselves into a pattern.

This superstition—and, again, it is the only superstition I have—goes back to the war. It is much too long of story to go into now, but the short version is that, only four days into Vietnam, on my first night ambush, a

Longitude and Latitude, with Attitude

volley of Marine artillery was fired over our position. I was brand new to the war and had never heard artillery fire, even in training. It was a very loud screaming over our heads, and, when the ordnance landed, the destruction was horrifying and total. Nothing survived. Everything was obliterated. As I lay on the ground in the dark with my rifle in my hands, I thought to myself, "God, that shelling is terrible. Even at the gun range I've never heard anything so loud and destructive. God, I sure am glad it's not coming in on us."

That thought would haunt me for the rest of my life because, no sooner had I conceived the notion massive Marine artillery started coming in on us, and Marine artillery was awesome, destructive, and very precise. For the next 40 minutes—the longest 40 minutes of my life—my unit came under barrage after barrage of Marine artillery, totally destroying everything in its path, obliterating every tree and plant, rearranging the earth that we clung to, face down. Wave after wave of destructive white-hot metal shrapnel exploded, ripped, tore, and mangled everything at our position, time after time, doing its best to kill us. Through some unaccountable or unexplained mishap, we had been mistaken for the enemy Viet Cong, and the orders were to kill and destroy them—*us*—with everything the Marines had.

Time and again the shells came crashing in, exploding, ripping, and tearing. We couldn't fight back. There was nothing to be done but hug the earth and wait for the inevitable. I couldn't believe I was going to die after only four days in Vietnam. I was the new guy going on my first night ambush, and the rest of the guys had said not to be nervous or scared because this night operation would be led by one of the most popular men in the platoon, Joe, a charismatic Mexican-American who "was the coolest guy under fire." What they meant was that, no matter how bad the fighting had ever been, Joe as a squad leader was always cool, calm, and collected—a natural leader for whom all the Marines in my platoon had great respect. Now here was Joe, "the coolest guy under fire," just 20 feet from me screaming over the radio, pleading and begging to have the Marine artillery stop. Screaming with emotion, when we were never allowed to even whisper during a night ambush, "Cease fire! Cease fire! Jesus Christ, stop firing or you are going to kill all of us!"

But the shelling did not end. The shells continued to come in closer and closer, to the point that I could feel the red-hot shrapnel cut across the top of my hair—and I had a short Marine haircut. The concussion from the exploding bombs, landing so close, had already given me a bloody nose, and blood was running out of one of my ears. I knew as everyone did that the next volley or barrage would be the end. Typical me—I felt more anger than fear.

Then it stopped.

After that, my rule was, "Never think of what you might fear and certainly don't speak it because without a doubt it will happen." It's my only superstition. And I think you can understand why.

"Never think that war, no matter how necessary, nor how justified, is not a crime. Ask the infantry and ask the dead."
– Ernest Hemingway

Nauru, the Tour

When I travel I often go out of my way to talk to people because it is a way to learn more about a country, plus I often gain tips or information that makes the trip more successful. I had ordered lunch—and, by the way, if I were you, based on today's lunch, I would avoid Chinese hamburgers—when I struck up a conversation with an Australian who happened to work for Nauru's airline, called "Our Airline." I suspect Nauru came up with this unusual airline name based on the results of their 1990s bankruptcy. The Australian banks and creditors immediately confiscated Nauru's entire airline because it was the only tangible possession they had (besides the dwindling supply of bird poop). Perhaps they feel a little more secure with the possessive "Our."

The Australian suggested hitching a ride somehow to go into the interior and see the actual phosphate mining and environmental disaster take place before my very eyes. He also suggested making a visit to the big Australian detention camp, where refugees were locked up behind fences, razor wire, and local guards from 5 p.m. until the next morning to discourage escape. (These precautions may sound like overkill, but the Australians apparently feel that these Asian refugees trying to get to Australia have already proved their ability to escape one country, so they have a bit of experience in this sort of thing.)

So, before my Shanghai burger arrived, I headed over to Reception and cut a deal for $35 to go into the interior. Off we went on my private one-man tour in the hotel van, which somehow included another 978 relatives, friends, family, children, and babies who needed dropping off at various points of the tour. On my private tour, I probably would not ordinarily have minded the two people who had to sit on my lap if they were hot babes, but one was an elderly wrinkled-up grandma, and the other a 19-year-old guy. The hotel guide took me (and all the others) to

Longitude and Latitude, with Attitude

the top of the island, where we saw both the mining and the detention center—neither of which were very interesting or offered much, if anything, worth writing about.

Eventually we dispensed with this circus of people, and the actual tour was on. Because the guide was a local gal with an accent difficult to understand, the radio was blaring country-western music, and I have poor hearing in the best of circumstances, I didn't glean much from her commentary. We did visit a beautiful tropical lake and a Japanese prison buried in the jungle.

By the way, these people suffered horribly under the Japanese during WWII. Back then, there were less than 2,000 of these people, and almost all of them were deported elsewhere as slave labor. Almost half of those never made it back and died as slaves on other islands. Many young people here tell of missing grandparents who died unknown and unmarked on some other island.

I'm sure it has nothing to do with the Japanese occupation, but one thing I noticed during my stay on Nauru is that the Nauruans seem to use hyphens quite a bit but don't always put them where they should, which makes for some unusual results. For instance, on the tour, we passed by "Bada-ss Service Station." I have no idea if the proprietor was indeed a real bad ass or perhaps just a dumb ass who did not learn the rules of hyphen use.

After my exciting two-hour tour of Nauru—and please don't even ask how a tour of a little eight-square-mile island made up entirely of bird poop took two hours (but it may have had something to do with the 978 other people who were chauffeured in the van)—I went for a walk on a different beach. Unfortunately it was similar to all the others not only here in Nauru but in most of the South Pacific islands. The beach was strewn with broken glass, trash, condoms, garbage, bottles, sanitary pads, cans, and other debris. A walk in Paradise.

Here's the good news though. Nauru's crime rate is 0%, even for petty crimes.

Earlier I reported that my former five-star hotel, except for a few rooms, had become a slum tenement for the poor and unemployed. At least, that's what I assumed, based on their poverty. However, I learned, after talking with my guide, that it was housing for government workers! After finishing the tour, I re-examined this place and found I had not exaggerated earlier about what a dump and slum it is. The living conditions looked like something out of a Dickens novel or modern-day Ethiopia. These workers lived in deplorable conditions! What surprised me most was that I had no idea Nauru was a part of America and was a Republican right- to-work state.

"The world is a book, and those who do not travel read only a page."
– St. Augustine

Nauru, Last Day on the Island

A parting observation: Perhaps it was because I knew. I have been on many islands but never felt so isolated and so far from my fellow humans as I did when I stood each evening watching the rolling surf of huge waves come crashing in with just nothing and nothing stretching out into the distant horizon.

My last morning on Nauru started off with three good cups of coffee at the Chinese restaurant, along with what the Chinese called French toast. It didn't look like or taste like any French toast I had ever had but was not bad, so no complaints on my part. To get that coffee and French toast, however, I did have to awaken the two local waitresses who were sleeping on the floor.

I was then involved in a bureaucratic chase-your-tail mission. When I had arrived three days earlier on Sunday, the immigration official—or should I say the old lady wearing a cloth wrapped around her waist, wearing a blouse with many holes in it, and walking barefoot—said I had to report to the Immigration Office the next day. I was not sure why, but thank God this island was a small one! I was almost tempted to skip doing it as a waste of time. Good thing I didn't; I would have never gotten out of this place.

The next day, the hotel van took me to the Immigration Office, and guess what. It was closed. It was also closed the next day. Again, I was tempted to just do whatever I had to do at the airport the day I was to leave. Good thing I didn't because I would now be emailing you from the island of Nauru telling you how lonely I am and how I miss you. So, early on the day of my departure, I again got into the hotel van and went to Immigration, and, in a bit of a surprise to me, it was actually open.

But now the government bureaucracy set in. They wanted to see my passport and visa-acceptance form. I produced both and then got a little surprise. They took both and said I would not get them back until I paid the $50 visa fee. (I had forgotten that I had a visa approval but had not paid for the visa itself.) No problem. I took out 50 Australian dollars—which was the fee for the visa and, I might add, a deal (a real steal) compared to the fee in many countries. A few years ago, I paid over

$1,000 dollars for a visa for Angola, and, I can assure you, Angola was not worth a $1,000 visa.

There was another problem or hurdle now: one does not pay the visa fee at Immigration; one must go to Revenue. Okay.

"Where's Revenue?" I asked. The lady pointed to a building less than 200 yards away, but getting there proved to be no quick and easy trip. It might be only 200 yards away, but it was on the other side of the airport runway, and no one is allowed to walk, run, or drive across the runway at any time, day or night, despite the fact that only two flights a *week* fly into Nauru. (And, by the way, the runway cuts across the entire width of the island of Nauru.) So we drove around the runway, stopping frequently to say hi to friends and family and make a few purchases at local shops, and finally arrived at Revenue.

That part went quickly because all they had to do was take my money, and they were very efficient at doing that. I was ready to head back to the hotel, but, no, there was one last thing to do concerning this visa. We had to drive back around the runway to go back to Immigration to show them the receipt that proved I had paid my $50. Only then would they stamp my passport and give it back. Finally, I was a free man and allowed to leave Nauru. Isn't it wonderful traveling the Third World?

I departed Nauru early that afternoon with my final destination being the island (country?) of Niue. It would take me four days and four nights to get there! To get there I would have to circumnavigate the earth a half a dozen times, make layovers in 163 cities, and finally finish getting there dog paddling on a balsa-wood raft. That last sentence might be a bit of embellishment, but the four days to get there is the God's awful truth. The immediate destination was actually Brisbane, Australia, so that I could get to New Zealand so that I could get to Niue—pretty simple eh?

The flight to Brisbane, Australia, went fine except for the food. I had forgotten to eat lunch, so my nutrition would have to be supplied by the airline, which was a scary thought in itself. (If God ever punishes mankind again through a Moses-like plague, it will not be frogs and locusts and death of the first born; it will be airline food and Marine C-rations—which, however, might consist of frogs and locusts... I'll stop there.) The cuisine was definitely Australian and appeared to be some sort of road kill, possibly platypus or dingo. Since Australians were the predominant group on the plane, the airline wisely did not serve beer, knowing the Aussies' penchant for that beverage and their behavior afterwards. There was unlimited wine, so, being the flexible guy I am, I quickly morphed from beer guzzler to wino immediately.

"The mouth of a perfectly contented man is filled with beer."
  – Ancient Egyptian proverb

Nauru Again (Actually Auckland, New Zealand)

I arrived in Auckland, New Zealand, which is a beautiful city, early in the evening. I checked into my hotel—and you won't believe this—it was actually a nice place; not a normal thing for Rufus. I cleaned up and did some reading and writing, and, as the hours went on, I did get hungry. What do normal people who are traveling do when they get hungry? They go to a restaurant and order and eat a nice meal. What does Rufus do in the same situation? He walks through the dark of night in a strange and unfamiliar city to a convenience store.

(Let me digress here a moment. Convenience stores are the same the world over. They are always shabby places with most of their goods looking like they have been sitting there long after their expiration dates. The guy behind the counter is always some weird-looking ethnic guy who can never speak the language of the country he happens to be in.)

I picked up a bag of those very nutritious Doritos (for $1.29), two large cans of a vitamin drink called Heineken, and, to aid my digestion, a Mars bar. This saved both time and money. My meal and two large beers cost less than one small beer at the hotel bar. Another factor in my fine-dining decision tonight was that the hotel restaurant menu offered Black Angus Eye Filet, 220g, for $44 and the Green Lipped New Zealand Mussels—which didn't sound good at any price.

Now let's talk about everybody's favorite subject—SEX.

Two stories to share with you on that topic: As I was walking back to the hotel from the convenience store, from a garage to my right, two young women—both with horrible physical disabilities that had disfigured their bodies so that they were all breasts and now did not have any other body parts such as legs, arms, hands, or a head—came into my sight. As it turned out, these two young ladies did have those other body parts, but I could not see them due to their greatly endowed chests that were attempting to escape from the tops of their dresses. Oddly, they seemed to have body guards or escorts, and I watched as they entered a nondescript building. There was a chalked sign in front that said, "The Easter Bunny May Be Gone, but Our Bunnies Are Still Available –with Private Rooms!" I walked back to the hotel, perplexed as to why anyone would want to spend time in a room with a little bunny.

Back at the hotel room, I wanted to watch the news, so I turned the TV on. (I should preface this story by noting how electronically challenged I am when it comes to computers and even TVs. If you were to spend much time around 813 Notre Dame, Grosse Pointe, Michigan, you would hear me plaintively calling for one of the boys to come down to the basement "to fix my TV." Twenty-two years with the same TV, I still have no idea how to record something, how to switch from movies to TV, or what half the stuff means on the remote.) I turned the TV on, hoping to get the news but ending up with movies—porno movies! Scampering across the screen of my TV were loads of young nymphs making strange sounds and seeming to be having a really good time.

As I was desperately trying to get the news to come on, I couldn't help let thoughts run through my head such as, "I didn't know you could do that!" I was not really too concerned about all these sexual goings-on (such as the fact that one guy was involved in an orgy with enough naked women to make a basketball team) until the most frightening occurrence: Suddenly a fairly large red sign on the TV screen started flashing, "For this movie, the charge will be $22.50." *If I have to pay $22.50 for this nonsense, the cleaning staff will find a dead body on the floor tomorrow morning; after all I'm the guy who had Doritos for dinner!* I mashed button after button on the remote and nothing happened—well there was a *lot* going on with all the naked women on the screen that I'd have to tell my buddies about later when I got home—but, in terms of changing the program, nothing. So there would be no news tonight—but some interesting stories to share with the guys when I got back.

The next morning I got up early and hit the streets of Auckland, spending most of my time down by the harbor. Auckland has a huge harbor that includes many creeks, inlets, drowned river mouths, and peninsulas, giving the city an awesome amount of shore line with direct access to the ocean. There are so many yachts and boats, you would think everyone in this city owned five or six watercraft. Breakfast was a special at a Chinese-run shop: coffee and a muffin. The Chinese seem to do a much better job with muffins than French toast.

During my wandering, I passed the Pride and Joy Ice Cream Shop. In front was a fake life-size cow named Joy with udders that, if pulled on, squirted a white substance which resembled milk. The little kids love it!

When I was little, my grandfather down in Tennessee would take me out in the morning for "milking." My Easter basket from the Easter Bunny one year was not a basket but a little milk bucket loaded with jelly beans and candy. I dumped the candy out immediately to go out "milking" with my grandfather. Well, he sure made it look easy. He had been doing it for a long time and knew all kinds of tricks, like the one where he had me stand back some distance with my mouth open, and he would squirt the milk right into my mouth, which I thought was fantastic. Then my turn came. At first I could not get the hang of it and became frustrated. At one point I hung from the udder with my body off the ground to no avail. My grandfather cautioned that to get results I should go easy and gentle, something my wife has also tried to impart to me.

Signs and wording in foreign lands always amuse me, so I was drawn like a magnet to "K Save Mart." Right down Queen Street, the main and busiest street in Auckland, is "Burgerfuel," a fast-food restaurant whose special is the "Greedy Bastard" for $13.90! It appeared to have about 13 beef patties on it.

In my morning wanderings, I already found my dinner spot and my drinking hole. Dinner would probably be at the Jewel of Bombay, an Indian-food place of very moderate prices that I checked out earlier. Good thing my wife, Monica, and my oldest son, Eric, were not with me. After our Himalaya trip to Sikkim, India, they both got so sick of Indian food that I don't think they would ever eat it again. It's still my favorite.

In terms of drinking, I thought I would, figuratively, go back to the homeland, Ireland, tonight. There was a Father Ted's Irish Pub down the street, and, based on their accents, the entire staff appeared to be very recent Irish immigrants. New Zealand was founded by the British with an overwhelming original population of English, Scottish, and Irish. These current Irish must be those that missed the boat 300 years ago. As for the name of the pub, Father Ted's, I don't know if referred to an Irishman who had a lot of kids or a defrocked priest who lost his flock and parish because he hit the bottle a little too hard. I hoped to find out tonight.

(I Googled it when I got back to my hotel room. It appears Father Ted's was named after an acclaimed TV series in England about some priests in Ireland. It sounded as if the series was the kind of light human-interest/humor series that one would see on our PBS. And I guess Father Ted was one of the priests.)

With a surname of McGaugh I seem to have a talent for finding Irish pubs in the most unlikely spots. Two years before, working my way down from a trek to the base of Mt Everest, 'way back in an alleyway I found a little Himalayan Irish pub—probably the only one in the world with Buddhist prayer wheels at the entrance door. A few years earlier I found an Irish pub in the little Moslem country of Azerbaijan in the Caucasus Mountains, of all places.

Early tomorrow morning I would fly to Niue.

"Why should I restrict myself to one corner of the world?"
- Xu Xiake, the most revered ancient Chinese traveler and travel writer (1587-1641)

Visiting the Fake Country of Niue

Fake Country or Not? (I Report; I Decide)

It was still the same trip; it was still April 2015, but I figured it was time to start a new chapter.

I flew from Auckland, New Zealand, to the so-called island country of Niue, which took three hours. As we flew in and the plane banked to make its landing, this island—from the air at least—did not look as though it would live up to its reputation as the jewel of the Pacific.

Let me tell you a little about this country and also why I call it a fake country.

Niue is an island country in the South Pacific Ocean, 1,500 miles northeast of New Zealand, and, even if you had one of the best maps on Earth, you would be hard pressed to find little Niue. (Try it.)

I call it a fake country for a number of reasons. First: it is not a UN member. Second: Niue is basically the Puerto Rico of New Zealand, meaning that it is possessed, ruled, controlled, and financed by New Zealand. Foreign aid, principally from New Zealand, has been Niue's principal source of income. New Zealand's annual aid to Niue amounts to about $11,000 per resident. Ninety-five percent of the Niuean people don't even live in their own "country" but live in New Zealand instead, where they can earn a living. (Niue's economy doesn't really allow for anything much for people to do.) Only 1,400 Niueans are left on this island "country"; all the others are in New Zealand working—with New Zealand citizenship there and on this island. So I say it's a fake country.

However, if you Google "Niue," the article at the top of the list on your computer screen is Wikipedia's "Niue, the Smallest Country in the World," so I decided to drop in and settle the Is-Niue-a-real-country question once and for all. I arrived at a verdict before I even landed: Niue is not a real country—but I feel duty bound to check out even fake countries, and so here I was.

Niue was both pretty and pricey—no $1.29 Doritos for dinner on this island but $30 fish and chips and $8 beers. The second night, there would be a barbeque buffet for $40. How I longed for those Doritos.

Time Zones, WiFi, and the Dolphin Phenomenon

I was having a bit of a time trying to orient myself due to the fact that I crossed the International Date Line—again. I left New Zealand at 9:30 the morning of April 11th and three hours later landed in Niue on April 10! While I was—where else?—at the pool bar, a New Zealand couple attempted to explain this dilemma to me, but I had too liberally taken advantage of happy hour and, despite being a social-studies teacher, was having great difficulty trying to figure out how I had ended up in the past. I figured I'd work it out tomorrow.

In 2003, Niue became the world's first "WiFi nation": free wireless Internet access is provided throughout the country. That fact was of interest because the fees the Matavai Resort was asking for WiFi were so exorbitant that I feared I would need to send a Western Union telegram—collect—requesting funds so I could get back home.

Sitting at the aforementioned pool bar (where I somehow squandered the whole afternoon and early evening), I witnessed something I have seen only twice in my life, and both times just recently: schools of dolphins playing and jumping out of the water. It really is an incredible and beautiful sight and, to my mind, pretty rare. The dolphins raced and jumped high out of the water back and forth in front of the resort. Big showoffs!

The first time I ever witnessed this phenomenon was on a cruise I made with my family, two years before, to Belgium, Spain, and Portugal. One early evening when it was still very light, I was standing out on the deck of our ocean liner. We were off the coast of Spain in the Mediterranean; the family had just had dinner together (out of 14 evening meals, I had had steak 13 times!), and, as I was standing on the deck, the porpoises or dolphins started swimming alongside the ship, literally playing with it. It was beautiful the way they leaped into the air. It was like watching a *National Geographic* Special except I was right there.

I had a major dilemma, however. I could stay where I was and observe a once-in-a-lifetime experience that I had never witnessed before or run like hell to collect the family to share it with them—risking the possibility that it might all be over before we got back, and all of us would be disappointed. Family won out—but I knew that gathering them together was going to be a nightmare of logistics because they were all over the ship, from top to bottom.

I ran to the closest person, my wife, Monica, who had gone back to our room, which was right around the corner from where I was standing. I got to the room—no key, of course—and started pounding on the door.

Longitude and Latitude, with Attitude

Monica yelled through the door, asking who it was. I told her and said, "Hurry up and get out here. There are dolphins swimming right alongside of the ship and jumping up into the air."

Monica replied, "I can't. I'm changing, and I don't have any clothes on."

Now, one would think, if my wife was in the room with the kids gone and no clothes on, this might be a good place for Rufus to be—rather than checking out dolphins. I was on a mission, however. She said she would dress and be out, and I said I was on my way to find my older son, Eric.

No problem or thinking there. I knew exactly where Eric would be—the ship's restaurant for his 63rd helping of food. I ran up and grabbed him, and we really did have a unique and wonderful father-son experience, watching the very rare sight of these dolphins, but I still had one more varmint to round up, and that was my younger son, J.T. As with his brother, I knew exactly where that rascal would be—the game room.

I found him, grabbed him, and tore him away from his game, and we successfully had a few minutes with the dolphins. Mission Accomplished—well, almost. As long as both the kids were busy and being entertained, and, seeing that the last I heard from my wife was that she was in our room with no clothes on—and the room was not an awfully long walk from where I stood—I decided to stop by and pay a visit.

And there she was—sleeping—and snoring. So I went back out to watch the dolphins.

Back to Niue

Flying on Air New Zealand demonstrated that much had not changed in the 30 years since I used this airline to travel to New Zealand itself. It is a good airline but cannot possibly be making a profit because its planes are often half empty, which is great news for the traveler who wants to push up four or five armrests and have a full bed to sleep on. This is the way it was over 30 years before, and it was the same way now.

On a plane that had nearly 200 seats for the voyage to Niue, there were only 28 passengers. There were two New Zealand film crews of about 11 people on this voyage because of a big story in New Zealand and a huge story in Niue. I'll explain that story in a moment. With the exception of the two cameramen, the rest of the film crew appeared to be reporters and television-type personalities—all young women. And, boy, were they lookers! (I couldn't help but notice.)

As we all know, to be on any of the television networks today, one must be young and good looking. Just as important, television journalists today must be intelligent—not counting Fox News, of course. Of the above three characteristics, I have no idea if these gals had the third one (intelligence), but they most definitely had the first two. It gets better—they ended up at my resort! Better yet, they all hit the pool in bathing suits that looked like nothing more than three Band-Aids. So of course I saw this as an opportunity to stroll down poolside to introduce myself and entertain these delectable young creatures with some stories and travel experiences. They just ignored me.

Once the poolside rendezvous ended in failure, my only hope was for the half-day tour of the island the next day. For the life of me I could not figure out why, with all the tours offered, there was not one that made a full circle of the island. The only explanation was that the islanders wanted to suck even more money out of me for a second tour. Somewhat reluctantly I signed up for the tour the hotel recommended, which was run by local people.

The next morning they put the film crew in a van and put three of us (the guide, me, and some guy who doesn't figure into this story again at all) into a car, and we were off. I was not expecting or hoping for much, but surprisingly the tour was pretty good.

There was a lot of beautiful coastal scenery, but I had the most fun with the oddities, such as visiting the world-famous—well, at least famous here in Niue—Washaway Café overlooking the ocean. It is open 365 days, 24/7 but the only day it serves food or has anyone working at the place is on Sundays. So, if you happen to be in the neighborhood, and you just happen to be thirsty, and it's not Sunday, you walk right in and pour yourself a drink or grab a bottle of beer, or a couple of beers if you have a terrible thirst, and then write down your name and what you had in the notebook that Willie, the owner, thoughtfully provides. Then, the next time you see Willie, which isn't hard on a little island of 1,400 people, you pay Willie.

Driving through Alofi, the capital, which consists of a very small number of buildings, I held everyone up to get two photographic shots I had to have. The first was of one of the smallest Parliament buildings on earth. The second was more in keeping with my peculiar sense of humor.

Washaway Bar and Café on the "fake" island country of Niue. Open only on Sunday but people can help themselves to a beer any day of the week and just pay Willie, the owner, when they happen to run into him.

During my research while putting this strange trip together, I discovered that little Niue did not have one single unique animal, bird, mammal, primate, insect, crustacean, fish, tree, bush, plant, vine, or tree. Everything on this pretty little island you can find somewhere else—except the Uga crab! (You gotta love the name!) Niue has numerous tours here to sight the Uga crab, catch Uga crabs, photograph Uga crabs, hunt Uga crabs, and barbeque and eat Uga crabs. My interest was so high I never even bothered to find out what they look like.

I did, however, want to see Crazy Uga's, a restaurant whose specialty is—what else?—the Crazy Uga. My research had incorrectly led me to believe that the Crazy Uga was a burger of magnificent proportions—43 meat patties, 19 pieces of cheese, 47 pickles, and two entire heads of cabbage placed on this monstrosity. Good thing I do my own research and exploring because the Crazy Uga ($22) is a breakfast! It consists of all the above ingredients plus a dozen or so eggs thrown into the mix.

Then we hiked to the Talava Chasm, which is a narrow limestone canyon right on the coast that fills with ocean water to create a miniature Norwegian fjord.

Next it was off to jail. Like the last South Pacific island country I just visited, Nauru, Niue too has a very low crime rate. Niue's crime rate is even lower than Nauru's, which, if you remember, is 0%. You are probably wondering how a crime rate can go below zero. There is no way I can explain this statistically except to theorize that the Niuean people—on the off chance, that someone on the island someday ever does anything bad—do a bunch of real nice things all the time just to offset the "evil"!

I was a bit perplexed, after interviewing numerous people on the island, how one ends up in jail on Niue, but it is a fact that occasionally someone does end up there. The jail is located right at the property line of the municipal golf course, and—because prisoners in jail are not locked in their cells (they are on the honor system)—prisoners have been known to play a few rounds of golf to alleviate the boredom of captivity. Nobody, including the police, has a problem with that. In fact, the prisoners are also allowed to make errand runs across the road to the liquor shop just in case they have developed a powerful thirst.

Returning to the resort after the tour, I went exploring on my own. As I set off on my walk, I got the usual reaction that I always get from people all over the world whenever I do it:

Local person (anywhere in the world): "What are you doing?"

Me: "Just going for a walk."

Local person (in Africa, Asia, or Latin America): "Where are you walking to?"

Me: "Oh, just anywhere, to see things and people."

Local person: "Mister, you are crazy to walk in this heat. Not even the poor walk in this country."

And there you go, travels with Rufus.

Sometimes the conversation goes into the next stage.

Local person: "Do you have lots of water?"

Me: "I don't have any water. I hate water and never drink it."

This last statement almost staggers people in disbelief. Just ask my family or friends; I never drink water unless hops are added, whereby it transforms itself into a wonderful beverage.

Continuing my walk, I met little nine-year-old Desmond—a girl, despite her name—who was on her bike and stopped to talk to me. Her first question was about my walking, but that then led into a question about where I was from. I made her guess, and she got it on her second guess. I congratulated her on being so smart, and she was tickled pink. I let the conversation follow its path, and she was really a cute kid, telling me about school and her family. She giggled over everything I said, so I must be a pretty funny guy over here in Niue—at least to nine-year-olds.

I just about got to the resort when an old man on a bike—his white hair a wild beehive Polynesian mat—stopped me to talk. He had been riding his bike with a machete in one hand and a cigarette in the other. Because he was so old, he was having a hard time articulating what he wanted to say and sometimes seemed a bit confused about how to proceed with the conversation he had started, so I just listened and joked with him.

After finding out I was from America and discussing the fact that no Americans ever go to Niue, he said, "You Americans probably think all the people of Niue are cannibals?"

I replied, "No, just those riding bikes with machetes," but he didn't get it, and I moved on.

Eventually, I got back to the room, stripped off my sweaty Brownell "Buck up, Broncos" t-shirt, showered, and put on my new "I Love Parcells" t-shirt (Thank you, Nan Sabella). For the next day's adventure I laid out my "Pierce [another Grosse Pointe Middle School] Athletic Dept." t-shirt (Thank you, Chris Clark). [Note: Another colleague, Jeannie Brousseau, emailed me about this same time to say she had another Pierce t-shirt for me. I already told her this, but I'm putting it in print now: "Don't give it away to someone else; you can never have too many shirts that don't have holes in them. And, if Pierce also makes pants, socks, shoes, or underwear, I'll take some of those too."]

P.S. Geez! I must be losing my mind! I forgot to tell you about the huge story that had brought two film crews here. It was all about the arrival of a very important visitor—no, not Rufus—Anjalee.

Anjalee is the elephant who had come ashore six weeks before from the Asian country of Sri Lanka (Ceylon). Nope, she didn't swim to Niue; she was flown in by the New Zealand Air Force, destined for the Auckland zoo. She was a beautiful animal, going through 12 weeks of quarantine on Niue before her flight to New Zealand. Once she got over her jet lag, she had a blast on Niue, running around in her enclosure, entertaining everyone, and getting lots and lots of treats from the local people and kids of this remote little island, who had never in their lives ever seen a live elephant.

A Little More about Niue

The first Westerner to discover Niue was Captain Cook. He called it "Savage Island" because the natives who first came out to greet him had red tattoos and red-colored faces. Cook thought the natives had painted their faces in blood. The original Polynesians called their island Niue which means, "Look! There's a coconut," which I happen to think is one of the dumbest names I have ever heard for a country or even a little island. As you will shortly see, naming things does not seem to be these people's strong point, whether it be the Uga crab or their first Christian king, Tuti-toga.

In the pages above, I discussed Niue's crime rate, which is below 0 %, and I struggled to try to explain to the reader how, if there is no crime there, anyone ended up in jail in the first place. Further research solved this mystery. It seems that one of the most serious crimes committed on Niue is letting your pigs wander. If the judge throws the book at you for this heinous crime and you are sentenced to jail, and are not too busy playing golf or running across the road to the liquor shop for beverages because jail cell doors are not locked here, you can work or cut the grass at the golf course, and the judge will shorten your sentence for good behavior. In the course of researching this subject, I again drove by the police station, only to find it closed, with no one there. I guess no one commits a crime in Niue on Sunday, not even wandering pigs.

On Monday, I rented another car, drove by the jail again, and again found no one there. A jail on Niue is a very lonely place. Speaking of car rentals, a car-rental contract on Niue is also a bit different due to its brevity. There are only three rules: "Drive safely," "Drive slowly," and (the most important; it was all in capitals and boldface print) "Do not park under a coconut tree."

Niue is supposedly the highest coral atoll in the world, and what happens is that the pounding ocean surf hitting the shore slowly wears the island away. At weak spots in the coral, the ocean waves have created many inlets or miniature canyons or fjords, called chasms. You can hike down to them, and that is just what I did many times, in over 90-degree heat. Once you get down into the chasm, it is very lake-like; the pale blue-green water is calm and looks nothing like the rest of the ocean that encompasses the island.

Niue may be a "fake" country but its beauty cannot be denied.

Longitude and Latitude, with Attitude

The rest of the island is surrounded either with high cliffs, where ocean surf crashes and creates huge white waves, or low, almost flat pink-orange coral.

With a car at my disposal, I was finally able to get over to the "forbidden zone"—the name that everyone at the resort laughingly gave to the eastern half of the island because no tours go there. (So they really weren't trying to suck money from me twice.) There is no shuttle service there. Locals tell you there is no reason to go there. No one will drive you there. What in the hell was that all about? Naturally, it was something I would have to check out. Off I went.

In brief, the eastern side of this beautiful island was even more beautiful and even less developed than the western side. It reminded me of beautiful, undeveloped state forest land in Michigan—but with tropical vegetation. I guess the Niuens are just trying to keep it all to themselves.

Burials are done a bit differently on Niue. When a family member dies, you walk across the street or road, dig a grave, bury your loved one, put a marker on top, and now you have an easy visiting place for family members who have passed on. You are only steps away.

The next morning I had to drive into town, Alofi, the capital, to fill up with gas before returning my rental car. In the process, I passed the police station, which was now open. I was relieved that the police were back on duty and I would no longer have to continue to worry about wandering pigs. As I drove past the jail for the third time, I hoped that, in the last 24 hours, there might have been an arrest and I would see a prisoner, preferably playing golf or drinking beer, but no luck. (And, by the way, on Niue, to keep your beer cold, you don't put it in an ice chest; you put it in a "chilly bin.")

After returning the car and going back to my room, I looked at the daily announcement sheet placed under my door, telling what was happening on the island. The biggest event on the island was taking place right at my resort that night, the Uga Crab Show!

Let me share with you the characteristics of this creature, as described by the resort. The Uga crab is also known as the Robber Crab or Palm Thief. (Even after three tries, the Niuens were still unable to come up with a name that was not insulting or silly sounding.) The resort's daily news sheet went on to say that the Uga crab "is the largest land-living arthropod in the world and is at the upper size limit of terrestrial animals with exoskeletons!" After reading this, I was not sure if I needed a spear or gun to protect myself.

Due to their delicious flavor, there are not a lot of them around anymore, and I had been offered the opportunity to have one for dinner that night to ensure that the Uga crab would not make it into the next century. The resort news sheet went on to say that Uga crabs have "branchiostegal lungs," which was getting 'way too scientific for me, especially if they were to be served up at dinner with lungs included. Finally, like just about everything else on this beautiful but peculiar island, these animals were a little different: "Uga crabs cannot swim and will drown if immersed in water"!

Let's see if I got this straight. The Uga crab lives on a tiny speck of land out in the ocean, thousands of miles from any other land—and it can't swim! It can't even float! Surely if I had one for dinner tonight (it depended on what the price was), I would be helping along the evolutionary process of extinction for a not-too-bright creature that also had three dumb names.

But all you animal lovers, pet owners, and environmentalists out there can rest easy and be at peace knowing that I did not partake of the Uga feast—not at $55 for the small portion! Once the wonderful wait staff at the resort picked me off the floor after I heard the price, I went in search of $1.29 Doritos.

The day before I left lovely Niue, I thought about joining the Niue Yacht Club, which describes itself as "the biggest little yacht club in the world." I do not own a boat or yacht and do not ever plan on having a boat, but the $20 lifetime-membership fee was very appealing to a cheapskate like me.

I arrived home from Niue with a beard that was pretty much all white. It was truly amazing how many people mentioned that I looked just like Ernest Hemingway—an Ernest Hemingway who had recently escaped from his nursing home and was off his meds!

Into Deepest, Deepest Africa: the Last Frontier of Africa

Day 1 and 2 (Jan. 22 & 23, 2016)

At 3:00 a.m., January 22, 2016, my good friend Mike, from the old neighborhood at the south end of Warren, was at my house to pick me up to take me to the airport for my two-week journey through the Omo Valley of Ethiopia. Anyone who'd pick you up at 3:00 a.m. on a cold winter morning is a good friend! But Mike is a really good friend! Driving through the dark morning at this insane hour, Mike revealed that he had not even gone to bed but stayed up and watched TV until blast-off time. Ironically, the day before he had gone through a sleep study at the VA hospital in Detroit, and they had discovered he had only slept a single hour during the entire night. So maybe staying up all night wasn't that much of a stretch for Mike, but I still appreciated his chauffeuring. I completed a psychological sleep program at the VA about six months before, and it was working out pretty well for me. Both of us, however, complained about sleepiness at the wrong times, such as when driving, attending meetings, or—in my case—any time my wife spoke to me.

My first flight was to Washington D.C., where they were on high alert and already closing some roads down for a projected 22 inches of snow. I definitely wanted to miss that and, once I arrived, was anxious to head out of Dodge (D.C.) as fast as I could—and did so. Luckily, my second flight was a non-stop to the capital of Ethiopia, Addis Ababa (it means "New Flower"), where I was expecting mild temperatures in the 70s, and much hotter—90s—in the Omo River Valley.

My good luck continued: I had two empty seats next to me (either that or the two Ethiopians sitting there were so thin that I didn't see them). I now had a bed I could lie on rather than trying to sleep sitting up over the next 14 hours. I would need the rest. The alarm got me up at 1:45 in the morning, and I was standing in my driveway at 3:00 when Mike arrived. It was an hour drive to the airport, a two-hour wait for my first flight, a two hour flight to Washington with a three-hour layover, and then the 14 hours to Ethiopia—22 hours, if I am counting correctly. The flight also allowed me to obtain two more unique airline barf bags for the already very large collection I have accumulated after 50 years of travel. These are unique because the writing on them is in Amharic.

(For those of you who don't know, Amharic is, as Wikipedia so nicely sums it up for me, "a Semitic language spoken in Ethiopia. It is the second most-spoken Semitic language in the world, after Arabic, and the official working language of the Federal Democratic Republic of Ethiopia.")

After disembarking, I endured a long line and a long wait to get a visa—a process that was not exactly done in high-tech fashion. At a booth with a glass façade, you must turn your passport over to an official who does something to it, and then your passport continues down through a gauntlet of other officials who each do something to it. The whole time, you're trying to keep sight of your most important travel document: your U.S. passport. The passport is briefly returned with a visa in it but not officially stamped. You now make a right-hand turn at the booth where many more officials sit side by side with a glass partition separating them from the public and again surrender your passport, which again begins another journey through thousands of Ethiopian hands and inked stamps. Finally, after an epic journey of some distance—and only if you deliver fifty U.S. dollars in nice, clean, crisp shape—you have a passport with a legal Ethiopian visa in it.

I continued my meandering journey through the Addis Ababa airport, being stopped and checked and inspected along the way by various official-looking government workers—no two of whom wore the same color or design of uniform. I decide to exchange some money for Ethiopian birr. For a man as cheap as I am, it is difficult to fork over good hard-earned U.S. dollars and, in return, get Ethiopian birr, which is not exactly one of the top or more valuable currencies in use throughout the world right now. As it turned out, it was difficult to get that birr, too.

The procedure took *a lot* of time. I can't recall the last time I saw humans actually using carbon paper to make copies. It may have been in the Pleistocene era or perhaps the 1960s, but I can report to you that carbon paper is alive and well in Ethiopia. Well, maybe alive but not so well because there seems to be an acute shortage of the stuff in Ethiopia. The teller had to use the carbon paper over and over to make the required 7,281 copies that are required for every currency transaction in the country of Ethiopia—even if some tightwad is exchanging only a twenty. I can assure you, if for no other reason than to save time, I vowed that—the next time I had to exchange money on this trip—it would be *forty* dollars!

At this point, many people who are reading this account may be prompted to ask, "Why would anyone exchange only twenty dollars for a trip that will last two full weeks?" This question can only be answered by

Longitude and Latitude, with Attitude

one who has been marked in life by a deep and abiding love of his money and does not want to spend it.

Anyway, I was on my way. I eventually found my driver and got to my hotel.

I hate to brag, but, with my exceptionally high I.Q. and my above-average ability to linguistically learn new languages quickly, I made amazing progress in becoming fluent in the Ethiopian language, which is Amharic. (See above.) I now speak like a native. The first word I conquered was *bira*, which means beer. Even when I slipped and said "beer," they gave me one.

Of course someone as talented as I am is not going to stay at that level for long, so, before you knew it, I was saying *"Yemiteta neger yet bira?"*—which, for those of you hopelessly unable to learn foreign languages, means "Where may I get a beer?"

As my skills and fluency in this difficult language expanded, the people no longer laughed at me and my mispronunciations—just at my clothes, as usual.

I did experience one minor problem almost from the onset of my trip, and that had to do with the date and time. Ethiopia uses the Julian calendar, which has 12 months with exactly 30 days for each month—except in leap year, when they add a thirteenth month of five or six days! And, for some strange reason, Addis Abba uses a very strange time which is not in sync with the rest of the country or the rest of the world. I have yet to figure it out.

My morning was free, but my afternoon was taken up with a tour of Addis Ababa, mostly of its museums and palaces. The palaces were once inhabited by the kings of Abyssinia, who ruled over what we now call Ethiopia. Perhaps the most interesting museum was the National Museum that holds the remains of some of the most ancient humanoids—creatures with human characteristics, part of the human evolution—on Earth today. More of these creatures have been found in Ethiopia than anywhere else, and that includes the much more well-known Olduvai Gorge in Tanzania made famous by Dr. Louis Leaky and his family of anthropologists.

The high point of the tour was when we got to view a cast of the actual full skeleton of "Lucy" in the museum. Lucy (Australopithecus), at 3.2 million years old, is no doubt the most famous skeleton in the world. This is despite the fact that the nearby African country of Chad, which I visited just a couple of years ago, has the much older, seven-million-year-old skull (Sahelanthropus tchadensis)—twice the age of Lucy—in its museum. Maybe it's all in the naming. Which one are we going to remember best in daily conversation or at a party or barbeque, Sahelanthropus tchadenis or Lucy? You see my point. And yes, the paleontologist expedition team did name Lucy after the Beatles song "Lucy in the Sky with Diamonds," which just goes to show how dumb our society and culture is getting to do something like that. (Why not name her after Lucille Ball? Then we maybe we could call Sahelanthropus tchadenis "Ricky.") The only dumber thing I can think of is when that dummy in a Presidential town hall meeting asked President Clinton if he "wore briefs or boxers."

I had my first meal in Ethiopia after 22 hours of eating or turning down airline food, which has to be the worst garbage on the planet to try to eat—not to mention digest! On the flight over, I passed on anything Ethiopian even though I wanted to try it, due to the fact that I would be eating Ethiopian for the next 14 days or so. At the remote spots where I would be stopping, there would be no choice, no menu, and, frankly, not much—period. But it would definitely be native Ethiopian (as opposed to what might pass for the same on an airplane).

I ordered a pasta meal of some sort with "normal bread." (I would hate to think of the alternative: "abnormal bread"?) It was all very spicy and very good. That first dinner gave me my first occasion to sample Ethiopian beers, so I started with a St. George beer, which was a delicious lager. The beer came complete with St. George slaying the dragon on its logo. There are a number of Ethiopian beers that have this exact same logo on the bottle. Evidently the Ethiopians don't like dragons—think Trump and the Mexicans.

The word from the tour came down: "Get your last emails sent out because, where we are going, there will be no email for the next 14 days." Hard to believe in this day and age that you can drive—not walk or crawl—14 days and not have access to email or phones. I emailed the family and let them know I planned on returning alive.

Days 3 & 4 (Jan 24 and 25, 2016)

Early on the morning of January 24, we started our day's journey, which would be a 400-kilometer-long drive from Addis Ababa in the direction of the Omo Valley. This unique and distant valley has been called "Africa's last frontier" by *National Geographic* magazine.

The whole point of this trip for me was to have a cultural experience. It is in the Omo Valley that some of the last tribal and primitive people exist. Many of these people are descendants of ancestors who have lived here for thousands of years and have been basically untouched by what

Longitude and Latitude, with Attitude

you and I would call modern civilization. So I was happily surprised that our long drive was through attractive and pretty landscape. The predominant terrain consisted of brown valleys reminiscent of California or Spain. The natives' huts were conical, sturdily built, clean, and well maintained. The settlements, adjoining farm land, and even the road were free of garbage or litter. This is in contrast to most Third-World countries that are plagued by the ubiquitous plastic bags strewn about by the millions, caught up in trees and littering the roads, the sides of the roads, and everywhere else, it seems.

For lunch, we stopped at a hotel and were entertained by a number of ugly-looking vultures sitting on the hotel rooftop staring down at us. I am not sure if they wanted our lunch or were waiting for one of us to croak. At one of our "pee stops" (at least, that's what my native guide called them), I asked if I could hand out a number of toothbrushes I had brought along to give away. The guide said no because the people did not know what a toothbrush was and would not know what to do with it. Here they used small twigs to clean their teeth, as they have for thousands of years. And we hadn't even gotten to the primitive areas yet!

We finally arrived at our destination: Lake Abaya, the second-largest lake in Ethiopia—encircled by high mountains and very beautiful. The next day we were scheduled to take some sort of boat ride on the lake. In the evening we ate Nile perch right from the lake while watching an amazing yellow moon appear.

Day 4 (Jan. 25, 2016)

After noticing the swarm of lurking mosquitoes hovering about the doorway of my room when heading to breakfast, I decided this trip would be truly miraculous if I didn't end up with malaria. I had avoided this deadly and sometimes fatal disease for 50 years so far, including when I served my year in Vietnam in both mosquito-infested rice paddies and the jungles of the Que Son Mountains. From the looks of it, avoiding malaria this time would be a huge challenge.

Breakfast was not particularly anything to write home about, but it sufficed. I was at least able to fuel up with coffee. A sign at this establishment claimed that Wi-Fi was available, but I think it was placed there by a very cruel and demented individual who just wanted to torment people and get their hopes up. Then again, perhaps the part of the message that read "to be available soon in the year 2095" may have faded away.

Our first activity of the day was a boat ride on Lake Chamo, the third-largest lake in the country, which adjoins Lake Abya.

I was very curious to see what passed for a boat here in these parts, fearing that this trip might be one of my more exciting voyages where I ended up drowning. Even better, the chief draw or attraction of the lake, outside of its incredible beauty, is its huge crocodiles of prodigious size. So if I got real lucky today, I could drown *and* be eaten by giant crocodiles.

You saps sitting home stuck in your tedious boring lives—I bet you are thinking at this very moment, "Boy, I wish I was more like Rufus and doing fun things like drowning and being ripped apart by man-eating crocodiles!" But it takes special and unique skills to have all the fun I have. I don't want to get arrogant or insulting, but the fact is that you are probably not as smart as someone like me who spends thousands of dollars to end up dying a horrible death either by malaria, drowning, or crocodiles—maybe all three. It takes someone very special to pull off this triple crown of hideous ways to die. I really hate to brag, but I can think of more stupid and idiotic ways to die on a trip than anybody I know. So, as you can plainly see, I am a very special person. And please don't—even silently in your mind—start thinking, "*'Special!* Yeah, 'special,' all right: *Special Ed!*" because that will only bring back horrible childhood memories for me.

A strange thought for me, a guy who couldn't care less about food, passed silently through *my* mind at the time: I wondered what we would have for lunch today. The crocodiles were probably having the same thought.

Well, we got to Lake Chamo by way of a dirt road that I am sure would have made even Daniel Boone or Lewis and Clark sit down and bawl like babies in anguish and defeat, but we got there.

The boats looked pretty old and not very seaworthy, but, hey, someone has to be the meat for the crocs! Now, when I say old, I mean *old*. On the inside of my craft I spotted the weathered initials "C.C. 1492," so this gives you a bit of an idea of what I was sailing on.

For the last 12 hours or so, I had been going incognito in Ethiopia. No matter where I went, no one could see me. That is because my body was usually covered in a giant swarm of flies that evidently found me a pretty interesting character and chose to hang out with me. Usually, as I went about on this trip, all one could see was a five-foot, nine-inch cloud of flies moving deliberately in whatever direction I chose to go. Getting on the boat and heading out into the lake, I had hoped I would get some relief from the flies. And I did—only to have the flies now replaced with scores of giant flying insects that on average were about the size of giant Condors.

This adulation of African insects for my American form was, of course, all taking place as I apprehensively and nervously kept glancing into the water for any of those man-eating crocs everyone was talking about. I ended up during this two-hour cruise actually seeing some amazing wildlife, such as eagles, hippos, storks, baboons, a number of interesting bird species that were unfamiliar to me, and, yes, some crocs—and they were big boys! All the while this was going on, I was bombarded, Japanese kamikaze style, by the giant flying insects who must have mistaken me for an aircraft carrier.

Bad News! The email was actually working. This meant I would have to talk to my wife.

Every time I leave on one of these adventures, my wife's immoral, unfaithful infidelities begin—not with another man but with the most precious thing I have in my life—my money. Evidently these trips of mine trigger the travel urge in Monica, and I am besieged with email after email about one family trip and destination after another. Her last email had her all excited and glowing over a Scandinavian/Norway fjord cruise for us and the two boys that was priced at $5,200 each and did not include the $1,200 airfare for each of us. The potential expenditure of over $25,000 of my money nearly caused me to have a stroke; the only thing that prevented it was my uncertainty about the additional cost of and procedure for shipping home a coffin and dead body from Ethiopia. (If it was less than $6,400, I would have come out ahead on the deal.) There's something about my absence that brings out that woman's insanity and craziness. Why she can't be happy shopping at Kmart like other women is beyond me.

But enough of my troubles. I survived the boat ride! I didn't drown, was not devoured by crocs, and seemed to escape malaria.

To celebrate my survival, that afternoon I surveyed a very interesting and colorful market at a place called Chencha. There, the Ethiopian women (these would be members of the Dorze people), with their fanciful and colorful clothing and headdresses, provided me with plenty of opportunities for some gorgeous photography.

After the market, I went into one of the Dorze people's village. The Dorze live in very tall beehive huts made of bamboo that are fashioned to resemble the head of an elephant—trunk included! The kitchen is in a smaller beehive hut, where the meals are cooked and beer each day is fermented and produced! (I immediately inquired about what it would take for me to be adopted into the tribe.)

The larger living hut for the family is divided into separate areas for children, adults, animals, and (in the most guarded section, complete with a wooden wall for protection) liquor. Strange that the greatest civilization on Earth is located in a very small region of Ethiopia inhabited by a people you have never heard of whose name you can't spell or pronounce—but it is a fact that cannot be denied.

The hut has a large wooden door that is kept closed at night to keep the hyenas out—which also explains why the domestic animals are kept *in* the hut. After we visited the village and walked into a number of huts, someone suggested that we sample some of the local liquor that is such a big part of the Dorze people's culture. I didn't have to be asked twice!

Perhaps it was the effect of the liquor—perhaps I was just losing it—but I suddenly couldn't understand or comprehend why in the hell I was living in the United State of America when, right here in Ethiopia, there was such a wonderful civilization with such happy people living in harmony with all their various liquors. Leaving this village, I have to admit I sobbed like a baby at the thought that I would probably never return to what an Irishman like me could only regard as paradise. Plus, these people do not have to live under the tyranny of Obamacare.

After getting back to the lodge (called Paradise Lodge—which I can assure you it is anything but), I had a pretty good dinner of Nile perch again. It was probably a healthy choice, but I was guided more by taste than nutrition. The meal again was accompanied by a number of St. George beers. St. George has become my new patron saint. St. Patrick is only a distant memory. This rivalry of saints was a no-brainer for me. One drove all the snakes out of Ireland, and the other is a delicious beer. No contest.

Day 5 (Jan. 26, 2016)

Today's schedule called for another long drive of seven hours or so. We were heading deeper into remote Ethiopia, hoping to see the Hamar people with their distinctive hair styles and colorful clothing. As we moved further and further away from the capital, Addis Ababa, it continued to get hotter, poorer, and more undeveloped. Even before arriving at our destination, I spotted a number of children completely naked, not out of tribal tradition, but due to poverty. There are not many places left in the world where you can see such a sad sight.

Despite the poverty and underdevelopment, the countryside was very pretty, dotted with small villages consisting of the Ethiopians' characteristic conical and beehive huts. From one valley to the next we

Longitude and Latitude, with Attitude

drove in our rugged four-wheel-drive jeep/truck. At all times we were surrounded by green/brown mountains (depending on the crop and harvest time). These smaller valleys are part of the Great Rift Valley—the longest valley on Earth, which stretches from Turkey to the very bottom of Africa! The elevation is very low, which makes it very hot. Other areas with such low elevations would be Death Valley in California and the Dead Sea in Israel. (Did you happen to notice the names for places so low and so hot—"Death" and "Dead"?) My driver and guide, both native Ethiopians, began complaining about the heat while I remained oblivious and enjoyed the scenery.

We finally arrived at the market, which was loaded with thousands of people selling, buying, trading, bartering, and socializing. These were the Hamar people, who have a number of distinctive hair styles and dress very colorfully. Some wear feathers in their hair, others skull-type caps made of shells or gourds. Some have shaved heads with a braid of hair across the top of the head, front to back. Others have shaved heads with multiple braids worn like bangs over the forehead. And still others have countless braids or dreadlocks cut and designed to look like a bowl. In the colorful-dress department, some women eve:n wear a long tail, resembling an animal's tail, made of goat skin or leather.

Hamar people of the Omo Valley, Ethiopia.

Hamar native, Omo Valley, Ethiopia.

Naturally I drifted over to the massive outdoor beer market where everybody was indulging in the local brew. I can assure you this was *not* craft beer, and one needs to develop a taste for it—or be suicidal and want to die an awful death from the worst-smelling stuff I have ever come across. Where was St. George when I needed him? I passed on the chance of dying of food poisoning in Ethiopia and said still another prayer that my patron saint, St. George, would miraculously appear in the desert with his delicious beer to keep me going.

There was not much of anything out here, so lunch consisted of some food we had brought with us, eaten under a beautiful mango tree whose branches sagged from the amount of fruit on it. It also offered some good shade. Unfortunately no St. George beer to accompany whatever in the hell it was that I ate—just water. Without St. George, I fear I was lapsing back into paganism.

We finally reached our destination, a little place out in the desert called Turmi Lodge. The place had little going for it except for being clean. (For example, while I was writing this account, the power went out and I had to use battery power only.) Surprisingly the bed had a mosquito net. Even more surprising, the mosquito net covered the whole bed, and there were no holes in it. The night before, I had had a mosquito net, but it left a small area open—about the size that a cow or an elephant could walk through—so I had to juryrig it with blankets to get some protection.

As you can see from the above description of my lodgings, this was another "Rufus five-star extravaganza." It was slowly starting to dawn on me why my wife, Monica, all my friends and colleagues, and all my past traveling companions passed on the opportunity to join me on this awesome adventure. I must have sent out over 200 emails asking people if they would like to come along with me to the Omo Valley of Ethiopia. I then sat at my computer like the Maytag repairman ("the loneliest man in town"), waiting for responses that never came. I can only guess that nobody wanted to make this trip because they'd read all those previous travel emails I've sent out and decided they preferred living a comfortable and enjoyable life rather than doing what I am doing.

There was a wild and crazy rumor going about that there would be some sort of food tonight. Even more over the top and outlandish was the word that this place had beer. So I decided to end my literary career at that very moment and mosey over to the building labeled "restaurant" and see if my prayers to St. George had been answered. If not, I figured I might have to start litanies and novenas.

*****

Well, I didn't have to start praying, but it was touch-and-go there, for a while. The Turmi Lodge may call itself "the desert rose of Hamar Village," but I think "stinkweed" might well be a better sobriquet for this establishment. I had to give the "desert rose" credit for one thing, though: my introduction to a new beer that was quite delicious. During, and after dinner, I had a number of bottles of this very good beer. It is called Habesha, and, on the label, below the name, is the description "Cold Gold." It makes me all warm and fuzzy just thinking of a beer that good. Better yet, the logo is of an angel—an Ethiopian angel at that! I didn't even know there were black angels. I just assumed they were all white. Hey, I live in Grosse Pointe, Michigan, and thought everyone in heaven was white, just like here in Grosse Pointe.

As I drank bottle after bottle of this delicious beverage, I had a lot of time to contemplate the picture of this angel on the logo of the beer bottle. No doubt about it—he was black and very Ethiopian looking. Previously, I just assumed all angels looked Swedish. I wondered what his name was. He certainly wasn't Michael the Archangel because Michael is white, or Swedish. He didn't look like Gabriel either. Not that I know all the angels or am on a first-name basis with them or anything, but this definitely was not Gabriel because Gabriel is white also. In fact all the angels in heaven are white. That's because all the angels were born in Sweden before the Civil Rights Act, and they were white. Black people like Obama were born in Kenya and are of course Moslems, so there are no black angels because nobody in heaven is a Kenyan or a Moslem. And don't argue with me; I have a Bachelor's degree in history.

Due to the fact that I am not prejudiced at all, I continued drinking these wonderful Habesha beers one after the other, despite the black Ethiopian angel on the bottle who was really a Moslem from Kenya. I made my way back to my room despite the dark and distance. Actually my room was attached to the restaurant and had an adjoining wall, but I had a hell of a time getting there—and especially getting the key in the door.

Day 6 (Jan. 27, 2016)

Because Ethiopia uses the Julian calendar that sometimes has 13 months and because their years are numbered differently, it gets a bit confusing. Traveling through this African country that uses some weird ancient Eastern Orthodox calendar makes knowing what day or month it is nearly impossible. Keeping all this in mind, I observed some amusing bumper stickers on vehicles in this country: "Travel to Ethiopia and be Seven Years Younger"; "Enjoy 13 Months of Sunshine in Ethiopia Every Year."

This morning, we were up early for coffee, pancakes—or at least what Africa thinks pancakes are—and honey. Then we were off.

As we got deeper into Ethiopia and Africa, the insects, especially the flies and mosquitoes, got ever more annoying—not to mention numerous. The black flies were especially persistent and found me especially attractive, so, once again, I often looked like a black cloud or a black sheet moving across the land. These flies simply cannot be swished away; you must physically brush them off your skin and body—and they put up quite a fight to stay right where they are, tormenting you.

Although I make it a rule never to put any liquid in my mouth other than beer, I did trek about Ethiopia with a water bottle in either my cargo pants or travel vest. This was a hot, tough, lonely-looking desert, and you just never know. There had been no internet for some days, and, as we went deeper into the country, electricity itself was also likely to disappear. Lodging continued to move down the scale too. We started with a hotel and then moved to lodges and were now heading for tents. The roads continued to deteriorate, from asphalt to gravel to dirt to sand—and today I could swear that I somehow ended up on the moon, based on the kind of cratered roads we bumped over. All the streams and rivers—with the exception of the Omo itself—were bone dry. Traversing these is more difficult in the deep sand than in water. Knock on wood; we had yet to get stuck. Better yet, no crocs! (Speaking of wildlife, we did see a rare and beautiful Abyssinian roller—a unique, incredibly beautiful aqua-blue bird.)

The bone-crushing, neck-breaking journey was to visit the Karo people who are renowned for their painted bodies and face decorations. This is the Africa you read about in the history books! Multi-colored necklaces, jewelry, and feathers adorn their bodies, and in most cases jewelry seems to be about the only thing these people seem to be wearing. Their bodies are painted with red stripes, their faces with pure white dots, and they sport various colorful feathers in their hair or through their lips! These people farm and raise goats and cattle, but they're a pretty aggressive tribe that takes its warrior status seriously. A number have traded their spears in for AK47s, making them look even more menacing. I made sure I tipped well. Up until recently these people also practiced infanticide, a perhaps "necessary" custom in this tough

Longitude and Latitude, with Attitude

desert country (though, when we were there, all the vegetation and trees were very green with the early rains).

Karo people, Omo Valley, Ethiopia. Note the feathers and jewelry.

Karo native with dotted face.  **Karo native with dotted face.**

One last thing that I can't stop myself from mentioning: the Karo people have a tradition and ritual of beating their women! Now, it's not quite as bad as it sounds—unless you happen to be the woman getting beaten. As a visiting bystander, I had no problem with it at all, but that's just me. (If you think I am going to be a flaming feminist supporter when a whole slew of big dudes are walking around with fierce war paint on their faces and chests and AK47s slung over their shoulders, you have a whole different idea about my courage than I do.) Just as in my marriage, the wife is not beaten for just any old reason. It's got to be for something extraordinary. In the case of the Karo people, a woman is whipped by her own family in preparation for marriage. In my marriage, it happens when Monica doesn't have beer in the fridge.

Day 7 (Jan. 28, 2016)

It is interesting to note that so many of the different tribes in this remote Omo Valley of Ethiopia have a very egalitarian system when it comes to the division of labor between men and women. The women are usually responsible for walking some great distance to a well or river (where, in the dry season, they must dig into the riverbed to find water), draw water, and then carry this great weight in large yellow plastic containers back to their home for cooking and even irrigation of their crops. (You did notice that I did not mention washing—either for clothes or the body.) The women are responsible for the planting, care, and harvesting of the crops. The women of course are responsible for building the hut, maintaining it, and caring for the children. The women do all the cooking. The women even make beer or other liquors daily. The men on the other hand do their best to hold up their end of the bargain: they do their share by drinking the beer.

Morning adventures included a visit to still another market. We then made a wide circle of travel and ended up at our lunch stop of the day before. So again I had the luxury of sitting under a mango tree laden with fruit. Dessert was only inches away—which was good, I first thought, because lunch was one of the least appetizing meals that I had on this entire trip. It consisted of a small bowl of greens drowning in greasy oil. At one point I thought I recognized a morsel of carrot but, not having bifocals, could never find it again. Accompanying this Ethiopian delicacy was injera (Ethiopian bread) sometimes called an "Ethiopian pancake" by Americans and Europeans (not to be confused with the so-called "pancakes" we had for breakfast on Day 6). It is a fluffy flat bread baked in a huge circle—think extra-large-pizza size. It is a bit sour tasting, so one eats injera with other foods. Only in this case the other food was pretty sour in itself. Ultimately, I passed on the free mangos just above my head after watching my driver in a fifteen-minute battle to get the skin off.

Just before leaving for our next long drive, I witnessed a minor traffic incident. A motorcycle accidentally struck a young child of about eight years old. She wasn't hurt, but she was thrown off balance, although her fall resulted in no real injury or damage. This scene took place right in front of hundreds of stunned pedestrians who were too shocked to react or move. I immediately ran over to the little girl to see what I could do.

If I do say so myself, I showed amazing grace under pressure, and my subsequent actions were beyond courageous. I immediately took command of the situation and, with my quick thinking, superior first-aid training, and experience with battlefield causalities, lifted the little girl's wrist to get a pulse. She had one. As I mentioned, she wasn't really hurt, but, nonetheless, I immediately placed two life-saving items into her little hand. One was a small business card that read "1-800 CALL-SAM—specializing in frivolous law suits" and the other another card that read, "Jeff Fieger, Law Offices, specializing in phony claims."

But this child did not heed my pleas to sue the Ethiopian Road Commission, the man who had bumped her, the Japanese motorcycle company who made the motorcycle, Japan, the U.S. Federal Government, Arkansas, and Wyoming. Unfortunately, this little girl merely continued on her way.

This is why Third-World countries remain Third-World countries: These foreigners just don't understand American capitalism.

We finally made it to Jinka, where we would be sleeping in tents.

Day 8 (Jan. 29, 2016)

The day started off great. There were crepes for breakfast. I love crepes, so I ate a slew of them. Perhaps having a meal like this now and then on this trip would prevent the usual outcome where I came home about 10 to 12 pounds lighter, with sunken eyes and shallow face. If I kept up eating like this, I might come back looking more like Porky Pig.

After breakfast, we took a long drive over torturous roads to see if we could find the Mursi tribe.

In terms of wildlife, the journey did not start off well. The only thing I was seeing were vultures, and that always makes me nervous because they always seem to be hungry and always seem to be looking at me. Later I did spot some baboons. We drove through the valley surrounded by deep green mountains for some unparalleled visual splendor.

To have any chance at all of finding any of the Mursi tribe, we stopped and picked up a park ranger. A park ranger in these parts plays many roles: ranger, policeman, soldier, social worker, and mediator to the tribes. He brought with him a rifle and ammunition—strictly for mediation purposes, of course. (The Mursi, like the Karo, are an aggressive people, and you never know what might go down.)

The roads were rough, and we had our second flat tire of the day, making three flats in the last two days. The vehicles were new Toyota Land Cruisers—eight-cylinder, four-wheel-drive vehicles, each with four new tires—but these roads put the vehicles through an endurance test. We finally arrived at a nomadic Mursi village. It was pretty small, maybe twenty huts at best, but there must have been 200 natives there—some perhaps from another village; I'm not sure.

The Mursi women are famous for cutting their lips to stretch the bottom lip out some distance and then placing a wooden disk or plate (about the size of a coffee-cup saucer) in the mutilated and stretched-out lip. To achieve this look, they have to have their bottom two (sometimes bottom *four*) front teeth pulled out.

Mursi woman with lip plate.   *Mursi woman with lip plate.*

Longitude and Latitude, with Attitude

Mursi woman with lip plate. *Mursi woman with lip plate.*

    The body enhancement or mutilation—depending on how you look at it—does not stop with the lips. They stretch their ear lobes at great length, and then with a knife cut a huge hole into the ear lobe, about three inches in circumference. Many Mursi girls and women find that even this is not enough and continue the beautification process by scarring their shoulders, arms, chest, breasts, back, and sometimes the face. This is done by cutting into the skin and then placing ash so as to make bumps, marks, or designs. I gotta tell you—it was a real Miss America Pageant!

    I hate to say it because it makes me appear to be culturally insensitive (not that that bothers me), but their lips are hideous-looking things. To form your own mental image, think of a juicy fat worm that has somehow ended up sitting out on the street, 'way too long, in a hot, blazing sun—like in Ethiopia where the Mursi live. Then really put your imagination to work and think of this very dehydrated worm being run over and over by many cars—no, make that Mack trucks—and you get an idea of what the bottom lip of a Mursi girl or woman looks like. It just kind of took all the romance right out of the Miss America Pageant I was viewing here, 8,834,492,667,217 miles inland in Ethiopia. I mean these lips are beyond the pale. These lips are 'way beyond any help that lip

[208]

balm or ChapStick could give—heavy-duty axel grease comes to mind as a remedy.

Mursi woman without lip plate.

Mursi women without lip plates. Notice the ear lobes and body scarring.

Eating with a bottom lip such as this is a real problem. Of course the lip plate comes out, so that now a long half-circle of lower lip hangs to the bottom of the chin or below. Having your bottom two front teeth—or, as mentioned earlier, your bottom four front teeth—removed for this whole lip-enlargement ordeal makes eating a very messy situation. As I watched Mursi women eat their sorghum or corn, I could see that—due to their distended lower lip, lack of teeth, or both—with every mouthful they took some of the food flew or dribbled out of their mouths. I hate to be cruel, but it was very much like watching my two boys at dinner each night.

I have now had the opportunity in my travels to see the women with lip plates here in Ethiopia; people with bones through their noses in New Guinea; the tallest people on earth, the Tutsi tribe of Rwanda; the shortest people on earth, the pygmies of Central African Republic; and people who cover their bodies with ugly, hideous tattoos in Michigan.

My guide fancied himself something of a jokester, and, once I had stopped taking what seemed like hundreds of shots of these unique people, he told me that one of the Mursi women had been attracted to me as a potential husband. I said thanks but no thanks. Kissing with a Mursi woman brings the art of kissing to a completely new level—and not a good one, to my mind. Besides, I already have a wife—with some pretty normal lips.

Despite my lack of interest, my guide brought the woman over towards me and claimed that her name was La-lu, which I suspect he made up on the spot. After looking at this woman, I can only say that the translation of her name into English would be "the ugliest female" (*La*) "in the village" (*lu*) The more I looked at her—and I tried not to—I began to suspect that *lu* didn't mean "in the village" but "in the *world*," and I said it was time to leave before I started having traumatic flashbacks to my dating life when I was single.

After leaving the Mursi tribe, we had a beautiful drive with spectacular views of the Great Rift Valley bordered by towering and imposing mountains. Leading up to the mountains was land terraced for farming whose soil was a brown-orange color. Small conical native huts dotted the landscape. We arrived at our next lodging to find no Wi-Fi, no electricity, and no water at the present. They did have beer, so I rated the accommodations five-star plus.

Day 9 (January 30, 2016)

Today we entered an 800-year-old village that is a UN's World Heritage Site. The village or ancient town is one in a series of 42 fortress-like settlements still existing here in the Omo Valley of Ethiopia. The one I entered is difficult to get in to because it sits atop a high hill for defensive purposes. It was built fortress- or castle-like, with enormous thick stone walls forming two complete concentric circles for defense. The walls are about seven-feet high. To get anywhere within the village or town, one must walk single file through narrow passageways—constructed thus as another defensive tactic. Here 2,000 Konso people live as they have for centuries.

Within the Great Rift Valley, 200,000 Konso people live their unique lifestyle. They speak an ancient Cushite language that is descendant of the great ancient Cushite Empire of Africa. Today they still live in their small conical huts and are expert farmers, herders, and weavers. Any time I stopped to work on my photography, the little children would approach and rub their hands on my arms. Most people in this area of the world have very little hair on their body other than their head. So when I entered these villages, the little kids—two, three, four years old—often rubbed their little hands across my arms to feel the hair where unfortunately I have more than on top of my head. They regarded me as sort of a furry pet ape that had come to visit their village. The fact that I am white and that some of them had never seen a white person added to the carnival effect. To all of this, add the ridiculous outfit—at least to them—that I was wearing: wide cargo pants with seven bulging pockets containing God knows what, travel vest with five more fully stuffed pockets, floppy sun hat, big oversized hiking boots, and all kinds of camera equipment hanging on straps around my neck and shoulders. I quickly become the Pied Piper of the village.

What most caught my interest were the unusual funeral practices of the Konso people, especially for "outstanding men"—a classification that would surely include me if I lived in this tribe. The most elaborate funerary rites are for heads of each clan. (The Konsos have nine clans.) These clan heads are considered to be direct descendants of the first Konso people, who lived thousands of years ago.

When one of these clan heads dies, his internal organs are removed, and the body is mummified and buried, only to be exhibited to his people nine years later! The bodies are pretty well preserved, considering, but it's still not a pretty sight! (I saw the photos!) After being dead for nine years—having first undergone the mummification process—the dead clan head looks like a Nazi Concentration Camp survivor—only dead.

Longitude and Latitude, with Attitude

Once a body is put on display, its missing eyes are replaced by egg shells, which give the corpse an ET-like appearance. I am assuming he looked a lot better when he was alive. Oh, and—by the way—the current head man of this village has five wives and 24 children.

Always ready to sink to the lowest level, even when I am supposed to be involved in something intelligent and intellectual, I was drawn to the wakas, the wooden statues placed over the burial sites of "outstanding men" (of which—I needn't remind you again, but I will—I surely would be one). The wakas, usually about four- or five-foot tall, are carved images of the "outstanding man." A waka usually depicts the eyes, nose, ears, lips, teeth, and sometimes the tongue of the "outstanding man"—and it always includes the penis, which is always of great size and length.

(This detail was my first hint that I might not fit in. My—if you'll excuse the term—"shortcomings" may preclude me from ever being an "outstanding man." I will say nothing further for fear of arousing a deep sense of inferiority within me.)

But it gets worse—as it always does with me: these statues not only have a penis of great size and length in the usual groin area but also have a huge penis of great girth on the forehead! I am now totally out of their league. (And, if size truly does matter, I have absolutely no hope of membership in this tribe.) What had started out as a good and exciting day ended with me leaving the village sad, lonely, insecure, worthless, humiliated, and defeated.

Walking about these villages inhabited by farmers and pastoral people with all their goats, sheep, cattle, and donkeys definitely had its drawbacks for my hiking boots. I hate to get gross, but—the next time you happen to have catastrophic diarrhea—take a quick glance, and then you will have an idea of what my boots looked like. And walking around under this sun had its drawbacks for my skin. Even though I was careful, the sun was so intense that I ended up with sunburn on my face and head.

The food on this trip hadn't been bad. I survived on peas, beans, squash, carrots, various greens with names I didn't recognize, bread, noodles, and Nile perch. (Actually, as I re-read that last sentence, it doesn't sound so bad now—in fact, it sounds kind of healthy!) In terms of lodging, the bottom line is (as I think I mentioned) that everything had been surprisingly clean. So far, there were no horror stories to report on this trip—which surprised the hell out of me.

I almost forgot. Today, January 30, is my birthday. The Great Rift Valley is one of the two strangest places I have ever celebrated my birthday. The other was Vietnam, where I celebrated my birthday deep in the jungles of the Que Son Mountains, soaking wet, hungry, just out of a hospital after being wounded, and surrounded by two divisions of the NVA (North Vietnamese Army). If I remember correctly, it was a pretty lousy birthday.

Day 10 (Jan. 31, 2016)

For my birthday meal the night before, I had a decent dinner with my new favorite companion, St. George—well, the beer that bears his name. We became quite an inseparable pair on this trip, despite his holiness and my paganism. Since every meal was served with injera, the "Ethiopian pancake bread," which is fermented in the process of making it, and usually accompanied by my bosom buddy, the St. George beer, I remained happy all day long, whether drinking or eating.

In this respect, I had gone native!

There was no danger of me coming home with a huge flapping bottom lip with a coffee saucer in it or a bone through my nose—no danger of me going animist. No, just in the food department, I went totally Ethiopian. No more "normal bread." From now on, it was injera all the way—and whatever the locals eat with it (which is kind of fun because it was always a big mystery as to what I was eating, and I was too chicken to ask.)

*****

On Day 10 I was up before the crack of dawn as usual, but here in Ethiopia you have an early rising even if you want to sleep in. That's because of the Moslem population in the country and their very loud call to prayer at daybreak. Unfortunately, Ethiopian Moslems either cannot tell time or do not own a wrist watch, so the call to prayer often takes place around the clock. It's especially bad about an hour or hour and a half before daybreak when the speakers are blaring from the various mosques. This raucousness is exactly why the good people of Tennessee don't want Moslems or Moslem mosques in their state. Even worse, the God-fearing folks of Tennessee know that Moslems in their good-ol'-boy state are just the first step on the road to Sharia law, and, before you know it, they won't be able to eat pork chops or drink moonshine. The fact that there can't be more than 17 Moslems in the whole state does not deter our fellow patriots one iota.

Speaking of Moslems, we drove through (not *over* them as the good people of Tennessee would like to do) a large Moslem region on Day 10, a region that looked no different than the other areas I had been through, and one would never know that it was Moslem rather than Christian—except that all the people there want to move to Tennessee. We continued to drive through the Great Rift Valley, now covered by savannah (treeless plains) with a few elegant acacia trees to add color or shade for the traveler on foot or camel. The river beds were dry and nothing but sand, but still the farming and husbandry of animals went on. At one point I saw a caravan of hundreds and hundreds of small wagons, each loaded 30-feet high with sugar cane and pulled by one or two little donkeys.

All this driving, distance, energy, and time that I spent in the last seven days had been to explore just one single valley in this country of great size. It is rough, hot land! The heat and the poverty and lack of hygiene were accompanied again by biblical multitudes of flies. At lunch, I lost my drink to the never-ending dive-bombing flies. There were just too many for one man to fight off.

Day 11 (Feb. 1, 2016)

Early in the morning, before anyone else was awake, I roamed the grounds of the lodge. I eventually settled in where the camp fire had been the night before, as the last dying embers still gave up a bit of warmth, and watched a host of monkeys play in the forest before me. It didn't take long before they came quite close and joined me, no doubt recognizing a distant relative.

After breakfast, we set off for a driving day even longer than the past few.

We had not been driving very long when we passed through a small town. Despite its tiny size and overall poverty, it actually had a painted pedestrian walkway across the road.

My driver was a pretty aggressive driver, as all drivers are in Third-World countries if they want to survive. My driver was also a pretty good-sized guy—a little over six-feet tall and well over 200 pounds. I was sitting in the passenger seat of the jeep as usual when I was jarred nearly out of my seat by his sudden stop. A gray-haired man with an umbrella—not quite directly in front of the jeep—was trying to cross but was hesitant to continue for fear of being run over. Normally my driver would have taken this opportunity to continue driving, but this time we stopped, and my driver made a sign of deference to the older man. The older man was not thankful or humble but rather very manly, standing his ground to cross. Then I spotted it. What I thought was an umbrella was the barrel of an AK47. My driver was adhering to one of my oldest rules: never get into a road-rage fist fight when the other guy has an AK47. We moved on—all smiles to the gentleman and his weapon.

*****

We drove into Texas today. Well it looked and felt like Texas, with huge open plains all yellow and brown this time of year. It was also hot as the dickens. The long-horn cattle were also present in these wide open spaces. The surrounding mountains were green and yellow. I even saw my first Moslem cowboy. He was on horseback but looked a bit peculiar wearing a Moslem sheik's flowing headscarf wrapped around his head rather than a ten-gallon hat. No six shooter, however. Evidently these backward natives do not have an NRA to protect their gun rights (except for the guys with the AK47s).

And then somehow we ended up in New Mexico or at least what looked like New Mexico, with yellow-topped mesas amid narrow canyons and valleys. We had moved from agricultural to pastoral.

We traveled higher up into the Bale Mountains. It was cooler there, and supposedly we might see some of the last safari animals in Ethiopia that had not yet been eaten by the people. When we finally arrived in these mountainous forests, we actually did spot a couple of warthogs and a number of beautiful antelopes called mountain myala, but that was it. Despite this pathetic "safari"—what would you expect in Ethiopia?—we were rewarded with the beauty of the surrounding countryside; think Tuscany or the amber wheat fields of Montana.

After all that traveling, we arrived at our lodging, which called itself a hotel, which made us anticipate that it would be a step up from our usual quarters. Unfortunately this "hotel" was a step down—'way, 'way down! For the next two nights, while I explored the Bale Mountain region, this ridiculous place would be home.

Even the name of the place was ridiculous: the Gobe-Wabe Hotel—pronounced *gobba-waaba*! Wait! It gets better—or worse, depending on your love of language. The above is the shortened version of the hotel's full name. The full name, phonetically, was *gobba-waaba-shababa*. Folks, I am not making this up. I don't have that sort of imagination. In any case this place was a five-star dump. It didn't even have running water! It had pipes and plumbing and was *supposed* to have water, but there was not a drop to be found anywhere within Gobba-Waaba-Shababa.

Day 12 (Feb. 2, 2016)

Yesterday my five-star Taj Mahal hotel had no water. Now this morning there was not only no water but no electricity or power. That meant that the one small flickering light bulb I had had in my room was just a memory. Little did I know that I was in for a fright.

I fumbled around for my flashlight, found it, turned it on, and saw my reflection in the large mirror on the dresser. I was covered from head to foot in tattoos! Bright red tattoos at that! Only Rufus could end up having one too many St. George beers and then wind up late at night in a tattoo parlor in Ethiopia! Believe me, this doesn't happen to everybody. Boy this was going to be a hard one to explain when I got home. Jesus, what had gotten into me last night to do such a thing? I had no idea because I could not remember last night—*anything* last night—except drinking a lot of beer.

The tattoos were all bright red and all circles. *Well*, I thought, *at least I'm consistent, even with a few too many beers under my belt*. The one on my right forehead was especially hideous, but none of them looked too good. If I was going to get tattooed, why pick red circles? Why not cover my body with a map of Africa or naked women? Slowly, because I don't think so well when I first wake up or especially when I've had too much to drink, it finally dawned on me that the big, bright red tattoos were not tattoos but the result of sleeping on an African-style mattress. Let me explain.

In many of the high-class places that I stayed at in Africa, like this current dump, the hotel bought or otherwise acquired old mattresses, and stripped them down to the springs. Then it stretched, very tightly, a very thin piece of cloth over the round steel springs. And that is exactly what I had slept on last night—a mattress that made a great impression on me. Happily, the bright red circles were slowly disappearing from my body—although (I hate to admit it) I was really starting to like the one on my forehead.

So, with great relief that I would not be coming home looking like something out of a freak show in the Barnum and Bailey Circus and wouldn't need to explain to my wife why I had returned from Africa covered from head to toe in bright red tattoos, I headed out to breakfast in pitch black with no lights. Two or three steps out of my room, I tripped over a body—not a dead body like the one I actually did trip over in 1984 during the famine, but a live body. It was the hotel's night guard, who obviously was not the most vigilant guard around. In fact, he hardly stirred even after I stepped on him.

I was heading for coffee. The hotel staff—if that is how you would like to refer to the two women and one man who wore hotel uniforms but spent an awful lot of time talking to each other, or going into a closed office where they often remained for great periods of time, or chatting on their cell phones, or gabbing to their friends who happened to stop by the hotel to visit, or running some great distances down the road to do whatever—had assured me just the night before that I could get some coffee at 6:00 a.m. They had sealed the deal with the most-frequently used expression in Africa, "No problem." This phrase evoked great dread in me because there are no words I fear worse in Africa than "No problem."

Let me help those of you who have never been to Africa understand exactly what those two words really mean. There are over 800 languages and over 2,000 distinct dialects spoken on this continent, and in every single one of these languages "No problem" means in the English translation, "There's no way in hell you'll ever, *ever*, see a cup of coffee tomorrow morning."

Nevertheless, after stumbling around in the dark and tripping over a body because there was no power or electricity—or water, I ambled down to the eating area to get some coffee. You'll never guess in a million years—no matter how many guesses I give you—what they didn't have.

It gets better. I couldn't really ask for coffee because the workers who might potentially be able to give me a cup (or tell me they didn't have any) were still asleep on the cement floor where they had worked all the previous day. (Just between you and me, I think there's some potential here for a union.) They were sleeping in the building because the doors to the hotel are locked every night, and no one can get into or out of the hotel then. The staff locks the doors because they know that the hotel guards on duty at night go to sleep every night and sleep very soundly. In fact, two of them continued sleeping as I tapped and knocked and yelled through the hotel doors that I would like some coffee.

There is some great irony in all this. As I walked back to my room in the dark, trying not to stumble over bodies, either dead or sleeping, I could smell the sweet aroma of Ethiopian coffee all about me growing on the plantations surrounding the hotel.

Since getting coffee was so difficult, I didn't even try for breakfast. Instead, I started out to explore the Bale Mountains. The Bale Mountains are spectacular in both beauty and diversity. This is high-altitude terrain, and it's cold—very cold. The second-highest point in the country is located here.

We got a good look at a lot of wildlife, including ducks, the blue-winged goose, prairie-dog-like critters, monkeys, baboons, and one of the rarest animals on earth, the Ethiopian wolf, a striking animal. The Ethiopian wolf is one of the five most-endangered animal species on Earth, and I was lucky enough to see one—actually two, together. The Ethiopian wolf looks just like a red fox here in America except it's bigger and definitely has the jaw and mouth of a wolf.

As we started to lose light, we headed back to the hotel, driving through beautiful coffee plantations, which only further reminded me that I had not had coffee this day.

Day 13 (Feb. 3, 2016)

Today our destination was the Great Rift Valley lake area. There are a number of lakes in this district, and the plan was to spend the night on one of them, Lake Langano.

Before blasting off in the morning, I watched in shock at the lack of hygiene displayed in the so-called kitchen of this so-called hotel. I did get my morning coffee, but, after watching the scene that took place before me, perhaps I should have skipped it.

I had assumed that drinking coffee, wherein the water is brought to a boil, would be the safest way to go. Unfortunately, the staff at that early morning hour used un-boiled water to make both the coffee and the milk to go into it. They then slopped the filthy water that they had been using to mop the floor into the sink with the dishes and cups.

Knock on wood—I have traveled to some of the most bizarre and dangerous countries in the world and have never gotten sick. I am assuming that is some sort of world record. In my younger, dumber days, with an attitude of invincibility caused by both youth and having survived a war, I took a devil-may-care approach when I traveled, drinking the local water even in places like India, Bangladesh, and Ethiopia in the eighties during the famine. When I did bother to eat, it was always at a roadside stand where food was cooked in greasy oil inside huge oil drums or garbage cans. You never knew what it was and, if you were smart, didn't ask. But it was cheap.

As the years went on, I didn't get any smarter, just more cautious. The price of travel kept going up, especially to the odd and unknown areas I was trying to visit. Most people have never heard of Vanuatu, Wallis and Futuna, Niue, or Nauru, but they are all places on the map and places I wanted to visit. I really didn't want a trip ruined or cut short after all the money, work, scheduling, and planning I had put into it. Gastronomical or intestinal sickness is something no one wants, especially while traveling far from home. So I now drink bottled water and, as a precaution, try to eat cooked food.

Vomiting or having non-stop diarrhea is not a fun experience. When I was in Nam during the war, many of us came down with dysentery, which is an infectious disease that basically is a non-stop diarrhea plus fever. They cut you no slack in the Marines; we just had to keep going. So (as I told you in my Vietnam chapter, but a gross story always bears repeating) most guys never bothered to squat to relieve themselves; they just went and went, soiling themselves non-stop all day and all night. We were already patrolling daily in Vietnamese rice paddies that the people and their animals had used as toilets for centuries for the fertilizing effect. Each day we patrolled through a thick brown soup of human and animal shit that, depending on the season, was ankle high, knee high, or neck high. Each night we slept three together under a small poncho, with the smell of human waste, body odor, and filth emanating from us, the Vietnamese and their water buffalo saturating our entire bodies. We averaged a shower about once a month. After going through an experience like that, I am one of the few people, probably on Earth, who take a special pleasure and delight from of the feel of a good clean pair of Fruit of the Loom underwear taken out of the dryer.

I tell this story only because dysentery or any of the traveler's diarrhea sicknesses have never struck me during my travels. I do carry a filled prescription of Cipro (Ciprofloxacin, an antibiotic used to treat various bacterial infections, including infectious diarrhea), but in writing this piece I just noticed that the expiration date on mine was 1979! Good thing I've been lucky. That is the only medicine I bring on these trips other than my daily cholesterol pill.

In an effort to travel light, I have a first-aid kit that consists of a single Band Aid. For anything more serious, I either use a Brownell Middle School "Buck up, Broncos" t-shirt as a bandage or tourniquet or bleed to death.

The above is my survival-health-care plan when I travel. And, as nutty as it may sound to you, reading about it, it has worked well for me all these years. However, even I have to admit that the adhesive on that one lonely Band-Aid that I have carried in my backpack since 1974 is starting to look a little frayed.

The only other item in the health department that I bring with me is mosquito repellent that is 99% Deet (diethyltoluamide). Mosquitoes love me, but that stuff keeps them away. I have been lucky in this area also, never having contracted malaria, which is a mosquito-borne disease—

even during the war—even when I tried! Like everyone else who ever served in Vietnam, I had times when I thought a break in a hospital on clean white sheets for three to seven days would be a welcomed respite from the rice paddies, jungles, monsoon rains, water-filled fighting holes, and filth. One of those times, I tossed away my malaria pills in hopes of such a break. But I couldn't get malaria even in Vietnam! Even when I wanted it! So I try to continue that trend and remain malaria free.

Malaria is a serious disease. It is debilitating and can kill, so I take my medication for malaria much more seriously. Checking the prescription box, I noticed that the expiration date was 2014—for me, that's pretty good.

Day 14 (Feb. 4, 2016)

On Day 13 we spent the afternoon at Lake Langano. As we approached what would be my lodging for the night, Lake Langano was clearly visible, despite the mist throughout the area. Most of the lake was covered by what appeared to be a brown liquid. I was afraid to ask. The area around the lake is very desert like. Trees were dry and leafless. The soil was sandy, and the weather was hot.

The lake itself is nothing special, at least to me—and I would sure like to know what that brown stuff is covering the surface. The birds are another story. Those birds that call this region home are unique and as splendidly colorful as any birds one could ever hope to see, with iridescent blues, pretty yellows, bright pure whites. There are a host of other birds colored ochre and magneto.

For the first time in nine or 10 days, we had Wi-Fi that actually worked. This meant I could finally send out an email to my family, letting them know I was still alive. Much later I received a return email from my wife: "So what?" You don't suppose the flame has died, do you?

I was admiring a beautiful sunrise over Lake Langano very early in the morning; the lake and its desert setting looked stunning. Suddenly I was attacked—by a swarm of pretty yellow birds. It was scene right out of Alfred Hitchcock's classic film *The Birds*—except these birds were polite and courteous. They wanted my breakfast, not my life. Seeing that my breakfast had not arrived and I only had coffee, they waited calmly and politely for their chance to steal it. Africa, no doubt about it, turns out the most polite birds on the planet.

Today would consist of the long drive back to Addis Ababa for the return trip home. Before my flight I hoped to take in one of the largest open-air markets in Africa, located in the capital. Meanwhile, the pretty yellow birds surrounding my table were now looking more like vicious, savage vultures as they impatiently waited to devour my breakfast. My manly, macho pride would suffer greatly if I had to come home and explain to everyone that I had been mugged by a bunch of cute little yellow birds.

Day 15 (Feb. 5, 2016)

When we left Lake Langano to return to the capital, Addis Ababa, we had another flat tire. The 6th flat we had in 14 days—with good tires! (We carried three spares—one in the jeep and two others tied to the top of the vehicle.) Considering the condition of the roads, it was almost like driving in Michigan.

Although the driver was an expert at changing tires and did it very quickly, we drew a lot of attention from the villagers every time it happened. First, there was the fact that a very big SUV/jeep had broken down, so that caused some interest. But it got a whole lot wilder when a white man stepped out of the vehicle. That action caused most of the village kids to run up to the vehicle to see what was going on. After that, it took about—I would say—one second before the entire village noticed what *kind* of white man had gotten out of the vehicle. This was no ordinary white traveler; this was Rufus—in an outfit the natives could barely believe they were seeing.

With my bulging cargo pants with stuff and equipment in every pocket, travel vest loaded with more equipment, big hiking boots, wide-brimmed bush hat, large aviator-style sun glasses, and my crowning glory, my Brownell Middle School "Buck up, Broncos" t-shirt featuring a wild raging stallion on the front, I cut a mighty fine figure, if I do say so myself. No wonder everyone in any village surrounded me.

On this particular occasion, most of the bystanders looked on with curiosity; a few smiled; and the littlest children as usual were drawn to rub their tiny hands up and down my arm to feel the hair. A pet ape had arrived at the village, and they enjoyed it. Some of the children were very amused by the bronco on my shirt, and one or two—always those in the age group I taught: 11-, 12-, or 13-year-olds (they're the most brazen, of course)—had to touch it.

Never shy about being the center of attention, I caused an even greater sensation by doing the unthinkable. I got out into the bright hot sun so I had good lighting for my photography. Even the Ethiopians have enough common sense to try and stay out of the sun in this region. They were all in the shade. They were now looking at me with utmost pity, sensing that the white man was mentally unstable and was choosing to stand in the hot sun to become even crazier. Despite the sun, despite their pity (or maybe because of it), I got my shots, made a few new friends—mostly under the age of 14—and we moved on. The tire was changed.

On the way back to Addis Ababa we stopped at Lake Ziway to see the bird life. This country has some wonderful bird life, and I saw a number of marabou storks, pelicans, egrets, white plovers, and a rare kingfisher. (Y'know, the more I stop to think about it, maybe something of Bert the birder, whom I accompanied on his bird-watching tour in Yugoslavia—and sort of into Albania—has rubbed off on me, after all. Despite the fact that I once told him that, for me, there were only big birds and little birds, I sure do notice a lot of our fine feathered friends, don't I?)

Rufus in an Ethiopian Strip Club!

When we arrived back in the capital, Addis Ababa, after two weeks out in the bush, my guide had a real treat for me, or so he said: dinner and drinks at a four-star hotel (note to reader: don't get too awfully excited about a "four-star hotel" in Ethiopia), an event that would also include a cultural show. I have to admit that folk dancing and singing is never high on my list of travel priorities, but the shows often have some spectacular outfits that I find interesting. So off we went.

The place was packed to the point of overcrowding. I ordered a St. George beer, so, to my way of thinking, things were off to a great start.

Immediately things began to head downhill. The food was "served" buffet style, which I hate, plus—even after two weeks in this country—I could not recognize one single item that lay in the pots to eat. So I passed on the food and ordered another St. George beer.

The band—yes, there was a band—continued to play the same song continuously for 35 or 40 minutes. And, even though you didn't hear it (for which you can be thankful), I can assure you it was not what we would call good music.

Finally, the native Ethiopian dancing started. It began astonishingly with five guys in baseball hats holding green glow sticks! I thought to myself, *I wonder what tribe this might be*. Five pretty young women then joined this peculiar ensemble. The young women danced, and it was kind of erotic, but of course they kept their clothes on—at least for now. One of the young ladies sang a horribly off-key song in Ethiopian, and one of the many Chinese who were packing this place came running up and somehow stuck a large currency note on her forehead.

What the hell! Was I in a strip club? I looked around for a bronze pole and wondered if a well-endowed blonde, always named Tanya, would start performing. Not that I've ever been in a strip club or anything, but I have been told that's what goes on in these places. (If at any point my writing seems to be a little off, awkward, or stifled, please keep in mind that my wife, Monica, reads these chapters.)

The number finally ended. I sat there, more confused than entertained. Minutes later, the group was back—all of them, the five guys and the five attractive young ladies. The women had not bothered to change their outfits because, I presumed, they were going to be coming off at any minute.

Representing yet another Ethiopian tribe, the young men now wore bright lime green/chartreuse polyester shirts and pants. What an amazing tribe! How did I ever miss this tribe while out in the bush of Ethiopia for two weeks? (They certainly would have stood out!) Despite this great cultural—nay, *anthropological*—event involving the men of the Lost Tribe of Ethiopia, I found it hard to keep my eyes off the young women, who were really getting into it now. It was hard to believe that one could do what they were doing with their bodies! Despite all the erotic movements by these young nymphs, everyone kept their clothes on, including me.

The third performance had the young men coming on stage—all of them—wearing white jackets, baggy white pants, and caps. I swear to God they all looked identical to the old Good Humor Ice Cream Men that I remember as a kid! But these Good Humor Ice Cream Men carried spears! How I would have loved it, when I was a kid, if the Good Humor Ice Cream Man had carried a spear! Even though I truly do love ice cream, spear or no spear, I found it hard to keep my eyes off the young women dancing because they were really going to town now. I continued to look around for that brass pole with Tanya on it but had no luck.

At this point I felt I had had enough cultural immersion for the night and told the guide we should head back to the hotel. At the hotel bar I nursed a St. George beer while I did some writing. For some strange reason I had a hankering for ice cream.

The Ethiopian people are a kind, gentle, and polite people. This last morning, walking about Addis Ababa ("New Flower," remember?) I was witness to that gentle politeness in dealing with the traffic congestion and confusion. Being a pedestrian in a Third-World country is not a pleasant or safe thing. Drivers are aggressive and reckless, yet, as I walked and attempted to cross streets, the Ethiopian drivers invariably made way for me with a smile and wave. Try that anywhere else in the Third World!

Late in the afternoon, we finally started off for one of the largest open-air markets in the world, located in Addis Ababa. The market was huge, crowded, colorful, and overwhelming. I enjoyed it immensely.

After the market, we stopped at a number of historic Ethiopian Orthodox churches. Ethiopian Orthodox churches are unique in that, along with an altar, there is also a replica of the lost Ark of the Covenant within each and every church. Moses and the Jews were commanded by God to build the Ark of the Covenant after the end of their slavery in Egypt. At the foot of Mt. Sinai, the 10 Commandments given by God to Moses were placed inside the box-like structure and carried before the Jewish people on their journey to the Promised Land. The Spirit of God resided within the Ark. It eventually was placed in the Temple in Jerusalem. The Bible tells us that the Ark went missing almost 3,000 years ago. Jewish tradition says it was a result of the sacking of the Temple in 586 BC by the Babylonians. Countless searches and expeditions have been launched to find the Ark of the Covenant—one of the holiest objects on Earth.

The Ethiopians have always claimed that the Ark is safely held within the Church of St. Mary's in Axum, one of Ethiopia's most ancient cities. The church is surrounded by a high metal fence and guarded. One Ethiopian Orthodox monk chosen for his personal holiness and chastity is assigned, inside the compound, to care for the Ark of the Covenant. This monk describes the Ark exactly as it is chronicled in the Bible. He has been quoted as saying that, when the "spirit of God" within the Ark of the Covenant makes itself known, it is a powerful and terrifying incident that only the monk himself has witnessed.

More and more religious scholars are now supporting this claim as the solution to the mystery of the Lost Ark of the Covenant. I think in the near future I need to verify this for myself. (Indiana Jones, eat your heart out!)

This particular trip ended with a visit to the Holy Land—no, not the one you are thinking of in Jerusalem and Israel, but *Ireland*, the ancestral homeland. The plane and Rufus both needed refueling—one with aviation fuel, the other with Harp, Ireland's national lager beer produced by Guinness.

Rufus in Dictatorland

North Korea, Part I: China

May 21, 2014. Surprisingly, considering that I was about to embark upon a voyage to one of the most closed, repressive societies on the planet, everything to date had gone smoothly. I'd booked my trip, procured my passport and currency, and packed my bags. My wife, Monica, drove me to the airport—and this is the point where, on many of my trips, things start to go off track.

Just a year and half before, as I stood at the airline check-in desk and watched the taillights of our Ford Focus station wagon pull away with Monica and the kids, the airline agent informed me that not one but *both* of my flights to Somalia had been cancelled. *Should I take this as a sign,* I wondered. *Should I pack it in, turn around, and go home?* No, I stuck it out, eventually muddling through that one, which involved an unexpected and unplanned landing in Mogadishu—with fireworks (i.e., *gunfire*) included for good measure.

Nothing like that happened this time. Having been tutored countless times by my older son, Eric, I was able to check myself in electronically at the kiosk, and I was on my way.

The big surprise was airport security. In just the three weeks since my family and I flew to India, some major changes and improvements had been instituted—namely, the TSA Pre-check that I, no doubt due to my superior intellect and wide-spread reputation, had earned. The Homeland Security guys ran the fingers of one of my hands over a piece of cloth (which, no doubt, contained some chemical) and then checked that in a matter of seconds. They didn't make me remove my shoes, which was always a major hassle, nor take my laptop out of its case, which was always a minor hassle. My backpack went right through the x-ray machine. For whatever reason, they wanted to further check my backpack, and that again took only seconds, and once again I was on my way.

This was the easiest and fastest I had gone through security in 30 years. I usually exited security looking like someone who has been blown up in a terrorist attack or just gone through a tornado: belt off, pants hanging down to an unacceptable level; unshod, carrying two boots in my hands; laptop, laptop case, belt, and the money belt containing my documents in my teeth for lack of a third hand.

Up until a few years ago, before the newer and better scanning machines were installed, I also had the added excitement of setting off the metal detectors' buzzers due to the shrapnel in my left leg and hip, which would always lead to a very thorough pat down that often looked like sexual assault, which would then lead to the authorities more closely inspecting my passport—and just guess what they found there? Visa and entry stamps to such family vacation destinations as Iran, Iraq, Afghanistan, Somalia, Chad, Bosnia, Kosovo, Lebanon, etc.

Passport inspection inevitably led to the opportunity for me to meet a fairly large number of employees who worked for Customs, Immigration, TSA, the Michigan State Police, and the FBI, all of whom I had to convince that I was a friendly, mild-mannered, nonthreatening middle-school teacher. Of course, the bomb fragments in my leg and hip and the—shall we say?—*unusual* travel destinations took some time to explain, but then I was usually on my way.

Well, sometimes there was one more delay. Now that the guys in nearly every Federal agency at the airport and I were friends, Immigration and Customs officials would ask me if I minded if they showed the new employees those visa stamps that they might not see much in their career, such as for Tonga, Burundi, Lesotho, etc. (For those of you who often ask, "Why do you arrive four and five hours before your flights when people flying overseas normally need only two or three?", the above description should answer that question.)

But this time I breezed through in under five minutes, waited for my plane, and, after a very boring 13 hours, arrived in Beijing, the capital of China.

The pilot announced the temperature outside was 93 and heating up. The tarmac was over 100 degrees, and all passengers were asked to pull their window shutter down so that the inside of the plane would not become a hot house. Not that it helped much. Not that it was any better when we finally got off the plane.

I walked around Beijing for a few hours, mostly to stay awake longer so I could try and get back to a normal sleep pattern. As I mentioned in an earlier chapter, the U.S., under President Jimmy Carter, on January 1, 1979, finally recognized mainland China after it had been closed to America for nearly 40 years. Six months later, as a member of a Wayne State University educational tour, I was one of the first Americans to visit China, which, at the time, was still very Maoist.

Since then, I had been going back to China on an average of once a decade, but the last couple of trips were unusual, to say the least, for, although they were fascinating expeditions that went to some of the most remote areas on Earth, they gave me little or no idea of what was going on in China proper other than what I read in the newspapers and books.

After the 1979 trip, the next excursion had been to Inner Mongolia, out in the Gobi Desert. The second had been to Tibet—as far west and different from the rest of China as you can get. (Traveling there was an adventure in itself. Instead of flying to Lhasa, the capital of Tibet, as most do, I took a jeep over the Himalaya Mountains from Nepal to witness some of the most breath-taking scenery that that mountain range has to offer.)

The most unusual trip had been the one I took just a few years before, and, again, getting there proved to be as unusual as the venue I visited. I went once more to the far west of China, this time to the Taklamakan Desert, one of the largest and fiercest deserts in the world. It is here that the Uighur people live. They are sometimes called the Chinese Moslems because Islam is their religion. Uighur women dress in the most conservative and fundamentalist manner of any Moslems anywhere. Their dresses go from neck to ankle; they wear a full scarf and head covering; and, to top it all off (so to speak), a solid piece of cloth covers their face as a veil—with no slit or screen as one would see in Saudi Arabia or Afghanistan. (One wonders how *they* see, but maybe their sight is immaterial.)

The Taklamakan Desert was part of the Old Silk Road, and the people and their way of life have changed very little since Marco Polo visited. I had about as hard a time getting there as he did! I flew into Kazakhstan and went through a very long, tedious, and painful process to secure entry into Moslem China (Xinjiang province). To leave the area, I had to go through Uzbekistan! So, bottom line, I had not been to proper or mainland China in quite a while.

I walked to Tiananmen Square, using a very poor Chinese map with few street names marked on it, but I eventually made it. It was a 10-mile round trip from the hotel in 94-degree weather.

The very tight security in place at the square—by both the police and the army—shocked me. The Square is completely fenced off to pedestrians. I waited in the security line for about 40 minutes just to get into a city open space called a square! My backpack was x-rayed twice, which made me reconsider my initial idea: to go to Mao's Mausoleum again. To go in and visit the dead tyrant, as I did years ago, I would have had to surrender my backpack and wait in yet another very long line. The duration of the wait didn't bother me as much as the thought that the busy and overwhelmed staff might lose my backpack, which contained all my travel documents and camera equipment. So one of the great murderers of history had to do without the homage of Rufus.

During my first visit in '79, China was still called the land of the bicycle. When I was there in '79, it was estimated that there were over

Longitude and Latitude, with Attitude

one billion bicycles on the roads and streets. No more. It now seemed that there were over a billion cars on the streets—and surprisingly a lot of American-made cars!

Another observation I couldn't help making was that, the more a poor country becomes modern and its income goes up, the more it looks like the U.S. I felt as if I were in San Francisco. It reminded me of the disappointment I felt on my first trip to Japan back in the 1970s. I came home telling everyone that Japan looked like Boston or Dallas, except that they had beautiful temples.

I wanted to check out the subway system, but, since there was security to go through and I was still carrying that backpack, I skipped it.

The Chinese cities were as clean as I remembered them (i.e., *very* clean), and they had done a marvelous job (as usual) of planting trees on every single street, like rows of soldiers, and into every nook and cranny, like a bunch of soldiers waiting in ambush—or a bunch of street vendors, waiting to ambush tourists' wallets.

The Wise and the wise guy—me, standing next to a statue of Confucius. Note my "Buck up, Broncos" t-shirt.

And finally, it seemed that every block sported two or three massage parlors. It seemed odd that a block would have even *one*, considering China's (until recently, apparently) puritanical attitude toward sex. I doubted that the Chinese suffered more than we do from back pain and sciatica.

[228]

For better or worse, I girded my loins for a Wi-Fi-less week or more, due to the fact that foreigners are not allowed to use the internet in China and there is no such thing as email in North Korea. My family and friends were going to have to do without hearing from me or receiving the daily reports of my travels. I hoped they could live with the suspense.

Well, I'm exaggerating just a little. North Korea *does* have a little internet service—but *very little* internet service—and very few of its people have access to it, mostly universities and the government. In any case, I wasn't exaggerating: foreigners are not allowed to use this service. And, anyway, there is no email in North Korea—for anybody. I wasn't able to file my impressions of the country until I was well out of it and back in China.

North Korea, Part II: North Korea

As far as I know, only a couple of tour companies in the world (located, I believe, in China and South Korea) have permission or a license to send travelers or tourists to North Korea. The one I was funneled through was called Koryo, which is the name of North Korea's national tour agency and national airline. As the oddballs of the world (present company excluded, of course) start joining up for a tour of North Korea, they are thrown together—which is good because at least these oddballs (not me, of course) realize that there are other peculiar individuals, just like them, in the world.

I was part of a group of 20 from all over the world: the U.S., Britain, Australia, Belgium, Ireland, Germany, the Netherlands, Canada, Puerto Rico, South Korea, and Romania: teachers, doctors, writers, Foreign Service officers, lawyers, business owners, and computer specialists. About half of the group no longer lived in the country they were born in or in the country they called home. All of us had one thing in common (besides being oddballs): the love of travel and the desire to see one of the most truly bizarre countries on Earth. (Well, maybe that's what *made* us oddballs.)

Because North Korea is so totalitarian and suspicious of everything, the North Korean government handled everyone's visa from beginning to end. (That was actually wonderful because getting a visa for most of the places I go to now is difficult, confusing, expensive, and nerve wracking.)They also offered us a series of "educational" seminars.

Before leaving Beijing, we attended a final seminar, at which we were re-issued the 12-page instruction guide to the "do's and don'ts" of travel inside North Korea—mostly *don'ts*, including the rule to never fold or make a crease in a picture or newspaper of "Dear Leader" Kim Jung Un. (When we finally did arrive in North Korea and were constantly being handed propaganda sheets, magazines, and newspapers that usually featured multiple images of "Dear Leader" on them, we had to walk around with these items folded in the most unusual and awkward manner so as not to disrespect "Dear Leader." The North Koreans seemed to be quite nervous and concerned about how we handled this situation. To just trash the paper or throw it in a wastepaper basket probably would have caused a collective nervous breakdown throughout the country—either that, or you would be reading my obituary now and not my reminiscences.)

Today was the big day; we flew to Pyongyang the capital of North Korea, the most isolated country on the planet. Naturally, we took North Korea's national airline, the aforementioned Koryo, and were served what I thought was a very strange lunch. North Korea is an Asian nation that has a long, well-established, well-respected cuisine. In addition, it is a bellicose and fierce enemy of the U.S. So the cold hamburger I was served was a bit of a surprise. A Happy Meal in the airspace of the most totalitarian communist nation on Earth!

Perhaps we Americans should learn a valuable lesson from this. Instead of spending trillions of dollars on defense and military budgets to oppose and fight our enemies, we should form shock brigades from Burger King, Kentucky Fried Chicken, and McDonalds to storm the beaches and invade. We couldn't beat them in the Korean War with bayonets and rifles, so perhaps we can overcome them with cholesterol and fat.

I have to admit there was a downside to this North Korean hamburger, and that was the taste. If my palate is any judge, I suspect that there were fewer stray dogs in Pyongyang after our meal was prepared. (So maybe serving us this adulteration of an American staple was a subtle, or not-so-subtle, act of war.)

Even before we landed, I counted the trip to North Korea as something of a minor success: I added a new, unique, and valuable barf bag to my collection. I have an assortment of over 200 airline-sickness bags from every airline imaginable. I used to make a giant bulletin board of them, and my students loved it. As I used to tell them, "Some people collect stamps. Some people collect coins. And Rufus collects barf bags." Of course, you need a seventh-grade mentality to really appreciate it, and all my seventh graders and I had a seventh-grade mentality.

After landing and taking forever to get our luggage, we made our first drive through the capital, Pyongyang. It is a big, well-planned city, and everything is perfect. There is no litter, trash, garbage, or graffiti. Every tree, shrub, bush, and—no exaggeration here—blade of grass is perfectly trimmed and maintained—everywhere! The people work six days a week, and on Sunday, their day off, they "volunteer" to pull weeds and clover from the grass on the boulevards, parks, and monument areas. I watched them do this in a pouring rain the Sunday I was there.

There are giant, monumental, over-the-top statues of Kim Il Sung and Kim Jong-il (the grandfather and father of the current "Dear Leader," Kim Jung-un) all over the city, indoors and outdoors. Imagine going to Washington, D.C., and seeing 40 or 50 variations of the Lincoln Memorial about the city—that'll give you an idea of what Pyongyang is like.

At all these larger-than-life monuments dedicated to Kim Il-sung and Kim Jong-il, there is subtle, almost subliminal music playing. It's a somber, martial, and a very patriotic kind of music that is guaranteed to stir one's emotions. I know I was so moved by it that, each time we left such a monument, I wanted to kill any capitalist that I might come upon.

And, by the way, even we foreigners had to stand in a perfectly straight line before any of these statues we visited and bow while our tour guide put flowers before the statues. I did not bow to those jackasses. It was the one act of subtle civil disobedience I committed in North Korea.

And I got to commit that act many times, for statues of those jackasses were *everywhere*. These gigantic monuments to the Kim dynasty not only define the city but dominate it and overshadow it. Not to mention the paintings, signs, posters, and pictures of the three tyrants throughout the city and country. Every room of every public building has two framed pictures of grandfather Kim Il-sung and father Kim Jong-il looking down from above. Every adult—no exceptions—wears a red lapel pin with the two past leaders on it.

There are few cops on the streets, and that's because there are *zillions* of soldiers all over and everywhere. Hard to believe, but I think I saw more military uniforms and soldiers in my five days in North Korea than I did in my two years in the Marines.

Speaking of cops, most of the traffic police officers are women. They wear bright powder-blue uniforms with matching hats that look like something out of Hollywood or a Broadway play. Polished black shoes with white stockings and gloves complement the outfit. In a land of no makeup, these gals wear lipstick, eye liner, etc. I am not sure of the requirements for males who want to become traffic officers, but it appears one of the qualifications for females is to have won three or four beauty contests.

Longitude and Latitude, with Attitude

This brings me to roads and traffic. I don't think anyone was surprised by how little traffic there is on the roads and streets of Pyongyang. As North Korea is both very poor and the most totalitarian communist state in the world, the lack of vehicular circulation makes perfect sense. What we never could figure out was why they built eight-lane roads in the middle of the city where you could lie down and take a 20-minute nap before a car or truck might come by in either direction! (But probably they need the space when all those zillions of soldiers goose-step down the avenue on May Day and "Dear Leader's" birthday.) We all took pictures of these roads that look like the L. A. Freeway after the Rapture, when everyone—people *and* cars—has ascended into heaven. A great site for a Hollywood movie!

One of our stops was an outdoor museum on which stood the house that was the birth place of Kim Il Sung (founder of the dynasty). Now, this is where it starts to get pretty farfetched. Because Kim Il Sung is god-like, the water from the nearby well obviously must have special powers. Our guide told us—with a straight face and in the most sincere tones—that drinking this well water would make a person 10 years younger. After some serious consultations with my hotel mirrors for the next four days I can assure you that this claim is another Commie Lie.

So far on the trip (except for the hamburger on the airplane), the food was actually pretty good. At one restaurant, called the Hot Pot, we individually cooked our own food right at the table, in a small pot of boiling water. We were given all kinds of vegetables and greens—few that I recognized—to dump into the boiling pot, along with a little meat, an egg, and all kinds of peppers and spices. That was good.

The next day at lunch we were offered a Korean specialty: dog stew. I passed and warned the younger members of our group that they wouldn't like it. And, sure enough, they didn't. I have eaten dog (China), monkey (Africa), snake (Nam and Burma), and rat (Burma), and the only one that was good was the snake. Since I wasn't having the dog, I amused myself by observing how the Koreans used chopsticks to eat foods you would never think could be eaten with chopsticks, such as a whole fried egg, and by watching them pick up a slice of bread with chopsticks and eat it that way.

Oh yeah, the best part of eating in North Korea was that, except for breakfast, all meals were served with complimentary beer!

Rufus McGaugh

Rare close-up of North Korean kids who normally will not even make eye contact or get near you, let alone pose. Fearful of the police and military, they quickly scattered after I took this picture.

Old North Korean farmer smiling wryly at seeing his image on a digital camera, probably for the first time in his life.

North Korean wedding with bride in a traditional Korean wedding dress.

North Korea, Part III: Public Transportation and the Pueblo

Every day, eating continued to be an adventure. Today it was duck hot dogs with fried sugared potatoes.

Pyongyang has a great mass-transit system of streetcars, buses, trams, and subways. The communist countries usually don't have a lot to brag about until you touch on the subject of transportation. Russia, of course, has the most beautiful subway system in the world. Every subway station is as attractive as a grand theatre or a palace, and every station is unique; no two are alike. In Russia the stations are walled in pink marble, gray granite, black granite, blue aluminum, copper, teak wood, rosewood, mahogany, etc. Russia is the gold standard that every country tries its best to emulate. Pyongyang is no exception, but, of course, it is a poor country and could never really compete. This made for a comical experience of sorts.

We were taken subway riding by our guide in order to see and experience the beauty of Pyongyang's subway stations. We were told to start by exploring Station Number 1; then get on the subway and ride to Station Number 2; check out Station Number 2; get back on the subway, skip four stops, and get off at Station Number 7. That seemed odd—until we did it!

Station Number 1 was made of beautiful white marble, with mosaic floors and multi-colored chandeliers. It was more like an opera house than a subway station. Station Number 2 was also beautiful; the walls were covered with beautiful murals and paintings. It was more like an art museum. However, as we passed by Station Numbers 3, 4, 5, and 6, it became obvious why we were not to get out. They all looked something like a West Virginia coal mine.

Next it was on to the main streetcar (tram) depot, which I found pretty boring until the guide announced that we were getting our own private streetcar for an exclusive run through the city. So off we went through Pyongyang while the city's other two million schmucks, who are usually packed like sardines on these things, looked at us and probably wondered who we were and what the hell was going on.

Now, say all you want about these dirty, godless commie countries, but this is the only country in the more than 200 that I have traveled to where a "beer bar" stop is not only included but mandatory. I have no doubt that, many thousands of years ago—somehow, some way—the Irish surely got here and spread their amazing culture. And, speaking of beer (which I often do), it's fifty cents a bottle or glass. My God, this is the Promised Land!

Outside of Pyongyang, everything thing is agriculture. One would think that North Korea could feed the world, since every inch of land seemed to be under cultivation, with all kinds of green crops growing at this time of year. I saw corn and beans and, of course, rice in the rice paddies. I didn't recognize anything else. Although I am the son of a Tennessee farmer, I don't have much skill in growing things. I cultivate a lot of weeds and crab grass on my lawn, but that's about the extent of it.

Much of the Korean soil is red, as it is in Tennessee and Georgia. When I was a kid and we drove to Tennessee to visit my grandparents, I was always amazed by this red soil. It seemed so different and unique. As a Mid-Westerner, I knew dirt was not supposed to be red; it was supposed to be black or brown! Of course, by the time we arrived in Tennessee, I was usually so car sick that the landscape looked psychedelic to me. My mom, in an attempt to cheer me up would say, "Well, the good thing about the way you get car sick so easy is that they will never take you in the army! Plus, you won't last five minutes on a ship in the Navy or in a plane in the Air Force, so you won't ever have to worry about being in a war."

I sure proved her wrong; I enlisted in the Marines. It seemed like a wonderful idea at the time because in the Marines there is little chance you'll have a problem with motion sickness because Marines love to walk and march everywhere—even when there are plenty of vehicles to get them someplace easier and faster.

I can't help remarking on the roads again, since all we did was to drive around on them all day, looking at gargantuan monuments. These roads resemble huge, deserted airport runways.

Today was an even more serious day than usual. We visited two very important sites to the North Korean people, the War Museum and the USS Pueblo. In 1968 North Korea captured the

North Korean kindergartner singing and dancing with her classmates—no doubt celebrating some humiliating American defeat.

USS Pueblo, which was an intelligence (spy) ship that they claimed was in their territorial waters. Over 11 months, the crew was beaten and tortured physically and psychologically. There was much debate in the United States as to what action we should take. The Vietnam War was at its height, and President Johnson decided that one war was enough. Naturally, the crew members were forced to sign confessions, and, after U.S. negotiators signed a statement of guilt and apology, the 82 crew members were allowed, one by one, to cross the DMZ (the demilitarized zone—the "no man's land" that divides North and South Korea) over the "Bridge of No Return" to freedom in South Korea. To date, the USS Pueblo is the only U.S. naval ship to be captured and remain in captivity anywhere in the world. For an American, it was a very moving and somewhat humiliating experience to tour this ship, view the brutal propaganda film they screen on board, and endure the smug attitude of the North Koreans about their defeat of "U.S. imperialist forces."

North Korea, Part IV: The War Museum

After concluding our tour of the USS Pueblo, we were escorted to the War Museum. If you are unfamiliar with the Korean War (1950-53), you might not know that the U.S. had a number of major setbacks militarily in that war. In fact, on a number of occasions it looked as though the American military along with the South Korean army would be pushed right into the sea. Not only did we lose many men (more than 36,000 killed, 92,000 wounded), but the North Koreans destroyed or captured a lot of military equipment (jeeps, tanks, helicopters, planes, trucks, artillery pieces, etc.), and it's all in the open-air section of the museum. Again, the last time I saw this much military hardware, I was in a war zone myself. It's a bit demoralizing even for a peacenik hippie like me to witness all this blown-up and shot-up U.S. military equipment. It's not only sobering but frustrating to see our tanks and planes with "U.S." painted on them being presented as war trophies—and the North Koreans had row after row of destroyed *materiel*.

Then (to add insult to injury, I guess) into the museum itself we went.

Here is a good place to mention that evidently the favorite (best?) way to kill American Imperialists is with a bayonet through the guts (always with the bloody entrails flowing out). The North Koreans not only had plenty of posters, paintings, murals, and statues depicting this evisceration but also postcards and stamps. It was about this time I started to get the feeling that they really don't like us very much.

In my Brownell "50 Years of Excellence" t-shirt ("Buck Up, Broncos" must have been in the wash), I pose with the military director of the North Korean War Museum. The museum celebrates North Korea's victory over the U.S. in the Korean War. (Hey! It was a draw, ending in a truce—but I didn't tell her that.)

That visit pretty much ended the day except for dinner with beer and then a ride to the "beer bar" for more cheap North Korean beer. I personally feel the beer makes this place more tolerable.

The next morning we were off early for a long drive down to the DMZ between North and South Korea. The DMZ, where- North Koreans face off against their American and South Korean enemies, is reportedly the most fortified border in the world. The everyday tension is almost unbearable, with troops on both sides always at the ready to attack or defend. Our guides, drivers, handlers, and even military officials were more on edge and nervous than usual.

To get permission to cross into the DMZ and then do it is a very ominous experience. We had to get off the bus, line up single file, and be marched over by a North Korean Army officer. We walked under a gigantic concrete arch surrounded by walls of concrete and logs, all covered by barbed wire. It was definitely over the top.

In this No Man's Land, in the little village of Panmunjom (no people live there now), we got to go in and see the site of the signing of the

Korean truce in 1953. (After all these years, there is still no peace treaty, only a truce.) The signed truce sits in the middle of the table with a North Korean flag on their side and a U.N. flag on the other side.

As it wound down, I reflected on my visit to North Korea. It was an "interesting" experience, to say the least. The trip had only three boring parts: going bowling, touring a bottling plant, and that tour of the streetcar depot—and did I mention bowling? Perhaps the main thing I noticed during my stay here is that the West (their governments and media) make North Korea out to be more bizarre than it really is. (You may not agree, considering what I have described above.) It is *definitely* different and sometimes over the top but not unlike the former Soviet Union and Maoist China, if that's any consolation.

I was able to get a few shots of me wearing my Brownell "Buck up, Broncos" t-shirt while in North Korea. The Brownell kids always get a big kick out of seeing their school represented at such spots as Antarctica and Mt. Everest. I realized, now that I was "retired" and substituting not only at Brownell but at Pierce and Parcells Middle Schools, too, that I was going to need Pierce and Parcells t-shirts for future journeys (which, as you probably can tell from this chronicle—specifically my trip to Niue—I have since obtained).

And finally: politics. Both sides in America would love this country of North Korea. For the Democrats, "Dear Leader" Kim Jung Un has provided the entire nation with Obamacare, complete with every Republican's nightmare: the death panels that Sarah Palin and Rush Limbaugh warned us about and how no granny in America would ever be safe again. For the Republicans, the state of North Korea is definitely a "Right to Work" state. From what I have seen, they work you pretty good here. And what about those pesky unions always wanting a pay raise? Go back a few sentences and read the part about the death panels.

At midnight, I bid a fond farewell to North Korea and its "Dear Leader" and returned to the relative sanity of mainland China.

North Korea, Part V: Back to China and Mao's Mausoleum

After leaving North Korea, I had a full day in Beijing. When I passed through China on my way to Pyongyang, I had arranged for a day tour upon my return. My request was to visit out-of-the-way sites because I had been to Beijing itself already. The one exception was that I wanted to re-visit Tiananmen Square.

As before (as always), security for anyone entering the square was very tight. We endured long lines, had our belongings x-rayed, and so forth. Once I passed through this gauntlet and actually made it *to* the square, I took a few shots of Mao's giant portrait at one end of the square and then handed over my camera and documents to my guide for safekeeping, for her return to me after I went through Mao's Mausoleum and came out the other end.

Security would still not let me enter the mausoleum because I had a camera lens in my cargo pants pocket. So I had to walk back some distance and turn *that* over to my guide, too, then start again, all to revisit the dead tyrant, whose preserved body I hadn't seen since the 1980s.

Big surprise this time: Mao did not look good! Well, he *was* dead, after all, but, compared to Lenin's corpse back in Red Square in Moscow, Mao's was decidedly second best. Mao's face looked like a job gone bad at Madame Tussaud's Wax Museum. The last time I saw the great mass murderer, he looked pretty good. This time his face was wrinkled, shrunken, caving in—and he definitely looked dead. Lenin, on the other hand, looks like he's napping and, if awakened, could sit up and have a conversation. (And Lenin died in 1924—52 years before Mao!)

The last and most important thing I want to mention about China is what an incredible economic machine it has turned into. You read about it. You know it. But, until you witness it for yourself, you have no idea of the changes and the pace of the changes going on in this country.

China is just not an "emerging economy"—it's already emerged, like a whale breaching! This is a country with a first-rate, world-class economy. Its people have always been hardworking and industrious, but now those traits are channeled, ironically, into one of the most powerful capitalist economic machines in the world. One sees it in nearly every facet of Chinese life: their new apartments, stylish attire (no more Mao suits), autos, consumer goods, and overall modernization. If things continue like this for them, I guess we'll have to make way for the New Chinese Century.

North Korea, Part VI: Desperately Leaving China

Well, it seems I can never have a trip without some adventure, screw-up, or disaster. I had made it through eight whole days without a problem when my driver, who was to take me to the airport, did not show up. I made several frantic phone calls, to no avail, as my flight-departure time drew nearer and nearer. I had no Chinese money left; no banks were open; hotels in China are not allowed to exchange dollars; and taxis do not accept dollars or credit cards, so I was in a bit of a predicament.

Desperate times call for desperate measures! When a taxi pulled up to the hotel to pick up a guest who was leaving with luggage, I ran out to the passenger and asked if he spoke English. He did. He confirmed he was going to the airport.

I said, "Hey, I'm in a bit of a mess here. My driver did not show up, and I'm out of Chinese money. Can I ride with you? If you take care of the driver, I'll reimburse you in dollars for the whole thing."

He thought about it for less than a second and said, "Hop in."

He was an agricultural specialist from Argentina, and he insisted I only pay for half the taxi ride. It was a long drive, due to the distance and the never-ending gridlock of traffic that is now a part of China. My share was $5. A lot of things are still very cheap in China.

After a full day of touring Beijing and then struggling to get to the airport, I arrived in time to board my plane at midnight and take a very long airplane ride with an odd flight pattern in order to reach one of the littlest countries in the world and the newest country in Asia, East Timor. (Up until a few years ago East Timor had been part of Indonesia.)

I flew six-and-a-half hours to Singapore, and waited three hours for my plane to East Timor.

There was much confusion among the airline employees at both airlines in both China and Singapore because none of them had ever heard of East Timor or even knew its location, and evidently airline computers knew nothing of East Timor, either. Neither airline I flew would at first issue an airline ticket because no one knew what the visa requirements were. I had to step back into my role as a social-studies teacher and explain, first, where East Timor was and, second, that Americans do not need a visa to visit.

North Korea, Part VII: Erupting Volcano Halts the Trip

And then, just about the time you think Rufus could not possibly add another wild adventure to his saga of travel experiences, the airline announced that a huge volcanic eruption was wreaking havoc right smack dab in our flight pattern. Giant waves, gale winds, turbulence, smoke, soot, flames, and—from the sound of it—the Apocalypse itself were taking place right in the vicinity of East Timor.

Apparently, the volcano, Mount Sinabung, had been erupting for quite a while by then. A CNN story from January 9, 2014, explained that "A volcanic eruption in Indonesia that has displaced more than 22,000 people is intensifying, local authorities say." By Groundhog Day, 2014, CNN was reporting that "volcanic ash smothers part of Indonesia, kills 15."

This volatile activity hadn't abated by the time I was set to leave. A *Daily Mail* headline for that date, May 30, 2014, read, "Flights in and out of Darwin Airport cancelled as ash cloud looms over Northern Territory coast after Indonesian volcano erupts": "Ash from an Indonesian volcano, known as 'Mother of Spirits,' has caused flight cancellations at Darwin [the northern-most city in Australia]."

I sat in a hotel room, stranded in Singapore (although, I gotta say, if you ever have to get stranded in a city, Singapore is about as good as it gets), hoping that we could fly out tomorrow or the next day. It all depended on Mother Nature.

Rufus in Non-Dicatorland

East Timor, Part I

Mother Nature took pity on me, and soon I was on my way to East Timor. (Since East Timor is one of the poorest countries in the world, I spent the flight wondering what internet service there might be like—if they even *had* internet service. Of course, I had to content myself with the fact that I finally *got* to East Timor, considering the volcanic impediment thrown in my path.)

As soon as I arrived, I re-worked my itinerary with the guide and the driver. We immediately decided to dump Dili, the capital (which didn't appear to be much) in favor of heading up into the mountains and the countryside.

The roads were pretty bad, but the rainforest covering the mountains was very nice. Four hours later, we entered Maubisse, a little town established by the Portuguese, the Western power that colonized this area.

My hotel (if you want to call it that; the Timorese call it a "pousada," from the Portuguese for inn or hotel) was a former Portuguese rest house or inn that had gone to seed—a dumpy little place with no hot water (and, of course, if you don't have hot water, you are not going to have internet service). The clocks didn't work, and the beer was warm. (But I am hardcore; warm beer is better than no beer!)

My room was not much to write home about (unless you wanted to write home to complain). It lacked toilet paper; the sink didn't drain; and there was a huge plastic tub under the leaky cold-water shower to catch the dripping water. I'd been in places much worse, so it was no big deal (i.e., not worth writing home about, even if I *had* had internet service). I had finished reading the last book I'd brought with me, so I was hoping that the group of six Australians who were behind me on the road would show up in time for some dinner conversation. I was also wondering, since I would actually be eating a meal in this place, whether the food would be as inviting as the accommodations.

It turned out that the food wasn't bad. The Australians eventually did turn up—dirty, tired, and hungry. One of their two vehicles broke down, so the one working vehicle returned to Dili (an hour-and-a-half ride back) to get another vehicle and driver. Quite frankly, I was amazed that a company in this little impoverished country had a backup vehicle because, as I mentioned, East Timor is one of the poorest countries in the world, and it looks it! Most people in this country survive on less than $1.25 a day!

The plane ride from Singapore to East Timor reminded me of my flight from India to Bangladesh many years ago. Bangladesh is one of the worst and poorest places on earth. It is a hell hole of poverty and despair with some of the worst living conditions on Earth. No one in their right mind goes to Bangladesh! The small plane that I was on to get to Bangladesh from India had eight passengers: a Red Cross representative, a worker for Save the Children, another worker from Catholic Relief Services, an Islamic Red Crescent representative, a poverty-relief specialist from the U.S. State Department, a U.N. representative from UNICEF, a World Bank anti- poverty specialist— and Rufus. The other seven passengers could not believe I was going to Bangladesh "to travel around and see things for myself." (I was originally going to tell you that there were *nine* people on the plane and that the woman sitting next to me was Mother Teresa, but I figured that would be pushing it.) Why did the plane ride remind me of that trip to Bangladesh? Well, maybe because, besides the six Australian travelers, there were currently two German travelers in East Timor—and me. Nine tourists in the entire country!

The beauty of East Timor comes through, even in black and white.

Besides its mountains and forests, the island country of East Timor has some very beautiful beaches.

The people of East Timor do not look Asian but more like the Melanesians of New Guinea, who look very much like black Africans. These people can also be a bit on the aggressive side. I guess that would explain why the Australian army (who fought the Japanese here, commando style, during WWII) loved these guys. The Timorese were daring and courageous fighters. It might also explain why these people—who possess only one half of an island (the eastern half of Timor) and have a population of a million people—took on the largest Moslem nation in the world (Indonesia, which spans 17,000 islands and has 250,000,000 people) in a fight for their independence—and won!

Male hair styles are bit different here. Many boys and men comb their hair from each side to the middle to form a low narrow Mohawk. It actually doesn't look bad over here but would probably look pretty silly back home. Always up for something new, I would have given this fashion a try—except, at this stage of my life, I only had enough hair for a comb-over, not a comb-together.

The next day, after eight or nine hours of traveling we ended up at a different pousada—one that was quite civilized, with air conditioning (that worked), hot water (kind of), internet service (that didn't work at all), beer (warm), and food which I had yet to sample. In other words, it was a five-star luxury hotel in East Timor.

As you may have guessed from my previous paragraph, the downside of traveling in this little country is that you spend most of your time driving and then driving some more. The roads are in very bad shape. It took two days to drive east from the capital, Dili, to the end of the island. If one were able to drive 70 miles an hour here, on an American-style freeway, it would probably have taken four or five hours.

In East Timor, the old saying "All roads lead to Rome" becomes "All roads lead to Dili." No road in East Timor forms a circle, and no road connects to another. Every road radiates out of Dili, so, to get anywhere else, you first have to drive back the same route.

Our travels took us to a number of more isolated villages that don't see much in the way of vehicles, so, as we drove in slowly (due to the poor roads), everyone had to check out the jeep—not to mention the white man (me) in the front seat, about whom they registered visible surprise and curiosity. For, if the people in the remote places to which I travel provide me with opportunities in terms of learning and photography (more often than not, I am visiting very hot, humid, and poor places throughout the world where words such as *hygiene*, *cleanliness*, *sewers*, *toilets*, *garbage pickup*, *sanitation*, *neatness*, *tidiness*, and *beautiful* appear to be unknown), I in a sense return the favor in the form of entertainment for them.

So, as I attempt to document the people by way of photography, the locals are always checking me out, and evidently I must be something of a comical site. With my cargo pants loaded with lenses, a flash, sun screen, a hat that I always forget to put on, maps, pens, notebooks, treats for kids (pens, pencils, and jelly beans), travel documents and passport, etc., I look something like a walking Sears tool box. My Brownell "Buck up, Broncos" t-shirt is matted to both my chest and back with sweat; my hair (what's left of it) is plastered to my head with sweat; my sun glasses are up on my head because the white sun screen on the lenses make them useless; and my feet are shod in over-sized hiking boots. A complete scene for cheap entertainment for the locals.

Another interesting thing about poor, Third-World countries is that they get it all mixed up, in my opinion, as to what should be hot and what should be cold. In the Third World, it's always warm beer and cold showers. I can live with that as long as I don't get thrown in prison (as happened in Zimbabwe), arrested (as in the old Soviet Union), detained by the police (again in the old Soviet Union), ticketed (Yugoslavia), chased by a gang who wanted to rob me (Venezuela), shot at (Nam and Somalia), robbed (Turkey), or denied service or beer (most American bars after 2:00 a.m.).

A number of people lately have been kind enough to compliment my photography. To be brutally honest about it, with no false modesty, the secret is, quite simply, dumb luck. If you work at it hard enough and take enough shots, you are just bound to get some good photographic material. Now, I am hoping everyone reading this noticed the words, "work at it hard enough" because that is exactly what I did that day in East Timor.

While my guide and driver spent an hour and a half having a nice, leisurely midday meal, I skipped lunch and stood in a blazing hot sun doing "people shots." I started by indicating to people that I wanted to take their picture—sometimes by asking them, more usually by gesturing. That approach got maybe one out of every nine people to agree to be photographed, which netted me about 5 photos.

East Timor boy mocking me, my outfit, and my photography.

Desperate times calling for desperate measures, I reverted to the fool-proof mode of shooting pictures sniper style: Hide behind a tree or building, take a shot of the unsuspecting victim, and then move on quickly before the locals raise a commotion or even start throwing rocks and stones at you. It works every time, except that you must do a lot of very quick walking to keep ahead of any angry locals who might decide to form a mob.

East Timor, Part II: Memories of Vietnam and Miss America

After another long drive, we arrived back in Dili, where I would finally have a half day of leisure at a small beach resort. The beaches in East Timor are very nice, sandy, and stereotypically Asian in terms of their beauty and tranquility.

The next day, before leaving on my afternoon flight, I toured Dili, which merely confirmed my original impression—that it wasn't much. In the entire country of East Timor, there are five traffic lights, and—from what I could tell—they were all in Dili within a few blocks of each other. Dili has two small museums, both dealing with the East Timorese's struggle for independence. At one of the museums, I had an unexpected encounter: I met— or perhaps I should say *saw*—Miss East Timor as she was making some sort of appearance.

Now, that brought back memories from many years ago when I actually had a date with, of all people, Miss America. It is something of a funny story for everyone but me.

I had my date with Miss America 'way back in December 1970. At the time, I was convalescing in a hospital after having been wounded a few days earlier in a firefight in the Que Son Valley of South Vietnam. (See "Shot Up in the Que Son Valley.") It wasn't much of a hospital and didn't look like any hospital I had ever seen. Basically it was a bunch of small, dirty tents. This is where they sent you if you were wounded but didn't look like you were going to die.

In my travels I have had encounters with three beauty queens: Miss Ivory Coast, Miss East Timor, and Miss Solomon Islands, pictured here. I also had a date with Miss South Carolina, kind of. (See text, "Memories of Vietnam and Miss America.")

I would guess that there were about 80 of us patients in these hot, hot tents, which lacked air conditioning, fans, or even ventilation—not to mention electricity, lights,

[247]

toilets, sinks, or showers. When I was medivac'd from the bush and placed in the hospital, I underwent the same treatment as everyone else. The doctors tended to my wounds, stopped all bleeding, and bandaged me up—but no one bothered to clean me or wash me. Like all the other grunts out in the bush, I was covered with weeks of sweat, dirt, and animal and human shit from walking through the rice paddies. I didn't look good. I didn't smell good. I didn't feel good, and I was in a lot of pain. In short, I was not in a very happy mood.

I was trying to get some sleep when a Marine Captain ordered all of us out of the tents for a formation, and nobody was very happy about that. The Captain was aware of our discontent, so he started off by saying, "I know none of you men are overjoyed about a formation, but I have good news for you." Even as dumb as most Marines are, I don't think one Marine fell for that one. From its founding in 1775 until the present, the Marine Corps has *never* had good news—at least, not for Marines.

He went on to say that Miss America was here on tour with a delegation and that two lucky Marines were going to be chosen to meet with her and spend some time with her. *Holy shit!* This changed everything, and the Captain definitely had everyone's attention now.

I don't know if anyone is aware of this, but, during the Vietnam War, if you were a Marine grunt, you were pretty much done with women for the next 13 months of your tour of duty. There were no women Marines in Nam, no female nurses or doctors, and only old grannies in the villages and hamlets. We could never figure out where the local villagers hid their daughters—a situation about which we used to frequently speculate. Some said they did orderly work for the Viet Cong; others said they had been sent to the cities. It really didn't matter; they were gone. And the bottom line for us was that this was a war we were going to fight like chaste monks.

Suddenly put Miss America in the presence of 80 Marines between 18 and 25 years old, and you have the makings of a world record for adolescent, impure, and lustful thoughts never to be equaled again. Every Marine had the exact same thought, "How do I get to be one of the lucky two out of 80 to be a part of this deal?"

Now Marine Corps history and culture tells us that Marines will fight to the death for their fellow Marines and that the Marines are most proud of their tradition of never leaving their wounded or even their dead behind. But that's combat and war, and right now the Captain was talking about something far more important than combat, duty, honor, and patriotism. He was talking about women—or at least one! And, in that case, an entirely different aspect of Marine culture kicked in: It's called "survival of the fittest" or "stab your buddy in the back" or "every man for himself."

Naturally, everyone wanted to meet with Miss America, but we were told that priority would be given to anyone from South Carolina because that was the state that this Miss America was from. The Captain asked if anyone was from South Carolina. Now, you are not going to believe this in a million years—in fact, it's something of a miracle— but every single Marine in that hospital was from the state of South Carolina—including me! Because Miss America hailed from South Carolina, I don't think I had ever been more proud of my beloved state of South Carolina than I was at that moment.

Now, this Captain, like most Marine officers, was not too bright, and he appeared to be shocked that every man in the hospital was from South Carolina. You could tell from the expression on his face that he thought *something* was fishy, but he couldn't quite make the mental leap to figure it out. Maybe he thought the Viet Cong had been given orders the week before to shoot only Marines from South Carolina—who knows?

Sometimes you have to think fast and move fast, and that's exactly what I did. While everyone was standing in formation yelling that they were from South Carolina, I simply walked up to the Captain, saluted, and said I was from South Carolina and would be proud to represent my native state. He immediately chose me as one of the two to meet Miss America.

At that point, the other 79 or so Marines were enraged and ready to kill me because the chance of one of them being chosen just dropped significantly.

I thought I was home free when one very angry Marine yelled up to the Captain—and I would like to use his exact words for the record— "Sir, that lying son of a bitch isn't from South Carolina! Just two days ago he told me he was from Michigan."

Now, this accusation presented a problem. The Captain looked at me sternly, and, without so much as a pause, I said, "Sir, that's not true. I've never set foot in Michigan in my entire life." I was in so deep now I didn't dare back down. I made this declaration with such seeming truth and conviction that the Captain believed me.

So we had one man ready to go (me, a proud South Carolinian if there ever was one) and one yet to be chosen—when, suddenly, things took a strange turn. The Captain was doing a pretty poor job of keeping his story straight, and somehow we figured out it really wasn't Miss America but a Miss South Carolina. There was some grumbling about being misled, but, hey, I didn't care if she had come in 50th out of the 50 states; it was still good enough for me, and I was still in.

Then still another strange turn. Somehow, we also figured out this gal was not the *current* Miss South Carolina. When we asked what year she became Miss South Carolina, the Captain hemmed and hawed and talked in circles. We then started doing the math (with Marines from the Southern states using their fingers and taking their socks and boots off so they could count better).

From what little information we received, we figured she had won her contest about 10 or 12 years ago, which would make her, like, 30 or 31. Collectively, in a less than a second, we were all out. Nobody, and I mean nobody, at our age would ever be so desperate or so hard-up as to go out with a wrinkled-up, over-the-hill old bag of 30 or 31! It just goes to show you what idiots we were in our youth. Every one of us imagined that a 30-year-old gal was in the same age bracket as our grandmothers! There is no other way to put it: the way we reckoned age at that point in our lives was adolescent and stupid.

Now none of us, including me, wanted anything to do with her. But I was stuck, and the Captain was exasperated with all of us, so he just volunteered another Marine to go with me, dismissed the rest, and then instructed us on what to do and how to behave. His last words were not to say or do anything stupid or we would pay hell for it, wounded or not.

Then the Captain dropped a bigger bombshell on us, "By the way, the delegation she's with is a religious delegation, so *no swearing*."

Damn, a religious delegation! That didn't sound good—especially with the way I swore all the time, especially at the time. Here I thought I was being so damn smart, and my scheme had backfired on me.

We arrived at the place where the Captain had sent us to find two old ministers, both with all-white hair, in all-black cleric clothing, and, along with them, Miss America—well, Miss South Carolina.

I don't know what we were expecting. I think we both were hoping that she was a hot babe and would be dressed in some outlandish, over-the-top, sexy clothing: at least a mini skirt—maybe even a bikini! (After all, it was hot as hell here.) It turns out she was pretty ordinary looking and dressed nicely but in nothing even close to the fantasies we had in mind.

She was nice and friendly to us when suddenly I caught it—her eyes. This poor girl had already seen 'way too much. She had volunteered for this good-will mission, had given her time for this good-will gesture, and the military had callously exploited that, dragging her to one hospital after another with guys in far worse condition than us (the walking wounded). She had seen too many horribly wounded and mangled bodies of 19- and 20-year-olds, and you could see it as clear as day in her plaintive eyes. I guess today you would say she was suffering from post-traumatic stress disorder (PTSD). In a weird reversal of roles, the other Marine and I tried to cheer *her* up.

Well I was actually feeling pretty good about myself. I did my good deed by trying to help someone who I felt was not in a very good mental condition. I had been polite and had even refrained from making my usual sarcastic or smart-aleck remarks. I started to take my leave when one of the ministers spoke up for the first time and said we should read a bible verse. I wasn't happy about that but couldn't figure any way to refuse his request. It was brief and not too painful.

I again attempted to escape when the *other* minister suggested we pray together. This situation was heading downhill real fast. I tried to weasel out of it by saying I was Catholic and didn't know any Protestant prayers, but he said, "Surely, as a good Christian, you know the Lord's Prayer". Damn! I forgot about that one, and so I was trapped again. I was tempted to tell them I was an atheist just to get out of this mess but thought the better of it. They would probably want to convert me, and that would take even longer.

So we said the Lord's Prayer, which is short, and I figured they couldn't possibly come up with anything more to keep me there when the first minister said, "How about we end this wonderful meeting of brotherhood by singing a hymn?" Now, I can't carry a tune to save my life. I sing horribly and don't know the words to any song except "Happy Birthday." I attempted to play my ace card again by saying that we Catholics were not allowed to participate in other religions, but that didn't work well either. The preacher said I could just hum along.

So the former Miss South Carolina with post traumatic disorder, the shot-up Marine, and two old preachers started singing—off key—some weird religious song I had never heard. I felt like a complete dork trying to hum along, just as I now feel like complete dork writing about it. It was embarrassing and pretty awkward. It did lead to another interesting discovering about myself and that is this: I not only can't sing; I can't hum either.

And that's how I got a date with Miss America (South Carolina), kind of.

*****

The year 2014 marked my 46th year of travel, and I had, in all that time, never gotten sick on a trip. Knock on wood. At this point, I had

Longitude and Latitude, with Attitude

only five more countries to do. Two (Cuba and Nauru) were difficult. The other three (Libya, Niger, and Mauritania) were currently impossible because of terrorism and al Qaeda. But I figured, if I could get into North Korea, I could get into Cuba. And if I could find my way to the out-of-the-way East Timor, I could make it to Nauru (which—as you already know if you've been reading this book from the beginning, straight-through—I did).

Rufus McGaugh

Rufus Travels to Cuba, and Comes Back a Commie Smoking a Cigar!

Day 1 and 2—Getting There

Going to Cuba was still illegal by U.S. law when I did it (22 November 2014 to 30 November 2014). To manage it, one had to first fly to a third country—in my case, Mexico. Just getting to Cuba was a hassle in terms of travel time. It took me all day to get to a country only 90 miles off shore of the U.S.

If I had waited a month or two, it would have been easier. As the website Legal Cuba Travel (www. legalcubatravel.com) explained it, "In December 2014 President Obama greatly expanded legal Cuba travel opportunities for Americans. On January 16, 2015 his Office of Foreign Assets Control (OFAC) issued regulations allowing nearly every American to visit Cuba without applying for a license." But time and Rufus wait for no man. What fun would it have been if it had been *easy*? And, anyway, I like to think that it was *my* trip to the island, my overwhelming American charm and good will, that "broke the blockade" and allowed Cuba travel for all.

My flight from Mexico to Havana was uneventful except for the breakfast meal provided by Cubana Airlines. It was some sort of breakfast sandwich with a meat patty that consisted mostly of fat, gristle, and whatever else may have been at hand. I suspect that, after they made this meal, there were several fewer stray dogs lurking about Havana. (So maybe Cubana Airlines had the same chef as Koryo Airlines—or they used the same *How to Stick It to Imperialist, Capitalist Dogs by Serving Them Dog* cookbook.)

After arriving, we were picked up by the bike-tour group. (Did I tell you I was going to Cuba to take part in a bike tour? Well, I was. Have I told you that I'm a glutton for punishment? Well, I am. I had suffered a bike accident at home a few months before, breaking my left collarbone. I was hoping it would heal sufficiently so I could make this trip and cycle Cuba. And it did. Pretty much. I went on the trip anyway.)

We headed to central Cuba, which consisted of a very long ride on a so-called freeway with little traffic. For, by the way, Cuba is a big country, relatively speaking. Most of us think Cuba's like most of the rest of the places in the Caribbean—a small island. But Cuba is 800 miles across, east to west! (For comparison purposes, it's about 700 miles to drive from Chicago to Washington, DC.)

At one of our rest stops, a nickel or dime in local currency gained you admittance to the toilet—with a bonus of 5 squares (approximately seven inches' worth) of toilet paper. I immediately started praying that my 46-year-long string of luck (not getting sick while traveling) would continue and that I would not develop any stomach problems on this trip.

Dinner that night was in the historic town of Santa Clara at a beautiful colonial edifice that was decorated with colorful ceramic tiles, plants, paintings, sculptures, and mahogany furniture from the past. The weather was beautiful—pleasantly warm and perfect, so we had our delicious meal of fresh locally grown food, with plenty of wine and *cerveza* (beer)—outside on a garden balcony.

This was an all-inclusive tour. (For those of you who don't know, "all-inclusive" means the price of the trip includes lodging, all meals and snacks, and beer, wine, and liquor. Unusually, the Cuba tour did *not* include beer, wine and liquor, but the bike-company owner usually paid for almost all our beer as a nice gesture.) The Cuban resort we stayed in initially looked like something out of the 1950s. Everything was clean, well-managed, efficient, and old fashioned, and everyone seemed to enjoy it that way. "Everyone" consisted of a dozen of us: me, my brother-in-law Tom, two Cubans, seven Canadians, and the owner/guide, Danny, also a Canadian. Thirteen years before, in Canada, Danny's parents had put Danny, who was 19 at the time, and his 14-year-old brother on a boat destined for Cuba, along with 30 bicycles to start this business in Cuba. And now look at him: he had Rufus as a customer!

Day 3: The End (Not of the Trip but of Rufus!)

After breakfast, we went by bus to a picturesque area, pulled the bikes out of the trailer, and started a 36-kilometer (or 22.5-mile) ride through scenic countryside dotted by small villages and towns. The final 10 kilometers took us straight up a beautiful mountain that is 400 times higher than Mt. Everest (or at least it appeared to be if you happened to have the bad luck to be on a bicycle doing the pedaling).

Elevation not only worked against us, but the climate was a co-conspirator. The official temperature this day was 105 degrees F! Having been there (and *never* being one to exaggerate or embellish), I would suggest the temperature that day was closer to 205 degrees F.

In any case, we all struggled to get up this dreadful monster of a mountain that just a few sentences earlier I was describing as beautiful. And now I must confess that, after all these years when no hill or mountain ever beat me, I had met my match. And to further my humiliation, I was forced to endure the ultimate shame of any biker: I got off my bike and started pushing it up that damn mountain. I lost my pride, my dignity, my bragging rights, my machismo, and my manhood—all to a commie mountain!

*****

The pause above was due to my sobbing over this great humiliation. It also gave me a chance to run downstairs and grab another beer!

Most people at this point would probably let go of this shameful indignity and move on, but that would be most people. So, instead of admitting total defeat and waiting for the bus to rescue me, I soldiered on, pushing that damn bike up Mt. Everest (which in Cuban Spanish is pronounced *Mt. Kill-a-Yankee*). The heat continued unabated. (Have I mentioned the heat, which was 305 degrees F?)

I continued pushing my bike upward when I came across my brother-in-law Tom, dead, on his bike. I mean he wasn't moving as he sat exhausted on his bike. But, by God, he was not going to dismount even if he couldn't move! (He was playing by biker rules: the cyclists' culture says you don't get off the bike even if you can't go forward.) So I passed him—neither of us having the strength to even acknowledge the other.

We leap-frogged each other a few times after this until, finally, I mustered my last reserves and was able to pedal to the finish—one of the few to do so. But, alas, it was too late to salvage my pride and dignity. Not that many of the other cyclists had any pride or dignity left. Most members of the group were a bit upset by or angry over such a difficult ride that most could not even complete.

We then had a lunch of good Cuban food, consisting of not one thing I could identify or had ever seen or tasted before.

The hotel we stayed in that night overlooked the pretty town square. Tom and I walked around the area, admiring the beautiful colonial architecture, all of which was painted in pastel colors, but in the afterglow of this phenomenal trip I would rather sing the praises of the beautiful and delightful local Cuban beer, Christel, which Tom and I indulged in throughout the trip.

Day 4: Easy Rider

The morning briefing described today's ride as an "easier one" than the Mt. Everest climb we made yesterday. Everybody was happy about that. The ride would be 60 kilometers (about 40 miles), and there was even a point where those who wanted to punk out or wanted an easier ride could bail out of the last 12 miles. However, the weather and heat were still a concern for most (especially the Canadians, who all seemed to be from some area of Canada colder than the North Pole). Yesterday's ride had already taken a toll on our group. Two people were down with heat exhaustion, including one of the guides.

We began the ride in the morning coolness—95 degrees F. Although, on paper, today's ride looked easier than the Mt. Everest ride of yesterday, just about everybody after 40 kilometers decided that they had had enough, especially with the temperature again rising to 105. Finishing the journey on an air-conditioned bus with a refrigerator stocked with cold beer seemed to be a smarter and more civilized way to end the day's journey for nearly everyone.

But there were a few fools who decided to gut it out all the way on a bike, no doubt due to some deep psychological issues involving machismo or masochism (I always get those two mixed up). And, of course, without reading any further, you have probably already figured out who one of those fools was. Yes, naturally it was yours truly, Rufus.

So the guide and I and three other knuckleheads set off for the fabled colonial city of Trinidad, which was only 17 kilometers away—a piece of cake even at 105 degrees F. Though temperatures were climbing, the landscape looked very un-Everest like, so off I went with what Mark Twain described as "all the confidence of a Christian with four aces."

I have to admit I was already pretty tired, but, since the landscape looked no different than the last 40 kilometers, I figured "no problem," and that naïve thought stayed with me until I arrived at what I could only describe as the Pike's Peak of Cuba. Perhaps the *Matterhorn* of Cuba might be a more apt description of what I was facing and would need to ascend if I wanted to get into Trinidad.

I did it! I even stayed on my bike the entire time in an attempt to salvage some of the dignity and manhood I lost back on Mt. Everest. I finished the ride looking pretty good—or at least that's what everyone said; I don't really remember any of it. I got off my bike and felt a bit wobbly and then started staggering around like a drunken Irishman (something I have a good amount of experience doing but usually not from riding a bicycle).

Day 5: The Best Lunch I Have Ever Had

Today's ride was through gorgeous green mountains on one side and the shoreline of the blue Caribbean on the other side. Lunch was at a little nondescript bamboo stall similar to all the others seen from one end of Cuba to the other (or, for that matter, which are pervasive throughout most of the poor Third-World countries). It was clean—and even had clean white tablecloths! And even more amazing it was probably the best lunch I have ever had in my life. The meal consisted of a grilled lobster with shrimp stewed in a thick garlic sauce, a filet of fish with fresh tomatoes, cabbage, cucumbers, white rice, and fried bananas.

Dinner tonight was interesting because we were taken to the restaurant in Cuban rickshaws.

Day 6: Crash Landing in Cuba

Arriving at our hotel in Havana, we discovered that our room had a small balcony that overlooked a central area of the city. It was the equivalent of having a room on the Champs-Elysées in Paris. Havana is truly an amazing and vibrant city, where one can overdose on some of the finest colonial architecture in the world.

The drive out of Havana went past one of the more interesting sites of the day: the Bay of Pigs, where the failed CIA-sponsored invasion of Cuba by Cuban exiles took place under President Kennedy in 1961.

Our bike ride today would be through a national park and included the most stunning scenery we'd seen all week. Unfortunately, I didn't get to see a lot of it.

We were on another mountain. But that was okay. As I said, the scenery was gorgeous, and the ride was going well—when, suddenly, my riding companion for the day, a Canadian doctor, swerved to avoid one of the many pot holes in the road and crashed immediately in front of me. I attempted to brake so as to not run her over.

My attempt to avoid injuring her led to my own accident and injuries. By braking so abruptly, I was thrown from my bike and over the handle bars.

The momentum caused me to continue tumbling down the mountain.

I first hit my right collarbone, then my left collarbone (the one I'd broken three months before and which hadn't completely healed yet), then fell on my right elbow, continued down the mountain, striking my left wrist on the pavement, and finally stopped—probably because there wasn't any other part of me left to hit.

I sat up but was stunned and somewhat in shock, unable to speak. I tried to get up, but my left arm was too weak from the earlier broken collarbone and the now-fractured wrist. When I attempted to use my right arm to push myself up I was unable to do so because of a fractured humerus (the bone which leads to the elbow). Oh, yeah: I had also fractured a finger on my left hand.

Our Cuban bus driver, the Canadian doctor whom I had been riding alongside, and another group member got me to my feet. They started leading to me the bus, but I said I would finish the ride, which was only another 12 or so kilometers. So I walked the bike about a quarter of a mile, got back on it, and finished the day's ride. Of course, at the time I did not realize I had all these broken bones and mistakenly thought I had dodged the bullet.

Later, I did a half-day walking tour of Havana, went to dinner, and drank a few beers. I slept a while, then got up at 3:00 a.m. for the nearly day-long return trip home.

The last leg of my 23-hour journey back from Cuba had me sitting next to a University of Michigan doctor. We struck up a conversation, and he proceeded to tell me that he was returning from a wonderful trip to Turkey, where he had attended a medical conference. Listening to him, you could tell he was still "in the moment," basking in the afterglow of what had evidently been a fantastic trip.

After he finished his tale, I figured I would share the events of my Cuba trip with him. As my story progressed and I got to the part about my bike accident, describing my descent down the mountain, banging one shoulder and arm after another until I finally stopped, I could see him becoming more and more distressed. "You need to seek medical attention as soon as possible once you get home" he stated.

"Nah! I'm okay, just banged up a bit." I answered.

The doctor recoiled as though he had been struck in the face. He gave me a look of incredulous surprise. "I think that right elbow is broken" he declared.

I gave it a cursory glance and said, "Nah. It's just bruised and swollen."

"Your elbow is the size of a cantaloupe, so I would think it might be fractured," the doctor insisted.

True, I hadn't been able to fit my right arm into the sleeve of my winter jacket because it had swollen to such a great size. Still, my total lack of education or knowledge of medicine and anatomy allowed me to cling to my belief that my left arm and elbow were simply bruised and swollen.

Again claiming that I was okay and assuring him that nothing was broken, I put on a demonstration to prove it by moving my broken arm over my back, around my back, and up my back to prove the point that my arm was functioning well and had suffered no serious injury.

The doctor, however, refused to be convinced. Not backing down from his airline-seat diagnosis, he said, "I don't care what you can do with that right arm, I'm sure you have fractured the elbow."

As it turned out, the good doctor's advice did not go totally unheeded. I was very conscious of the fact that I have a pretty good threshold for pain and therefore may have been ignoring or not quite feeling the seriousness of my condition. So, at the end of my 23 hours of travel, after arriving at Detroit Metropolitan Airport, I took one more trip—to Beaumont Hospital's Emergency Room, where they confirmed the doctor's diagnosis and fitted me for an uncomfortable brace and cast, a hometown souvenir of my Cuban voyage.

*****

As you may have guessed by now, when I have a project or mission, my drive and focus are very intense by anyone's standards. My will to succeed and to accomplish my goals under the most grueling conditions might well be my strongest personality trait.

Consider my stint in Vietnam—that enforced "vacation" which either instilled in me my wanderlust or, more likely, stoked the fire of a yen for travel that had burned in me since I was 10. When our chopper was hit on its rescue mission and I got shot up in the leg and hip, along with those two other unfortunate Marines, I still joined my gun team in the fire fight that followed (thus sustaining my second and third wounds), and only at the end was I medevac'd to a hospital.

When I was being patched up, a Navy corpsman who was treating me kept looking at me in an odd way (kinda like that doctor on the plane), and finally he asked, "Weren't you on the chopper with the other two Marines who got shot up?"

"Yes," I answered.

"Then why didn't you just *stay* on the chopper like the other two wounded Marines did?" he wanted to know.

"It never occurred to me" I replied.

I would just like to add that my enemies—and I have many—will tell you that both of these stories show a man with more guts than brains.

Guilty.

Getting Eric

Of all the stories in this book, the most precious one, and the most important one, will be this one. This story involved traveling thousands of miles, spending more money than I had ever spent in my life (significantly more than what, for many years of my life, I earned in an entire year), and navigating through a formerly hostile country whose language I did not speak. At times it was nerve wracking and fraught with potential diplomatic disappointment.

This story too had all the usual misadventures and problems we seemed to have on every trip, but in this case it was no laughing matter, then or now. Failure in our endeavor would be devastating; success would bring great joy. I am talking about the trip my wife, Monica, and I made to Russia in 1996 to adopt the love of our life, baby Eric.

We were married in 1993 when I was 44. My bride, Monica, was 40. It seemed as if we tried everything under the sun to have a baby but with no luck. We then turned to adoption, which is not an easy or foolproof solution, as we found out—especially at our age. The age factor pretty much disqualified us for a domestic adoption, so we began to investigate foreign adoptions, and it was very complicated. We went to meetings and checked out adoption agencies and did our research.

In 1996 the four countries that stood at the top of the list for couples actually ending up with a baby were China (almost entirely baby girls), Guatemala, Russia, and Romania. Each country had its own unique problems, issues, bureaucracy, and cost, which on average was $20,000.

We ultimately decided to use an adoption agency out of Texas called Los Niños. The founder of Los Niños, Heinrich Erichsen, was a former German soldier whose service in World War II would alter his whole life dramatically. After the war he dedicated his life to humanity and attempted to make the world a better place.

Los Niños worked in Russia, so it looked like our adoptee was going to be a Russian baby. Partly because of that, we were fortunate to have Heinrich's daughter-in-law Trish living only two miles from us in the same community. Trish was a great person, very bright and energetic, and—most important of all—a fluent Russian speaker and writer.

We filled out the reams of paperwork, forms, and applications and waited. We were told it would be a year and half before getting a baby—if we were lucky. I tipped off my principal at school that at some point I would be taking a two-week leave of absence with very little prior notice. All we could do now was sit back and wait.

Nine months later we received word that there was a baby available; were we interested? We were, sight unseen! Four heads, nine toes, or six eyes, it didn't matter; we're not the fussy type. Plus, I always figured, kids are kids. Then we received a grainy video of the baby that lasted all of three or four minutes, showing a nurse holding the baby and trying to get him to do something—anything. The baby, however, didn't seem too interested in participating in this dog-and-pony show. Monica immediately fell in love with this six-month-old baby, but she's a total sap who would fall in love with any baby. My impression was, well, it was a baby.

The little guy didn't look as if he would win any beauty contests. His face was covered with what looked like big, brown warts. However, I thought, *Even homely kids need a mom and dad too*, so I was okay with the warts. (We would discover later that he didn't have warts; he had mosquito bites. But a blue medicine had been put on his bites, and the video was of such poor quality that it turned the blue bumps into what looked like brown warts.) Every once in a while God rewards me for doing the right thing, and this time, as it would turn out, I would win the jackpot. So we continued to wait for our baby.

The Russian Parliament was in the process of changing foreign-adoption laws—again—and Los Niños was concerned that, if the age for parents was changed, it might disqualify me. So Los Niños went into overdrive to make this adoption happen.

A short time later—it was a Friday—I came home from school, where I had been working late; it was well after 5:00 p.m. Monica, too, had been home for only a little while. She was sitting at our dining-room table with a huge stack of papers from the adoption agency. The instructions accompanying the forms to be filled out included an important alert that they needed to be completed and mailed by 5:00 p.m.!

Monica was devastated and at her wits' end. I was sanguine and philosophical about it: if not this baby, then another. To this day, I wince every time I think of that episode and my cavalier attitude. I might have been philosophical about it and ready to move on, but the future mother, who had bonded with her baby, by way of the worst-quality video ever made, was not giving up. For the next few hours, Monica answered every question and filled out every form in that mountain of paper work. But we were too late; it was 'way past 5:00, and FedEx then was not what it is today. We had one of the least-appetizing dinners of our life that night, poisoned by the perceived loss of that child.

The next morning Trish Erichsen called from Russia and said to FedEx the documents; it was not too late. Now, even God was working overtime. (Of course, it dawned on me that this beneficence was probably not God rewarding me but the other half of this marriage, the one who actually bothered to go to church on Sunday.)

It was Saturday, and the only FedEx open in Detroit was downtown by Tiger Stadium. I drove Indianapolis-500 style all the way, and the documents were sent. *Whew!*

There was a catch, though: the documents were on their way, but we were not. We had to leave Monday to be in Russia, on Tuesday—and this was Saturday. Holy shit! We were totally unprepared and in near panic.

The first thing I needed was two flights to Russia—to some weird city that I had not only never been to but had never even heard of: Saratov. I do a lot of traveling, and I had a great travel agency, Greatways of Grosse Pointe, and a super travel agent, Margaret Harms, whose son Marty was currently sitting in my 7th-grade social-studies class. I called Margaret, and she leaped into action. She drove to the closed office, arranged our flights, and brought them to the house. Talk about service! I next called my principal and said I would be out for the two weeks, and, I hoped, when I returned, we would have a baby (because it was still an iffy proposition). His only words were, "Good luck!"

Monday arrived, and Monica and I ran around making last-minute purchases for a baby. I was kept busy in the money department. The adoption would cost $20,000. It would be paid piecemeal to a variety of courts, government agencies, and provincial courts on the spot in Russia. No credit cards, travelers' cheques, personal checks, or even Russian rubles would be accepted. It was all to be done in American cash, brand-new U.S. one-hundred-dollar bills no more than two years old.

I knew that last part was going to be the killer. But off I went, first to my credit union to withdraw $20,000 dollars, and an extra $2,000 for expenses. While I was at the credit union, I garnered up as many brand-new one-hundred-dollar bills as they had.

As it turned out, the Detroit Teachers Credit Union didn't keep a lot of brand-new one-hundred-dollar bills lying around, so I left with only a few. That's when I started my tour of local banks within the Detroit Metropolitan area.

Initially, despite every bank and every teller going out of their way to assist me, especially upon hearing my story about adopting a baby from Russia, things were not going real well in the "gathering-up-one-hundred-dollar-bills-in-excellent-shape-no-older-than-two-years" department. But, finally, after visiting many banks and credit unions, putting another 10,000 miles on my car to accomplish this feat, I had $20,000 in brand-new one-hundred-dollar bills and another $2,000 in smaller denominations. The thought crossed my mind: *Is everything in Russia one hundred dollars? Doesn't anything cost five, ten or twenty dollars? If everybody is dealing only in hundreds, how do you get change?* I guessed we would get the answers once we got there.

We were now ready to roll. Well, not quite. Little Miss "I Have to Eat or I'll Faint" had to have lunch—based on the flimsy rationale that I had ruled out breakfast that morning because of all we had going on. It's really difficult trying to live with a very unreasonable person who wants to eat all the time—sometimes as often as three times a day!

We went to our very favorite Greasy Spoon, Travis'. Whenever we felt the need to elevate our cholesterol level, this was our favorite place to do it.

As we walked into the small restaurant, I spotted an old colleague, Don Dungan, who had recently retired. Seeing me, he was (I could see) wondering why I was there in the middle of the school day. After our hellos, that's exactly what he inquired about. "Well, Rufus, did you take a personal day today?"

"Yes. In fact, I took 10 personal days," I replied.

"Really!" He was surprised.

"Yeah, in about three hours my wife and I are flying to Russia for two weeks."

"Really! You're going to Russia during the school year?" he asked in almost alarm.

"Yeah, there's a six-month-old baby there, waiting for us to adopt him."

"Really!" he replied again. Don was silent for a moment, shook his head, and then said, "You know, Rufus, it's always a little different and unusual talking to you."

Well, that's one way of looking at it.

Our cholesterol elevated to the desired level, we took off for the airport.

We had a long flight to Moscow and then a connecting flight to Saratov on the Volga River in the very heart of Mother Russia. We landed in the evening in total darkness. Notwithstanding the lack of light, we could see, through some perverse miracle, that this airport looked much worse and more dilapidated than any airport I had ever been to back in communist times when just about everything in Russia looked like hell and ready to collapse. Right off the bat, my alarm system was up and functioning.

Longitude and Latitude, with Attitude

Prior to this trip I had twice been to Russia when it was the U.S.S.R., a communist state, and I had also traveled to a slew of other authoritarian dictatorships in Africa and Asia and Red China. I knew from firsthand experience that breaking the rules or laws in such places could be met with Draconian measures frequently resulting in prison time. I often push the limits and skirt the rules a bit, but I like to think that I am never reckless or foolhardy or, even worse, stupid. But we had been advised—a number of times—that, when going through Customs in Russia to lie about the amount of money that we were carrying.

I had a problem with this. I am a traveler and would be a scholar, if I were smarter; but I am not James Bond or working contract for the CIA. This whole lying-to-the-authorities thing gave me the heebie-jeebies. My goal was to end up with a baby, not in a prison cell. The adoption agency insisted that fibbing was the only way to go, so we fibbed—and it actually worked. I can't remember how much money I told Russian customs I was carrying, but it certainly was nowhere near the $22,000 I had scattered all through my body, clothes, shoes, and backpack.

Leaving the terminal, we followed the Russian crowd, which seemed to be as hesitant and leery of its pitch-black surroundings as we were. We just kept moving forward, hoping to be greeted by someone or to see someone holding a sign with our name on it—anything. We continued walking through what appeared to be airport tunnels that were barely lit and reeked of alcohol and urine, with 'way too many shady and tough-looking characters eyeballing the lambs of prey walking by. Every crook, thief, and hoodlum in Russia knew that every Westerner, American, or Japanese businessman or tourist carried cash, and probably lots of it.

This was not looking good. It got worse before it got better. Eventually, we were walking outside in the darkness, where many people, including us, were tripping over the broken walkways and sidewalks, which were all in a horrible state.

At least a few people appeared to know where they were going, so they went, and the crowd started to thin out somewhat, but the rest of us in this ever-diminishing herd kept on ambling, clueless as to what direction to proceed in.

A man, a pretty big guy, approached us and said he was from the adoption agency. Monica and I met this news with relief on the one hand, but on the other I was still on guard. Who was this guy and was he really who he said he was? Should I trust this big, bearded, sloppily and ill-dressed bum or con man? I hate to say that, but that's what he looked like. The more I looked him over, the worse it got. His shoes looked exactly like the dirty, flattened-out, and worn-out shoes one sees on a wino or street person in our big cities. I started looking around to see if there was anyone else that might be there to pick us up—I mean the *real* person the adoption agency had sent out rather than this opportunistic criminal.

I couldn't see anyone. I had little choice but to follow this guy who seemed 'way too eager to carry our luggage. I declined his offer, stating that I was very physically fit and strong and well capable of carrying my own luggage. That declaration was meant to send a message to Hercules, towering above me, that he was not dealing with a pushover. Even Monica declined the offer from this chivalric Sir Lancelot. She too, without saying anything to me, must have sensed the danger and the oddity of our greeter.

Nevertheless, like captives, we followed this huge hulk of a man to a distant corner of the airport parking lot. (Why was his car 'way off in no man's land when there was row after row of totally empty parking lanes?) After putting our luggage in the trunk of a junky little Russian-made Lada, an auto often describe as a communist-inspired motorized roller skate, we got into the vehicle to discover another pretty-good-sized guy, silently sitting in the driver's seat.

Now (as I explained to you in an earlier chapter about what I had to deal with the year before in Turkmenistan), the one problem that marriage had brought to travel was that I obviously felt protective toward my wife. This meant that one option—flight—from a bad situation was always out of the question. That left the other option—fight. I don't want to get all macho or anything, but I can stand my ground and fight with the best—or worst—of them. But I also like to think that I am no fool. If I can get out of a bad situation and save my money—or my camera, or myself—by running, I am more than willing to attempt to break any and all speed records by fleeing as fast and as far as I can. However, I couldn't expect Monica to be able to sprint with me. And I certainly wasn't going to leave her behind to the tender mercies of these Russian linebackers.

The very large man who had picked us, and had somehow defied all the laws of physics by squeezing into the front seat of the tiny tin can of a Lada, now turned to Monica and me in the back seat. He told us his name was Sasha. As it would turn out, in this two-week trip, we would meet a whole bunch of Sashas, both men and women. He seemed friendly, but I was definitely on guard. I could tell Monica was not at ease either. He made small talk and seemed amiable enough—people who rob other people tend to be the friendliest humans on Earth.

After what appeared to be a long drive, we pulled up to what turned out to be old Soviet public housing or apartments, and Sasha directed us to get out of the car. I did so but kept scanning the area looking for any confederates of this guy or anything suspicious. My vigilance never ended until after we were led into a building and up two flights of stairs. Sasha knocked on a nondescript door, and a blonde woman of about thirty answered the door. She did not speak a single word of English but did seem to be expecting us. She motioned to all of us to enter.

We had now just entered, not the Twilight Zone, but the classic, stereotypical, Russian apartment from back in the communist days. It was beyond cramped. My barracks' space in the Marines and then my skid-row housing in the ghetto of Detroit during my years at Wayne State as a struggling student looked palatial compared to this habitat. The poorest Japanese family living in a cramped tenth-rate apartment in Tokyo would feel they had been downgraded in this place. The main room of the apartment, the living room, was so small that the four of us could not fit into it standing—nor sitting, which would have been a pointless exercise because there was only a single piece of furniture in the room, a small love seat that would accommodate two people. While Sasha was speaking to the blonde woman, I was physically forced into the hallway; there simply was not enough room for me in the room. Later, when Sasha began to leave and was giving last-minute information—he had to stand in the hallway while I took his spot in the main room of the apartment.

Sasha and the woman talked in Russian for some time before he explained to us that we would spend the night here. Tomorrow someone would contact us—or maybe the next day. Then he turned and left. Great! Two days in a cramped Russian apartment with a woman who didn't speak a word of English! We were a bit stunned by the sudden desertion. We hadn't been robbed or assaulted, but what in the heck was going on?

When we finally collected ourselves and our thoughts, we turned to the woman. She smiled at us. We were at a total loss. In desperation, we attempted to get some information or make sense of this situation by conversing with the English-deficient woman, but it was useless. To every question or enquiry, she would smile and say "Laura," which appeared to be her name.

Then she guided us to our bedroom, which in our country we call by another name: a closet. It had a simple, single twin bed—just like the little bed I slept in upstairs in the finished attic when I was twelve years old and growing up in Warren, Michigan. How cute! Except I'm a lot bigger now. And have a wife I usually sleep with. However, as my wife,

Monica, can well attest, we have been in worse lodgings—especially on my travel budget.

The next ten, eleven, or twelve days were nothing but a blur.

We would get up in the morning and out of our tiny little twin bed. The bed was against the wall, and, from the bed, I could touch the opposite wall. That wall had the only other piece of furniture in the room, a tiny chest of drawers only about two-feet high! It looked as though it were made for a doll house or play house.

Taking turns, we would head for the bathroom. You are probably already expecting or imagining a very tiny cubbyhole—and you are not wrong. The door to the bathroom was on its last legs and would not close, and the wood was rotted out from about two feet on down. One person could get into the room but only by squeezing and leaning to and fro to get his or her complete body in. The room had a toilet, sink, and shower—not over a bathtub but over a small, round porcelain tub about the size of a sink. Every fixture had two things in common. Everything in the bathroom was waterlogged and everything was orange—from the rust. Everything—toilet, sink, and shower—also leaked.

After our morning wake-up rituals in the bathroom, we headed to the kitchen for breakfast. The kitchen was six-by-six feet! I'm five feet, nine inches. That meant I was in a room just slightly longer than I am tall! It had a small sink, a tiny, miniature refrigerator, and a stove for midgets. I have been on camping trips with Coleman stoves that were larger than what blonde Russian Laura was trying to cook on!

The only other item in the room was a breakfast table that is surely listed in the Guinness Book of World Records as the smallest in the world. Two small, beat-up, wooden chairs accompanied the table. It was quite romantic to sit at that table and hold hands with my lovely wife. We held hands not out of any latent romanticism that had been re-kindled in her or discovered in me. No, we held hands because, if we both put our hands on the very small table, our hands would touch whether or not we chose them to.

Prior to our stay at the Hotel de Squashed, I had never really noticed or paid any attention to what a very beautiful face my wife had. Now as we sat 1.3 inches across from each other, within intimate-kissing distance, I noticed. (I also noticed that the left lens of her glasses had a scratch on it.) The table was so small that it could only hold two small plates. This meant that I had to balance my plate on my lap so that there would be room on the small table for my cup of tea. It was either the small plate or the cup of tea—not both.

We survived. Laura continued to smile and worked like a slave to prepare us a totally unrecognizable meal. During this first meal, we were happy to find out that Laura was learning English—meaning she knew one single English word, "lunch," which she used to call us to all three meals. I was sure that, with this sort of linguistic progress, by the time we left in two weeks, Laura, a true polyglot of language, would be reciting Shakespeare.

Los Niños, the adoption agency, which had a staffed office in Saratov, was helping us navigate our way through the sea of Russian bureaucracy—government and various courts—and meal-preparer Laura was our Captain Cook. (Ha-ha: a little pun there. But Laura as Captain Cook did not exactly fill me with confidence, as you may remember what happened to Cook on a certain Polynesian island. The natives killed him.) It just so happened that nobody, in any of these tens of thousands of rows of apartments, throughout this big city, had a phone in their dwelling. Not that it would have mattered. I knew neither how to operate a Russian phone or speak Russian, so the phones were basically useless to me (and I to them). So Laura's biggest role was to act as the "telephone person," a task nowhere near as easy as it sounds.

The only phone for our use—actually Laura's use—was a public phone two or three blocks from the apartment. Since nobody had a phone, these few phones were for the use of everyone in the city. The amazing thing about this is how little the Russians used phones back then. Think about it for a minute, and it becomes clear why that was so. For all intents and purposes, the public-phone system was really only good for making calls. There was really no way to receive phone calls, unless you wanted to spend hours or days standing next to a phone booth in the hope that perhaps someone might call you.

So Laura would make frequent journeys to the public phone to get our schedule and her marching orders, return to the apartment, and then guide us to a car, commandeered by a driver (and, usually, Sasha), to get us to the various courts or ministries to sign papers and documents. Once we arrived, waiting for us would be a very friendly and competent Los Niños representative to translate and help with the paperwork and documents. Then we'd get back into the car and return to the apartment.

Sometimes Monica and I met the ministry officials together, and at other times we were split up, to sign away our lives and fortune. After being separated and eventually returned to the apartment, we would then compare notes about where we had been dragged off to. The usual question we asked each other was, "Did you understand any of the Russian documents you were signing?", and the usual response was, "Nope." This went on for days.

Sometimes I would be needed to talk on the phone, and this is when we learned that my star pupil, Laura, had added one more word to her increasing English vocabulary: "Rufus." In a decade or two this woman would be fluent.

We were doing a lot of running around, signing a lot of documents, and seeing a lot of the city from the back seat of junky little Ladas—but no baby. It was about this time we made four new discoveries. Three good and one bad.

First, there was another woman living in this tiny apartment with the three of us. Even crazier, it was an American woman, Laurie, from Texas, who was also adopting. Now, this apartment was smaller than the tiniest New York City micro loft that ever existed. It wasn't really big enough for one person when Monica and I had arrived—and now we had four. Actually Laurie had been there for about a day and a half, going through pretty much our routine, and somehow our paths had not crossed until now.

We met Laurie, and she was a great person and everything, but she happened to mention that, since she was single and unmarried, she had brought her mother with her from Texas. Holy Moly! The population of this little apartment just nearly doubled in the last minute or two!

Before any of this had a chance to sink in, another guest and dweller showed up—Laura's husband! I didn't even know she was married! It gets better! In a day or two, two new, little six-month-old babies would join the fray! This was going to be very interesting.

Laurie and her mother had a room identical to ours, so Laurie gave the tiny bed to her mother and slept on the floor. Laura, our Russian host, did the same in the living room with the new mystery husband, who couldn't even say "lunch" or "Rufus." Now, at night, save for the short hallway, every single square inch of floor in that apartment was taken up by sleeping bodies. Where were we going to put the babies when we got them?!

We were not yet done with guests. The last guest turned out to be a real problem for me. The husband had brought home a fairly large fish, and it was placed in a pail of water in the kitchen as it flopped around in its death throes. So, at each meal—as I gazed across the 1.3 inches of space separating us into the eyes of that lovely person I had married—out of the corner of my eye, I had to witness the demise of that damn fish. That was bad enough, but I don't like fish—I mean eating fish (although, since my recent trip to Ethiopia, I have acquired a taste for Nile perch). So I sat at each meal in mortal fear that the Moby Dick in the pail was destined to be one of my dinners. And still no baby!

My wife, Monica, has few character flaws and is a pretty easy person to live with. If I had not yet figured this out, I certainly had enough people in our family and among our friends reminding me of this fact. But patience is not her forte—especially when it comes to getting a baby! As the days went on, Monica questioned and enquired more and more, "Where's the baby?"

Finally the big day came—for me, not her. It was time to do the payoffs. I would have to let loose with every one of *my* precious babies, in denominations of one hundred!

I have been through a lot of strange situations in life. I've fought in a war. I was imprisoned in Africa. I have entered countries illegally. I've been lost in a remote canyon in Mexico and shaken hands with a president. Even in financial situations I have had some different experiences—with hyperinflation in Nicaragua, dealing in the black market in communist Poland, and once getting two cocoa beans as change in Africa. The financial transaction for the adoption of our son Eric may well be the strangest on record—anywhere!

Early that morning, as we had been previously advised that they would, a car, a driver—a very, very big driver—and Sasha showed up at the apartment. (Sasha was about twice my size and the driver was about twice Sasha's size.) At first I didn't realize the driver was the driver, and then couldn't believe he was going to be able to fit in the Lada. He did get into the Lada, but it was an amazing entry. He hurled himself in, head first, so that his upper torso was primarily on the passenger side of the car, and then heaved in the bottom half of his body. After the driver straightened himself out, Sasha got into the passenger seat. We then took off for our destination.

The bulk of these two men in the front seat was such that it obliterated the entire windshield for those sitting behind them—like me. There was a tiny, little, narrow telescope of front window not covered by the driver's and Sasha's imposing shoulders and heads. Sasha, at one point, attempted to turn to us in the back seat. A big man trying to move or maneuver in a Lada is quite a scene because there is just nowhere to go with one shoulder pressed to the window and the other to the driver. Finally Sasha settled for turning his neck as much as possible. He then informed us that we were going "to pay for the baby." Fair enough. He also informed us that the person collecting the money was a Russian woman by the name of Sasha.

Did everybody in this country have this same name? Both boys and girls, men and women? I refrained from asking what the driver's name was because I just knew without even asking that it was going to be

Sasha, too. But I did ask who this other Sasha was and what her full name was. I thought it might be helpful to know the last name of a strange woman whom I had never met before I started turning thousands of dollars over to her. The answer that Sasha (the original Sasha, with whom we had been dealing all along) gave was terrifying—at least when you are talking about my money. Our Sasha said, "Sasha is just a woman and does not want you to know her last name."

There is a word in our language (I'm sure they have the same word in Russian, but I'd have to ask Laura): "speechless." It's a word not much used because—*come on!*—how many times have you or someone you know ever really been *speechless*? I was speechless. We were speeding through the city of Saratov, Russia, a hitherto unknown (and, for all I knew, *mythical*) city, where I was to give thousands of dollars to a Russian woman who had the same name as the other 148,000,000 people in this country (except Laura), and whose job description and professional title was "just a woman." I had to entrust all this money to a woman who didn't really want me to know her last name.

I was now convinced that I was on my way to doing the dumbest and most reckless thing of my life. I looked to my wife for moral support in my time of need—meaning me being separated from all I loved: my money! This situation didn't seem right or legit. The concerned look on my face was sending out warning vibrations—*"Maybe we should back out of this scam or at least go to the adoption agency's office and check this all out!"*—which Monica couldn't or wouldn't pick up on.

This normally intelligent and bright woman was sitting in the back seat of this death trap of a Lada with a serene look on her face, content and happy. There was no turning back! She didn't give a shit about the money, the scam, or anything else! She was going to get a baby!

I was desperately trying to think of a way to escape or cancel the deal when—believe it or not—things got worse. Sasha said to me, "Do you happen to have $18,000 for Sasha?"

What I wanted to say was, "As a matter of fact, I just happen to have $22,000 dollars—but—NOT FOR SASHA! I AM REALLY NOT IN THE MOOD THIS MORNING TO GIVE ONE OF YOUR CITIZENS WHO HAS THE SAME NAME AS EVERYBODY ELSE IN THIS CITY—NO, THE SAME NAME AS EVERYONE IN THIS *COUNTRY*—AND DOESN'T WANT ME TO KNOW HER LAST NAME, $18,000 OF MY HARD-EARNED MONEY UNTIL I GET A BABY!" But I wimped out because I really didn't have any other choices or options, at least none that I could think of at the time. I resigned myself to my fate and tried to be optimistic that somehow and some way this would all work out and we would go home with a baby.

The car finally stopped, parking along the curb of a very busy street in Saratov. That was another thing: I didn't even know the name of the street I was on. When it came time to report to the Russian police the scam and theft of my money by con artists, I wouldn't even be able to tell them where it happened. Monica and I sat and waited, both perplexed as to what was going on. Finally I summoned up enough will power to ask (and instinctively I knew I was not going to be happy with the answer), "Why are we just sitting in the car here?"

"We are waiting to meet Sasha in her office" our Sasha replied.

"Where is her office?" I asked.

"She likes to meet her clients in a car, so you will meet Sasha in this Lada," our Sasha explained.

No shit! Sasha's office was this very Lada we were sitting in. (At $18,000 a pop, you'd think she could afford a bigger office, like a Volkswagen.)

So we sat.

Suddenly there was a flurry of activity. Sasha was arriving! In size, the female Sasha was bigger than our Sasha and looked very much like a player for the Green Bay Packers. Our Sasha and our driver got out of the Lada to make room for the newly arrived Sasha. She got into the passenger seat while the rest of the Green Bay Packer team, consisting of the driver and our Sasha, surrounded the Lada, both standing at attention, forming a defensive line to protect the quarterback. They struck identical poses, hands folded in front of them, facing out with stern, ominous expressions on their faces. I can state this authoritatively because I was there: the crowds of Russian people immediately starting hurrying away from our area. What had been a busy, city street scene was now avoided like the plague.

Once settled in the Lada, Sasha was all business, meaning she wanted my money. "For district-court costs, it is $3,000," she announced. I reached into my money pouch and pulled out thirty brand-new, United States hundred-dollar bills and surrendered them—reluctantly.

Sasha's next request was, "$5,000 for the orphanage." I reached into my front pocket and pulled out 50 more one-hundred-dollar bills and handed them over.

"The provincial government fee is $6,000," announced Sasha. Sixty more hundred-dollar bills changed hands. This six thousand came from the inside of my two shoes.

"There is a $1,000 fee for the Russian Federation," Sasha said. I reached into my underwear for these ten bills.

Sasha then announced that she needed another $3,000 for her agency—the name of which I didn't quite hear (and she ignored my two or three requests that she repeat it)—so I shelled out another 30 brand-new U.S. one-hundred-dollar bills, which made for a grand total of $18,000—but who's counting or cares?

Now in possession of $18,000 of my hard-earned money and without another word, Sasha managed to get her bulk withdrawn from the Lada, albeit with some difficulty. Once out of the Lada she turned and put her face very close to ours, as we sat in the back seat and said, "Tomorrow, you get baby."

She walked into the early-morning crowd of thousands of other Russians heading to work (or just getting away from our Sasha-protected Lada) and was slowly being swallowed by the mass of humanity. My first impulse was to jump out of the car, chase after this woman, tackle her, and retrieve my stolen money. But I just sat there immobilize by indecision. She disappeared.

As much as I missed my $18,000 ($2,000 more would be eventually paid to someone, somewhere in this country, but in the trauma of what had transpired, I forget now who got that $2,000), believe it or not I was more concerned about my wife, Monica. She sat there in that piece-of-shit Lada, in the failed state of Russia, surrounded by scam artists, actually believing we were going to get a baby tomorrow. She may have the higher IQ and be the brighter of us two, but I am far wiser and far much cynical in the ways of the real world. War alone taught me at a very young age what mean, worthless, pathetic things we humans are. Against the very teachings of my faith and church, I can never believe that humans are the highest and greatest creation of a God. Humans are very capable of lashing out more cruelly than any carnivore created by a Supreme Being. Although humans can act with great love and self-sacrifice, it doesn't take much stress or turmoil to turn them into the basest savages. I wasn't setting any odds, but things did not look too promising that the end result of all this time and effort and expenditure would be a baby.

The next morning we were off to pick up the baby—supposedly the same one we had seen in the video a few months earlier. That was another of my concerns: bait and switch; who knew what child we would end up with—or if we would even end up with a baby, period? The drive was very long, about two-and-a-half hours, and actually took us out through farm land into the middle of nowhere. (The long ride just made things more agonizing for me, wondering how it might all play out and how Monica would take it if it ended in failure.)

Longitude and Latitude, with Attitude

It snowed! It was the first week of October, and it was snowing! Russia was living up to its stereotypical image as one big giant frozen Siberia. To be sure, it was just snow flurries, but snow it was—and there already was snow on the ground from a previous snow. I couldn't help myself; I'm a history major, student, and teacher, and I felt I was experiencing what Napoleon and his French troops had gone through and then the Germans in WWII.

We finally arrived at a building I recognized, at least by association, because it looked pretty much like all the other factories one would see in my home town of Detroit. When one describes an orphanage looking like an old, dilapidated Detroit factory, you just know things are not going to go too well.

We got out of the taxi as the driver sat silently, unmoving, ignoring us, and we walked into the building. We were greeted by a number of people—office workers and care takers who wore old-fashioned nurse-like outfits that seemed to be out of the 1800s. Everyone smiled and seemed polite and gave a good shot at attempting some English. Only one woman, the director of the orphanage, I assumed, could really convey any sort of message. I now started to get my hopes up but still feared what they would present to us as a baby, only because I had heard and read of the horror stories in situations such as this.

After signing a few documents, every word in incomprehensible Russian, we were informed that only Monica would be allowed to go back into the babies' and children's area. That was strange.

As surreptitiously as I could, I had been doing my best all along to catch glimpses of this back area. Each time the door would open to that area, I would take in as much of the scene as possible—and it was not good! Parts of the cement floor were covered in pools of water. I could see toddlers standing in what looked like iron-clad cribs of steel bars—prisons for babies! It was noisy back there!

So a group of orphanage workers led Monica off to find our kid. She would later tell me that it was heartbreaking to see not only the horrid conditions but the younger children who grabbed her hand or clothing in a desire to go with her— go with anyone to get out of that place!

I don't know what took so long—at least it seemed like a long time— but Monica was back, without a baby. (To this day we have no idea what this little walkabout in the orphanage was all about.)

Before I could ask her what the deal was or what was going on, the director or whoever she was announced, "A nurse will now bring your baby out!"

Well! This was taking a turn for the better! A few moments later, a nurse brought a bundle of rags out and placed them on the long rectangular table we were all standing around and gave us the nice smile. The rags were of various colors, patterns, and sizes. They appeared to be very outdated textiles resembling some of my old sixties apparel that somehow had not yet been discarded or was being used as basement rags for cleaning chores. Everybody now looked at us with beaming smiles.

Evidently this was baby clothing or swaddling apparel that was being donated to go home with the baby. I was going to make a smart-ass comment or joke—something along the lines of, "Thanks for the used awning patterns you're giving us, but, when we get home, we plan on putting our baby in real clothing rather than the used Ethiopian hand-me-downs"—but then thought better of it. However, everyone kept smiling and looking at us, and it was getting awkward and a bit unnerving when finally someone motioned to the pile of rags.

Not knowing what was expected of us, and not wanting to seem unappreciative, I profusely thanked the staff and orphanage for the rags—I mean the baby clothing. Now they were smiling even more, and one of the women walked over to the pile of rags and motioned us over closer. (Did they want us to admire each piece of cloth?) The woman started sorting through these small rags and pieces of cloth when—OH MY GOD! THERE'S A BABY IN THERE!

There he was, little baby Eric as he would now be known. My first impression of him was that he was not cute so much as he was goofy looking! And that would be great, because he would look like me! Of course, in all fairness, anyone wrapped up in used canopy remnants and old dish towels would probably look pretty goofy. Adding to the comical atmosphere of our first born being delivered, or at least presented to us, was the Barnum and Bailey Circus clown suit he was dressed in. Gee, he even dressed like me!

This was love at first sight and the best damn idea I had ever come up with. Monica remembers it a bit differently. She claims I did not want to adopt or even have kids. She claims that I said that retirement was only a short time away and that kids would do nothing but get in the way of travel and having fun. But Monica is such a damn liar that you can't really believe anything she says. All I knew is that this was the single greatest and happiest moment of my life. Once uncovered and freed from his cocoon of ancient Soviet rags and debris, little Eric was on the move, with all four limbs going in different directions. He really did have a silly smile and seemed amused by whatever we did to him or for him.

The staff insisted that Monica—not me—undress Eric and then re-dress him in the baby clothes we had brought with us from America. The undressing was the easiest; the rags literally fell off Eric. Shockingly they wanted these rags back; no doubt these castoffs would be used to cover another poor orphan. Monica then put a diaper on him and a baby outfit, resulting in a normal-looking baby.

Boy was he a tiny little peanut! As it turned out, when we got him home to a pediatrician, the doctor informed us that Eric was malnourished and very small for his age. He, like all the other babies, had been surviving on five bottles of sour yogurt a day—that was it. A nurse would walk around the room of metal-barred cribs, stick a bottle of sour yogurt in the baby's mouth and then, when she reached the end of her round, immediately start collecting the bottles back, starting with the first that had been feed. These babies would have to suck like no-tomorrow to get their full bottle. This malnourishment was one of many issues that would have a lasting effect on Eric.

We wrapped him up in blankets we had brought, said our farewells to the staff, and they assured us Eric was the very favorite in the entire orphanage among the staff. I took that with a grain a salt. My mom had always told me I was her favorite. Years after her death, I came to find out that she had, separately, told my sister and my brother the exact same thing. We walked to the waiting taxi and we were on our way.

The orphanage had given us one very important item that, among adoptive parents in Russia, is the Holy Grail of survival, sanity, and peace—the Russian nipple! It seems that Russian nipples are different than American nipples for baby bottles, which meant that—besides the normal complexities of feeding a brand-new, not-used-to-us, six-month-old baby—we were soon to be confronted with the double-whammy of switching him from the sour yogurt that he had become accustomed to and, even more radically, from the nipples that were the conduit to that nourishment, an action that many babies revolted over.

"Revolt" might be too mild a term to use. There were stories of Russian babies screaming, crying, and becoming hysterical over the nipple switch, especially on the long flight home to America. We had heard, read, and seen the YouTube videos of screaming, hysterical Russian babies being transported home as angry passengers and flight crews berated the hapless new parents to do something about the uncontrollable infant. But that was all in the future; right now I was holding a very inquisitive baby in my arms in the back seat of a Russian taxi. For two-and-a-half hours, this little guy wanted to see all and everything. This was a very intelligent child, even though he didn't say a word. He didn't talk—and wouldn't for the next two years.

Upon returning to the apartment, we discovered another guest had decided to make his home here, at least temporarily. Laurie from Texas had also come back to the apartment with a baby. We had a real Russian-style Babies "R" Us going here.

At some point we went off to our palatial closet—I mean bedroom—with the single twin bed crammed into it, taking up about 95% of the room. Up to this point, the twin bed had been responsible for re-kindling the romance in our marriage by placing us in this replica of my boyhood bed closer and tighter together than when we had sex! Now we were joined by the newest member of the family, who had clocked about six hours of seniority within the family. Despite that measly six hours, even a visitor from Venus would have been able to see who the undisputed king of the family was and around whom everything revolved.

Where were we going to put the baby? There was no room in the bed. We were both terrified of sleeping in the bed with him for fear of rolling over on this little guy. Likewise, we were afraid to give Eric the whole bed while we slept on the floor for fear he would roll off. If necessity is the mother of invention, I was the Thomas Edison of the moment. I pulled out the bottom drawer of the dresser and placed blankets in it, and—*viola!*—now baby Eric had a wonderful bed—except he didn't like it! It was too confining I guess.

Our second attempt was to pad the bedroom floor with blankets, away from the door—we had not yet realized that Eric at this point not only could not crawl but could not even turn himself over—and try that. It kind of worked, but not great.

The next two days consisted of Sasha shuffling us to and from nearly all the places, ministries and courts, that we had once been to—but this time with the baby, to more or less physically prove that there was one mom, one dad, and one Russian baby ready to leave the country as a family.

These trips were quite stressful on everyone, including Eric, who was constantly being jarred awake to go to all these sites. We had him in a car seat that we had brought, and he was quite comfortable in it. But, no matter how careful and delicate I was getting in and out of taxis, the movement would awaken him. He was not used to being moved. Upon opening his eyes, he would not recognize his environment, so different than the one room in the orphanage where he had spent his whole life. There was a mixture of curiosity and alarm in his eyes. He didn't like it. He wasn't used to it. Monica or I would have to hold him to comfort him. That worked up to a point, but he was exhausting himself from lack of sleep.

Happily, we were getting to the end. The next day we would fly to Moscow. There we would check in at the U.S. embassy and register the newest American citizen, Eric Austin McGaugh. I am certainly prejudiced and biased, but America is the better for it! No passport, however! That would have to come later, when we arrived home. I was somewhat concerned about that, but there was nothing I could do about it. That meant Eric would fly home with us to America bearing a red Russian passport with the old communist hammer and cycle on it. I was going to hear no end of this from my right-wing friends who always accused me of being a commie-pinko. Not only was I adopting a little Russian, but he came complete with a hammer and sickle.

Once in Moscow the never-ending visits to bureaucratic offices were non-stop. One errand required a visit to the KLM office to re-confirm our flight home. This trip, including baby, already had enough stress factors built into it that no others were needed. So, when a very snotty KLM employee at their very small office—travel to Russia at that time was scant—informed us that we did not have a reservation for the connecting flight home from Amsterdam to Detroit, the argument began. It went back and forth, with the agent blaming my travel agent, Margaret Harms. That accusation particularly infuriated me because I knew of all the last-minute sacrifices Margaret had made, on her day off, to get us here. I went ballistic, but it did me no good. Amsterdam to Detroit would be standby, just to add to the stress.

Because of our Herculean effort to secure the baby, along with all of its attendant problems, not to mention the excitement and sheer novelty of the situation, we had not really thought through our move back to Moscow. Now that point would be driven home very clearly. A driver dropped us off at an apartment with a Los Niños representative. We were ushered into yet another tiny Soviet-era apartment that, for whatever reason, was deserted. That was the good news.

The bad news was that there was no one else there to help us. Laura with her two English words of "lunch" and "Rufus" was back in Saratov, hundreds of miles away. The Los Niños representative regretted to inform us that, when she left us—alone—she was done, and we were on our own until we got home to America. That was a bit chilling to hear. Yes, a driver would be dispatched to pick us up the next day to take us to the airport, but, from this point on, we were on our own with a brand-new baby, who didn't speak English—in fact, didn't speak anything!

Having to fly standby tomorrow, when the snotty KLM agent said there was little or no chance the flight would have room for two people and a baby, didn't exactly make for a rosy picture. Suddenly, a little—

and I do mean *little*—old gray-haired lady appeared at our door, smiling. The Los Niños representative said this grandma lived in one of the apartments below us and had volunteered to answer any questions or help with any problems we might have while we stayed here. That, however, didn't seem to improve the situation a whole lot, considering this lady's inability to speak or understand a word of English. Then the Los Niños representative left, deserting us to Mother Russia and one little granny who continued to smile. She too eventually deserted us.

Tonight was going to be the big night for all of us—especially baby Eric, who had no inkling of the historic event that was to take place. This was the big one that we heard about, read about, and dreaded. Tonight we would run out of the last bottle of sour yogurt and switch to the formula that we had brought with us from the U.S.

The bigger and more prominent issue was the nipple switching. As I mentioned, Russian nipples are different than American nipples—the ones on the bottles, I mean—and previous adopters' experience had shown that many Russian babies had great difficulty giving up the former for the latter. Some of these babies couldn't figure out how to work their mouths around these Western nipples, and so they cried, would not eat, or became hysterical. On a plane—well anywhere, but especially within the confines of a jet, for many hours up in the air—this could be real problematic for those sitting anywhere near the baby; a wailing, inconsolable infant at 30,000 feet was perhaps one of the most stressful events for the new parents.

When it came time for this first feeding with formula and an American nipple, things didn't seem to be going real well. Better safe than sorry, so I immediately headed down a floor to find Granny. Once down there, I discovered there were many apartments, and I had no idea which one belonged to the old lady who I was hoping could help us.

On my second try of banging on doors I found her, and as usual she was all smiles.

Up against our language barrier, I began one of the more bizarre conversations I have ever had in my life. Here I was discussing nipples with what looked like a 93-year-old Russian woman. Usually when I am talking nipples, I am sitting in a strip bar, shitfaced, hoping a neighbor doesn't come in and recognize me, as I attempt to shove even more of my children's college-education money down the thong of a skinny 20-year-old dancer, usually with a name like Bambi or Ruby.

Trying to get the concept of "nipple" across, I did lots of gesturing and hand signs attempting to demonstrate what a nipple looked like or at least the nipple I was enquiring about, but to no avail. The old lady simply smiled, and then, as I attempted to get her to follow me upstairs to see for herself what I was talking about, she didn't follow. No doubt, if you are a 93-year-old woman, going to the apartment of a man who seems to be infatuated with nipples doesn't sound like a smart move.

By the time I returned, little-old-ladyless, to Monica, the problem had been solved. Eric was demonstrating what his true love was and would always be: food. He's never stopped eating. Well, I was relieved because now I could concentrate all my worrying on the issues that would face us tomorrow: our flight, or lack thereof. I think all three of us actually got *some* sleep that night.

The next day, as the Los Niños representative promised, a man was at our door to take us to the airport, which he did.

I usually don't brag, but I could write the book on how to travel light. With over 40 years of travel under my belt, I carry only a small day pack—not even a full backpack. On the smallest planes, my day pack is allowed as a carry-on. Not on this trip, that was for sure. We had luggage, formula, baby bottles, toys, a car seat, stuffed animals, and suit cases. As agreed, Monica took Eric, and I handled the Mayflower-Moving-Van-load of accessories.

Everywhere in the Moscow airport, people smiled at the beautiful baby, offered us cuts in lines, and helped carry or move the massive amount of luggage we had. It was a night flight, and all three of us were whacked, so we were especially grateful for the help.

Once on the plane, Monica handed Eric over to me, and collapsed in exhaustion. I held him all three hours and never allowed myself to sleep for fear of dropping him. I had asked the stewardess to let me know when we were out of Russian air space. The adoption was not set in concrete, in my mind, until we were out of Russia. When the stewardess came and told me we had passed out of Russian air space, I looked down at this beautiful human being and knew he was ours forever.

We landed around midnight in Amsterdam, dead tired. The entire plane disembarked, and every single person on that plane walked through Dutch Customs and Immigration, taking only seconds to do so. Then we showed up, flashed our American passports, started to be waved through until the red hammer and sickle passport came up, and were stopped immediately. The Dutch officials were very kind but also very thorough. Eric's passport received great scrutiny. Finally, the Dutch official released us and wished us well. We caught a hotel bus, checked into our hotel, ordered a crib, and slept very fitfully, knowing that we did not have a confirmed flight for the following day.

Arriving at the airport the next morning, I reported to the counter and began my begging for seats, using my trump card—a new adopted baby.

It worked for everyone in the airport except the airline. We were on standby, and that was that.

It didn't look very likely that we would make this flight or the flight the next day, but—ever hopeful—we waited. After the final boarding call and then countless repeats of that same message, and with only minutes before takeoff, we were given two boarding passes. Hooray for KLM.

Well, hold off on the applause until the end. KLM was to demonstrate that they were not at the top of their game on this flight. After we were seated, the stewardess attached a small crib to the bulkhead in front of us. We were able to look down and across at Eric, and he seemed fine with that, so I felt we had escaped the worst. I politely informed our stewardess of our situation and that at some point we would probably need hot water for the bottle and formula. I was given a snappish answer that they would do their best, but it was a full flight and we shouldn't expect instant and immediate service. I had not implied or requested "instant and immediate" service, but I let it go.

As it turned out, we needed little from the KLM staff other than that hot water, and, the few times we asked for it, they provided it—maybe not instantly and immediately, but soon enough. So the thirteen-or-so-hour flight to Detroit went relatively smoothly. Once or twice Eric got a little fussy, but it was nothing serious or stressful. However, Eric did demonstrate that he would not be a happy camper unless he had the full attention of both Monica and me, so there was no sleep to be had over the next 13 hours. The perfect preparation for a parent's first year or two with a baby.

We landed in Detroit and ended one journey to begin a life-long journey with one of the sweetest kids you ever want to meet.

Eric is definitely not the malnourished little peanut we picked up in Russia in 1996. He's much taller and bigger than me. Monica and I always feel we won the lottery when Eric came into our lives.

Postscript, February 4, 2016:

We as a family were planning a trip to Norway this summer. We were attempting to include Russia in the itinerary so that Eric could see a bit of the country of his origin. Below is an email Monica received yesterday from Trish Erichsen, the woman from the adoption agency, who was so helpful in bringing the adoption about.

> *I am a little worried about anyone taking advantage of you and Rufus and Eric.*
>
> *There is a new law that all adoptees can only travel in and safely get out of Russia again with a Russian passport along with their American passport. It sounds really strange, but I can see that this is another attempt by the Russians to tap into American families for more money, since the adoptions have stopped. It is another fee they can charge.*
>
> *The process isn't easy. I think the parents have to send the original Russian passport to Moscow.*
>
> *A lot of people are unwilling to do that because they are afraid they won't get it back, or that it will be lost. Apparently, the officials in the region where the child was born have to work in conjunction with the officials in the federal passport-registry office in Moscow. Doing it long distance is difficult. But, if you go without the paperwork in order, you may not be able to leave. A Russian federal prosecutor told me that they can even fine you now, retroactively, for not having the Russian passport periodically re-registered and that it can even include jail time!!!*
>
> *I am sure that is an empty threat to try to exact extra fines, but it is disconcerting to hear that they have passed a law requiring this registration to take place on a particular schedule and can hold you to it, if you try to travel there. You may be able to find out more about all of this on-line.*
>
> *Blessings,*
>
> *Trish*

So we didn't include Russia in our itinerary after all! We went through too much to get Eric in the first place and love him too much to ever do anything that would endanger him or cause him to be detained or imprisoned. There will be no family trip to Russia in the near future—perhaps ever.

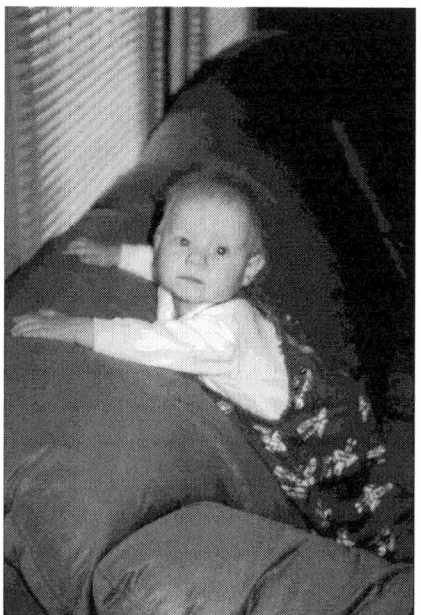

Baby Eric, our son, shortly after we returned with him from a grueling 10-day trip to Russia.

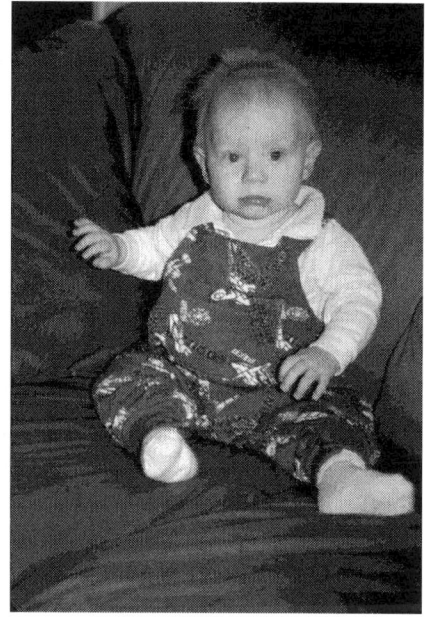

Eric was six months old when we adopted him—very small and malnourished from his time in that horrible orphanage.

*****

As for me and my travels, I've got one more country to go: Libya. To date, the best plan for that one is to parachute in and run like hell out. When I'm visiting and teaching at middle schools, even the 6th- and 7th-graders feel this is not a very wise plan.

So I Came Up with *Another* Plan: Rufus in Libya

Just learned today (May 25, 2017) from Ihab Zaki, who planned and organized the flights that took me to Libya, that I was the first American to get into Libya since the fall of Gaddafi in 2011! Not only that but talk about good timing, lucky timing, or a combination of both! Look at this headline from The Washington Post *for May 26, 2017: "A day in Libya's capital, just as the civil war reignites."*

Libya (Part I)

As you might imagine, getting to Libya was a very interesting process, to say the least. Since Libya is often described as the most dangerous place in the world to visit, it took some work to get there.

The Glitch That Almost Spoiled the Plan

I had been quietly planning this mission, operating surreptitiously and under the radar so as not to invite the interest of my good friends and pals (ISIS and Al Qaeda in Libya) when, nine days before I was set to leave, local TV crews descended on my home—cameras and microphones blazing—to report the big story that a local man was heading to Libya to finish his quest of visiting every country in the world. Talk about having your cover blown! It was at that very moment that local terrorist groups in Tripoli starting measuring my neck size on their satellite-TV screens to see what sword would be best for the beheading. Nevertheless, as usual, "All Guts and No Brains Rufus" was not to be deterred. This was the last country/land on my list (number 251), and I was going to make the trip with or without a head.

I would like to say that it was kind of nice—really touching in a way—that so many family, friends, colleagues, and former students expressed their concern over my safety if I went to Libya. I *would like* to say that. To tell the real truth, absolutely no one was concerned about my safety or well being but instead made countless tasteless jokes about my chances of survival and what a beheading might feel like—which goes to show that most of my friends are just as stupid as I am.

The Glitch That Didn't Spoil the Plan

Oh—there was one other minor development that came up before I left. I had kidney cancer. At least that was what the internet claimed when I plugged in my symptoms on Google.

My family wanted me to stay home or go to Emergency, see a doctor—whatever—but I put my foot down and said I was going to Libya, the last country on my list, even if I had to pack one or both of my kidneys in a duffle bag and bring them along for the tour. Besides, how could anything possibly be wrong with my kidneys when I had done such an amazing job all these years of lubricating them with my special elixir of hops, water, grain, and yeast?

Well, we compromised. I did visit a physician, just to keep my family happy. (It may have had something to do with them trussing me up while I had my foot down, tossing me in the car, and forcibly taking me to said physician.)

My amazing doctor, Dr. Tesch, despite having a fully scheduled workload of patients, took me in for an exam and urine test and then used all her mighty clout to get me an ultra sound within 20 minutes. We waited.

The conclusive medical opinion of the radiologist and the St. John Hospital medical staff was—wait for it—it was definitely something. No one was quite sure what that something was, and the opinions ranged from gall bladder to muscle spasm, but—heck—it wasn't cancer and thus wouldn't prevent me from traveling. I now had three new drugs to ingest on the trip to make me even more crazy than what I usually am. I was off to Libya.

The Flight

To get into Libya I had to fly through three continents and three countries on airplanes that got progressively worse—from one that was merely rickety to another that looked more like something out of Dogpatch (you remember *L'il Abner*, don't you?) to a last "plane" that appeared to have just completed a murderous bombing raid and gotten the worst of it.

The Ruse

To enter this war-torn and terrorist country wherein every other citizen belongs to ISIS, Al Qaeda, a terrorist cell, or a militia, I used a visa that stated I was a Chinese engineer. Now, those of you who know me are aware that I look no more like a Chinese person than I do an

Ethiopian. Even more alarming are my engineering skills. I can't get a door knob back on or operate a microwave. I did little preparation to pull this scam off other than to practice, each day before I left, saying "chop suey" with an Oriental accent.

For those of you out there who have been disparaging my intelligence all these years, let me just tell you that I pulled off the impersonation with all the grace and aplomb of Sherlock Holmes or Batman in disguise. Although it might be more accurate to say that Libyan officials were too incompetent to notice and also didn't give a shit, but, just the same, I got in to Libya.

The Master Plan

My next plan, besides touring about a bit, was to keep my head, figuratively and literally, and not let the local thugs end up having Rufus' noggin as the new neighborhood soccer ball.

First Night and Day in Libya.

At around 4:45 in the morning, my fitful sleep was disrupted big time when the mosque right next door made the call to prayer over huge speakers, most of which were aimed directly at my room. Groggily I greeted both Allah and Mr. Mohamed but did not get up to worship. Rather, I stayed in bed in an attempt to get a few hours of sleep before beginning my exploration of Tripoli, Libya's capital city.

A few hours later (before the next call to prayer), I was awake and up and making my first discovery: my hotel was an ancient structure which dated back to when the Ottomans used it as a caravanserai—a place of lodging for the caravans that once plied this route—a rest stop for both the camel drivers and their animals. After a quick breakfast (with no camels), my Libyan guide and I were off.

Tripoli was pretty disappointing and didn't have a whole lot to offer. Despite being oil rich, Libya has had almost 50 years of misrule—first under Gaddafi, then under various succeeding governments. Tripoli looks like a rundown Rome—in a poor state and in need of repair. Trash and litter cover the streets and sidewalks. Most of the more undesirable jobs are filled by black Africans from countries to the south of Libya. I watched these garbage men tear apart each plastic bag of garbage they collected (so that the rotting and spoiled contents now added a gross aroma to the setting) as they looked for anything of value that they could salvage.

Driving to our first point of interest, my jihadist guide went into a lengthy and heated lecture about a small monument that commemorates the Barbary War (1801-1805) fought against Libya by the United States. The Barbary pirates, who controlled what is now Libya and Algeria, caused this war, attacking and capturing U.S. ships in the Mediterranean Sea. President Thomas Jefferson sent the Navy and Marines to stop it—and they did, at least for a while. With great anger, my jihadist guide related the story of U.S. Marines storming the Barbary beaches and recounted what a destructive force the Marines had been, both to people (mostly by shooting them) and to property (mostly by burning buildings to the ground). He was really getting worked up about how brutal the Marines were and how successful in defeating his people, causing great suffering. I decided this was not a good time to mention that I had been a lance corporal in the Marine Corps. I also made a mental note to stop humming the Marine Corps Hymn, especially the part "from the halls of Montezuma to the shores of Tripoli."

It only took Mr. Jihad a few minutes to get to our next site, which was another monument. This time it was the turn of the U.S. Navy, rather than the Marines, to take the abuse. This lecture was a more gleeful one, at least as told by my suicide-vest-wearing guide. This second monument commemorated the capture of the USS Philadelphia by the Libyans during the Barbary War. I was starting to get the idea now that these people don't like us very much. I was tempted to blurt out that, unlike back after our Revolutionary War, when the U.S. really didn't have much of a navy, our modern Navy of today, could probably kick Libya's ass not in years, months, or days but in minutes or seconds. I decided to let that one go unsaid also. Good thing too because Mr. Al-Qaeda turned out to be a pretty good guy once you got to know him and got him off the subject of his country's conflicts with the U.S.

On the outskirts of Tripoli we visited a very run-down, poorly supported museum that had some great Punic (Phoenician and Carthaginian) funeral relics, tombs, and artifacts.

To be honest with you, I really didn't see all that much of value—that is, until I arrived back at the hotel. That's when I spotted it. On its outside wall, the building next to my hotel had a gigantic painting of a huge exploding grenade blowing infidels to kingdom come. No doubt this was the local meeting place for jihadists of the city. My goal now was to be out of Tripoli before their next meeting.

And, finally, I experienced an interesting situation, one which happened a number of times there on my first day. When I talked with Libyans (at least those who spoke English), they always ended up telling me what good jokes I told and how funny I was. I would have been flattered by this assessment—if not for the fact that I had *not* been telling any jokes or trying to be funny. Well, at least their reaction was better than people's in the States, where most folks either walk away or fall asleep when I talk.

Driving in Libya.

I don't want to sound critical or superior when I call the driving in Libya bad or chaotic, but that first day I did witness a guy driving in the wrong lane against oncoming traffic and another guy doing the exact same thing in the lane next to him but in the opposite direction. They passed each other—both in the wrong lane against traffic— with ease.

Those two drivers perhaps experienced no problem, but all of us driving in our correct lanes in both directions nearly had a heart attack as we watched two speeding cars coming toward us against traffic. Typical Libya: everyone survived; no one was killed; there wasn't even an accident—but, for a few moments, many of us on that highway thought we were watching our doom play out in real time.

My driver/guide, Mr. Suicide Vest, had very relaxed ideas of driving and highway rules. He seemed to think that red lights to stop are for suckers and tended to ignore them unless a huge semi or rig on the cross street happened to have the green light and didn't show any inclination to slow down or stop.

Libya Part II

Leptis Magna, a Declared UNESCO World Heritage Site: Supposedly the Greatest Roman Ruins on Earth

Next day. Did Leptis Magna live up to its reputation as the greatest of all Roman ruins? I would say yes.

Well, a conditional yes, because, if one were to consider all aspects (size, number of ruins, condition of ruins, and variety of ruins—how many unique and different types of architectural buildings and structures there are), then, certainly, Leptis Magna might very well be ranked number one among all the Roman ruins that exist. The Roman ruins at Baalbek in Lebanon are by far more beautiful, and Pompeii has better Roman art, but Leptis Magna has it all. The list of architectural structures is staggering: triumphal arches, temples, a forum, shops, homes, a coliseum, a theater, arches, a basilica, shipping port, mosaic art, and a well preserved and huge oblong circus (the Roman race track for chariots), and of course my dearest favorite of all, the famous Roman toilets.

The only group to love Roman toilets more than Rufus was the Romans themselves. Roman men would spend hours there—not due to diarrhea or constipation but out of the love of a place where they could talk politics and sport and gossip by the hour. With their artful stone statues and large fountains (filled with huge, strategically placed bullfrogs to disguise the gross noises men often make on the toilet), it was hard not to become enamored of them.

Ancient Rome set the gold standard for toilets, making them of expensive marble. This ostentatious display of wealth on the part of ancient Rome did however cause one problem. The eternal dilemma that humans have faced since Adam and Eve is this: what is to be done with a very cold toilet seat when we come created with a naturally warm butt? Hand it to the Romans to devise an ingenious solution. When a Roman had to make a trip to the toilet and it was chilly or outright cold, he simply brought his slave along, had him yank his toga up, and then with his bare ass, sit down on the icy marble toilet seat and warm it up. A minute or so of this, and it was now ready for the master.

Amidst my commentary on fountains and marble, the fact should not be lost that the Roman toilets at Leptis Magna were the Mother of all Toilets! I checked one out that was a fifty seater! A two-seater outhouse used to be considered by some in our country as a luxury or extravagance. But the mighty Romans could comfortably seat 50 at a time—with amenities.

While I'm on the toilet—er, on the *subject* of toilets—I might also add that the Romans had the equivalent of flush toilets over 2,000 years ago. Below all those Roman toilets was a drainage canal made of bricks with a constant flow of water. That's the good news. The bad news is that all those human feces from all those defecating Romans drained right into the beautiful blue Mediterranean Sea.

Libya, Part III

Last Day

Breakfast this last morning was not the sumptuous feast of the previous two mornings. Today's breakfast was a few end pieces of bread and—are you ready?—two slices, in plastic, of Velveeta cheese. They must have figured out I was an American and didn't like me anymore. After that miserable breakfast, I spent my time walking around a huge Roman triumphal arch which was only steps away from the hotel.

Leaving Libya

Ali, my guide, had warned me that the Tripoli airport was probably the worst disorganized mess of chaos of any airport on the planet. There were no signs or monitors and when they did bother to announce a flight, they did so in Arabic only. *Great!* I thought. *I'm never gonna get outta here!*

We arrived to find an airport that had nearly as many broken windows as those that still stood undamaged. When Ali could go no further with me into the airport, he passed me off to a local, making him promise he would get me on the flight. The local man swore upon the holy Koran to both Mohamed and Allah that I was under his protection and he would get me on the flight one way or the other. Two minutes later the local ditched me never to be seen again.

Now to get on this plane on my own I would have to use all my intelligence, skills, and wits—a very, very scary thought. But I was up to it, and things were going fine—except the plane was late, which in Libya is the norm rather than the exception.

Suddenly I was approached by a very mean-looking man followed by a posse of other pissed-off individuals. Evidently they had had time to think, and, after all that thinking, decided that Rufus did not exactly fit the profile of a Chinese engineer. Jeez! I wondered how they came to that conclusion. It must have been the engineer part of the story. Although I have to admit they were also a bit skeptical about me being Chinese.

This was not a friendly group I was surrounded by, more a lynching-mob group. They were really angry and seemed to think that I was up to some scam or that my visa information was untrue. They as much as told me they thought I was lying to them about being Chinese and an engineer. What could I tell them? How could anyone doubt such a plausible story?

That's when things turned real ugly. The lynch mob confiscated my passport. Now I was going to have to explain not only how I happened to be Chinese and an engineer, but why I had an American passport.

During the interrogation that followed, I was tempted at one point to tell the mob of officials that Rufus was just my Shanghai nickname and my real name was Ching Lee but then thought the better of it. It was about this time that I really started to regret not doing more preparation for this aspect of the trip other than practicing just the word "chop suey" and wished I learned at least a few other words in Chinese.

We went back and forth about my identity for some time, with me always sticking to my story. Although they did trip me up a few times. I blame that on the fact I was telling so many lies so fast that I couldn't keep my story straight.

Minutes before my plane was to leave, the lynch mob of officials, for whatever reason, gave up, and I got my passport back. (Maybe they'd seen that local tv-news report and didn't want to be the spoilsports who prevented a guy from achieving his goal of seeing the whole world. Maybe they didn't want to give my family and friends the satisfaction of saying "I told you so" to my beheaded corpse.)

After all that, I couldn't wait to get back home to Shanghai and my career as a mechanical engineer. I had taken on a mob of Libyans and won. Ronald Reagan would have been proud of me. His two favorite activities while he was President were clearing scrub and trees on his ranch and bombing Libya.

Bottom line. It was a great trip!

And, almost (but not quite) lost in my enjoyment of traveling, making a trip, seeing new places, learning more and then sharing that knowledge with students, was a momentous event: I finally did it. I completed my quest to see it all—every country in the world. Perhaps the very short email I sent out (below) after completing this trip sums it up better than anything I could say or write at present.

Mission Accomplished!

On Sunday, May 21, I flew out of Libyan air space after a three-day visit to one of the more dangerous countries in the world, thus completing the travel goal I had set for myself nearly 50 years before: to visit all 50 states, all seven continents, and the 251 countries/lands thereon. I started this journey when I was 19 years old with an attempt to drive to Alaska and ended it in a dangerous area of North Africa.

It has been a wild ride and an amazing odyssey. I have traveled in the midst of famine, war, poverty, political upheaval, and natural disasters. At the same time, I was able to witness most of the great wonders and sights—and some of the greatest beauty—that our planet has to offer. The tales of the events I've experienced and the people I've met could fill a book (like this one)—maybe several books.

How can I celebrate this achievement?

... Well, I was thinking of making a trip.

Longitude and Latitude, with Attitude

Yours truly, wearing my "Buck Up, Broncos" t-shirt and flashing a "Buck Up, Broncos" bookmark in Antarctica. Never made it to the South Pole. A story for another book…

Printed in Poland
by Amazon Fulfillment
Poland Sp. z o.o., Wrocław